Lessons in ESSAY WRITING

Derek Soles

Camosun College

Prentice Hall Inc.,
Scarborough, Ontario

To Mary

Canadian Cataloguing in Publication Data

Soles, Derek A. J., 1949-
    Lessons in essay writing

ISBN 0-13-525296-2

1. English language - Rhetoric. 2. Essay. I.Title.

PE1471.S65 1997   808'.042   C95-930009-3

 © 1997 Prentice-Hall Canada Inc., Scarborough, Ontario
A Viacom Company

Prentice-Hall, Inc., Upper Saddle River, New Jersey
Prentice-Hall International (UK) Limited, London
Prentice-Hall of Australia, Pty. Limited, Sydney
Prentice-Hall Hispanoamericana, S.A., Mexico City
Prentice-Hall of India Private Limited, New Delhi
Prentice-Hall of Japan, Inc., Tokyo
Simon & Schuster Asia Private Limited, Singapore
Editora Prentice-Hall do Brasil, Ltda., Rio de Janeiro

ISBN: 0-13-525296-2

Acquisitions Editor: Rebecca Bersagel
Developmental Editor: Karen Sacks
Copy Editor: Shirley Corriveau
Production Editor: Lisa Berland

Production Coordinator: Sharon Houston
Cover and Interior Design: Julia Hall
Cover Image: Photonica/Daniel Root
Page Layout: Phyllis Seto

1 2 3 4 5   CC   01 00 99 98 97

Printed and bound in the United States

We welcome reader's comments, which can be sent by e-mail to
collegeinfo_pubcanada@prenhall.com

Credits

p. 74, excerpt from "Boomtown Jitters," Tim Falconer, *Report on Business*, November 1995, reprinted with permission from the author. **p. 75**, excerpt from "Spring Flings and Seasonal Sorrows," George Koch, *Ski Canada*, Fall 1995. is reprinted with permission of the author. George Koch is a Calgary-based freelance journalist writing about business, politics and skiing. **p. 76**,excerpt from "The 21st Century Belongs to Canada" by Andrew Coyne first appeared in *Saturday Night*, October 1995, and is reprinted with permission from the author. **p. 83**, excerpt from British Columbia Medical Association, "Steroids," December 1993, reprinted by permission of the BCMA. **p. 89**, excerpt from "My Journey With Cancer," Elizabeth Simpson, *The Saanich Review*, 1995, is reprinted with permission from the author. p. 100, excerpt from "Wired Women," Elvira Kurt, *Flare*, November 1995, is reprinted with permission from the author. **p. 109**, excerpt from "Bone Up on Exercise," Beth Thompson, *Chatelaine*, November 1995, reprinted with permission from Beth Thompson, Chatelaine. **p. 117**, reprinted with permission of Scribner, a Division of Simon & Schuster, Inc., from DEATH IN THE AFTERNOON by Ernest Hemingway. Copyright 1932 Charles Scribner's Sons. Copyright renewed © 1960 by Ernest Hemingway. **p. 212**, "The Dead", from DUBLINERS by James Joyce. Copyright 1916 by B. W. Heubsch. Definitive text Copyright © 1967 by the Estate of James Joyce. Used by permission of Viking Penguin, a division of Penguin Books USA Inc.

Table of Contents

Preface

TO THE TEACHER

For the past twenty years, I have taught written composition at a college and at a university. I have learned from this experience that a good text book, designed to help students improve their ability to write clearly and intelligently, has four characteristics. It is concise; it uses relevant models to illustrate the principles of good writing; it reinforces what is taught, using a wide selection of exercises, assignments, video interviews with professional writers, summaries, definitions, and helpful hints; and it teaches writing as a recursive, not as a linear, process.

I have kept *Lessons in Essay Writing* brief because only part of the time students spend in a writing class will be devoted to learning *about* writing. In the contemporary writing classroom, students spend as much time in groups—brainstorming, "peer conferencing," discussing assignments, writing collaboratively, and evaluating each others' drafts—as they do listening to a teacher lecture about the qualities of good writing. The aim of *Lessons in Essay Writing* is to give students the information they need about the elements of good writing to guide them through their own writing assignments and to help them work effectively with their teacher and their classmates.

To illustrate the principles of good writing, this text contains many model sentences, paragraphs, and essays on topics relevant to students' lives. There are models about popular culture, current events, and personal experiences. But there are also models relevant to the academic and technical subjects that students study at college and university. Since written composition is one of these subjects, there are, in this text, model paragraphs and essays about writing and language. In some lessons, in fact, a passage from the text itself serves as the model. The various models used—some written by students, some by professionals—not only provide examples of good writing but also reinforce the material covered in the text and in class. *Lessons in Essay Writing* is the ultimate "process approach" to teaching composition.

Lessons in Essay Writing contains a wide selection of questions, exercises, assignments, definitions, summaries, and helpful hints. Each lesson incorporates the following elements:

- Brief assignments after each main section
- Questions for study and discussion
- A comprehensive set of supplementary exercises
- A summary of the main points covered in the lesson
- Clear definitions for all key terms related to effective writing
- Helpful hints that highlight key aspects of the writing process

In addition, marginal icons are used throughout the text to direct students' attention to certain special features. The computer-mouse icon, for example, tells students that information relevant to writing with a word processor is featured in this section of the book.

A videotape that complements *Lessons in Essay Writing* is available to instructors who adopt this text. The videotape contains interviews with such prominent writers as W.O. Mitchell and Sharon Butala, who give helpful advice about the writing process while they discuss their own work. Introductions to the video interviews, along with exercises and writing assignments based on the interviews, appear at the end of Lessons Eight, Eleven, Sixteen, and Eighteen.

Finally, the text emphasizes the recursive nature of the writing process. Naturally, all of the usual characteristics of good writing are covered: find a thesis; come up with ideas to support the thesis; compose an outline; write a draft; revise the draft for content; revise the revised draft for paragraph structure; and revise again for sentence structure, grammar, and mechanics. But the text reminds its readers that these elements of the writing process rarely occur in a prescribed sequence, that students might find their thesis *after* they have written a draft, that they might think of a good introduction while writing the conclusion, and that they will revise sentences and paragraphs throughout the whole process of doing a writing assignment. In this text, writing is viewed, in the best possible sense of the phrase, as a form of organized chaos.

There is a sound organizational structure to *Lessons in Essay Writing*. The first five lessons deal with the essay as a whole, focusing on the overall content and structure. Lessons Six through Ten focus on writing effective paragraphs. Lessons Eleven through Eighteen focus on writing effective sentences. Lesson Nineteen presents a summary of the preceding lessons and, in the process, brings the text full circle by illustrating how to revise the essay as a whole.

Within this structure, however, there is also flexibility. Each lesson is a self-contained unit. Teachers who want to discuss citation at the end of their writing classes can easily do so. Teachers who want to begin their classes by discussing the characteristics of effective sentences, then move on to effective paragraphs, and conclude with overall essay structure will find no difficulty in re-arranging the lessons to suit their needs.

Lessons in Essay Writing ends with two appendices, a glossary of important terms, and two answer keys: one that answers the objective Assignments from within the chapters, and one that answers the objective Supplementary Exercises from the end of each chapter. Appendix A presents a detailed analysis of one of the model research papers in the book to give students a clear idea of the process they must go through to write an outstanding research essay. Appendix B presents three versions of two essays with comments explaining how each version would likely be assessed and graded by an English teacher. This will help students understand how and why they get their grade on the essay they have worked so hard to create.

TO THE STUDENT

While I was writing *Lessons in Essay Writing*, I tried to keep in mind what I know, or think I know, about you.

You are probably a busy person, taking several college or university courses, working part-time, perhaps, and trying to enjoy at least some semblance of a social life. For these reasons, I have done my best to keep this text as short as possible, while recognizing the need to cover all important aspects of the writing process.

You already know a lot about writing and language. All errors that college students tend to make—in grammar, sentence structure, paragraphing, punctuation, and diction—are discussed in this text, and methods of overcoming these errors are prescribed. But errors that college students rarely make are not covered.

You probably prefer to read about issues that are interesting and relevant. There are many model paragraphs and essays in this text that relate to the subjects (including written composition) you are studying. There are also model paragraphs and essays about popular culture and current social issues.

Finally, you probably work the way most writers do. You start with a basic plan and a basic idea about what you want to say, but you change, reshape, revise, and refine the structure and content of your essay *while* you write it. *Lessons in Essay Writing* advocates this method, called the "recursive" writing process, over the sequential, step-by-step, or "linear" method of writing.

I hope that *Lessons in Essay Writing* will help you improve your skills in written composition.

Derek Soles
1997

ACKNOWLEDGEMENTS

My editors at Prentice Hall and some colleagues across the country provided me with excellent suggestions and sound advice while I wrote and revised *Lessons in Essay Writing*. I want to thank Marjorie Munroe, Karen Sacks, Lisa Berland, and Shirley Corriveau for their professional expertise. I must also thank my colleagues who reviewed the manuscript or sections of it and who generously shared their wisdom and experience: William Armstrong from the University of British Columbia, Emmy Miser from Wilfrid Laurier University, Joan Pilz from Humber College, Roger Ploude from the University of New Brunswick, Jacqueline Ballhorn from Algonquin College, Jean Huntley from Marianopolis College, John T. Lucas from Dawson College, and Jennifer A. Waterman from Algonquin College.

Getting Ideas

Get the Idea!

Ask Questions
Freewrite
Keep a Journal

Make Up Analogies
Talk It Over

In Neil Simon's screenplay *The Odd Couple*, an awkward and recently divorced Felix Unger is trying to make conversation with two young women whom he and his roommate, Oscar Madison, have invited for dinner. One of the women asks Felix what he does for a living. He tells her he writes the news for a TV station. "Oh, how fascinating," she replies. "Where do you get your ideas?"

The young woman's question is hilariously illogical, but her instincts are good. She intuitively knows that writers need ideas. Of course, newswriters have a readymade source for their ideas, but even newswriters could benefit from the strategies described in this lesson.

When you are writing an essay or a report, you must try to make your work interesting and informative. Your teachers value and appreciate writing that contains sound, well-developed, and intelligent ideas. Writing that is interesting and informative does not, unfortunately, flow naturally and spontaneously from your mind onto your paper or computer screen. It takes effort to gather the ideas, information, facts, anecdotes, and details you will need to interest and inform your readers.

To complete many of the essays assigned to you in college or university, you must do library research. In Lesson Two, you will learn how to find information in your college or university library efficiently. However, before you visit the library, there are five strategies that can help you begin to assemble information that will be useful as you work through a writing assignment. This lesson describes those five methods of acquiring insights and information.

ASK QUESTIONS

The first thing to do when an instructor gives you a writing assignment is to consider certain key questions that are related to the assigned topic and to the writing process. These questions get you started on your assignment, help you to determine what you already know about the topic, and establish what you still need to find out in order to complete your assignment successfully. Some of these key questions depend, to a certain extent, on the nature of your assignment. There are two questions, however, that you need to answer in order to help you get going on any writing assignment.

First, ask yourself as follows: *What does my reader want from me?* The answer to this question helps you discover what to say in your paper and helps you develop a **style** appropriate for your reader.

Style: the level of vocabulary, length, complexity, and structure of sentences that a writer uses.

Suppose, for example, your literature teacher asks you to write a paper in which you are to analyze one of the short stories on your reading list. If you take time to consider what your reader (in this case, your teacher) wants, you will probably reach several conclusions that you will be able to incorporate into your essay. First, you realize that your teacher has read the story and knows it well. This, in turn, should tell you that your teacher does not want you to retell the story. She wants you to discuss characters, themes, style, and point of view, but she does not want a detailed plot summary. By considering the needs and expectations of your reader, you begin to develop the content of your essay.

HELPFUL HINTS

Always know who your audience is and what your purpose is before you begin to write an essay.

You also begin to understand the style you should use when writing this paper. You are not writing to a friend; you are not writing for twelve-year-olds; you are writing for your English teacher. She expects a certain level of diction, a certain sophistication in sentence structure, and good grammar, spelling, and punctuation.

Suppose, on the other hand, she asks you to recommend a novel to your classmates and to explain to them why you think they would enjoy reading this book. Consider your readers now, your classmates. You cannot assume they have read the book, so, without giving away dramatic twists or surprise endings, you have to talk about the plot of the book in more detail than you would if the assignment were written for your teacher. Your style will also change. You are writing for a less specialized audience, so your words and sentence structure can be somewhat more informal.

Content: the ideas, information, and arguments in an essay.

Both the **content** and the style of writing change as the audience changes. Taking time to consider the needs and expectations of your readers is a vital part of the writing process.

ASSIGNMENT 1-1

Write an essay of approximately 500 words in which you describe "the typical reader" of one of the following:

- *Playboy* magazine
- *The English Teacher's Journal*
- *Sports Illustrated*
- *Ms.* magazine
- *The Star Trek Newsletter*
- *The Financial Post*

- *Chatelaine*
- *Cosmopolitan*

Select a magazine or a journal you are familiar with if you are unable to complete the assignment using one of the magazines listed above. Include, in your essay, such information as the gender, age, interests, and personality of the typical reader.

Rhetorical modes: the three subcategories into which written discourse can be divided.

There is a second question to ask when you are beginning a writing assignment: *What is my purpose in writing this essay?* Your answer to this question provides you with more information for your writing assignment. It should also help you discover the most effective organizational structure for your essay, because it will help you determine in which of the three **rhetorical modes**—informative, persuasive, or expressive—you will be working.

The Modes of Discourse

Informative Mode

Informative mode: subcategory of written discourse that presents factual information to the reader.

Most college and university essays are written in the **informative**, sometimes called the *expository*, mode. The purpose of the informative mode, as its name suggests, is to present information to readers. If your history professor assigns you an essay on the causes of the Russian Revolution, she is asking for an informative essay. If your literature teacher asks you to compare and contrast two poems, two characters, or the writing styles of two authors, he wants an informative essay. If your biology professor asks you to explain the process of photosynthesis, he also expects an informative essay.

Persuasive Mode

Persuasive mode: subcategory of written discourse that attempts to convince the reader the writer's argument is valid.

Some college and university essays are written in the **persuasive**, sometimes called the *argumentative*, mode. The purpose of this type of essay is to persuade the reader that the writer's views on a particular subject are the correct ones for the reader to adopt. Persuasive writing is more subjective than informative writing. Whereas the purpose of the informative essay is to give the reader information, the purpose of the persuasive essay is to convince the reader that the writer's opinion is correct. Informative essays indulge the reader; persuasive essays indulge the writer.

If your history professor asks you to explain the foreign policy of Elizabeth I and to discuss whether her foreign policy stabilized Europe or increased hostility and tension, he is asking for a persuasive essay. If your literature professor asks whether you think Hemingway or Fitzgerald has a more effective style for setting the scene of a story and describing a story's characters, she, too, is asking for a persuasive essay. And if your biology teacher asks whether you think the spotted owl is an endangered species, and wants you to support and justify your answer, she, too, wants a persuasive essay.

Expressive Mode

The third rhetorical mode is the **expressive**, also known as the *narrative* or *descriptive*, mode. Not many college and university assignments are written in the expressive mode, unless the course is one in creative writing. In expressive writing, the focus is at least as much on language and style as it is on the information you present. The purpose of expressive writing is not only to say something important, but to say it by exploiting the artistic dimension of language. Poems, short stories, and personal essays that contain a lot of description and anecdotes are examples of expressive writing. If the attention of informative writing is focused on the reader, and of persuasive writing on the writer, the focus of attention for expressive writing is the text itself.

Many of the essays you write as a college or a university student contain elements of two, or even all three, of the rhetorical modes. One mode usually dominates (most often the informative mode, but occasionally the persuasive, or rarely the expressive), but characteristics of the other two modes might be present. It is perfectly acceptable, sometimes even advantageous, to combine rhetorical modes in an essay.

It is important, then, to determine your purpose before you begin writing. This will establish what mode suits your purpose best. Here are some questions you can ask yourself:

- Why am I writing this essay?
- Do I want to educate my reader(s)?
- To inform them?
- To let them know how much I know about this topic?
- Do I want to persuade my reader(s)?
- To convince them that my views are the ones they themselves should adopt?

Before you begin an essay, write out the answers to these questions. Often, your answers give you a place to start. If you ever suffer from writer's block, you can usually push through it by freewriting, discussed next, and by taking the time to determine your purpose. Determining your purpose can help you get started and can also help you access ideas that you can use in the body of your essay.

ASSIGNMENT 1-2

Choose a topic of interest to you.
a. What writing assignment, related to that topic, could you design that would result in a predominantly informative essay?
b. What assignment would result in a predominantly persuasive essay?
c. What assignment would produce a predominantly expressive essay?

Purpose: the reason a writer is writing a particular piece for a particular audience.

By considering your reader and determining your **purpose**—in other words, by asking "why" and "for whom"—you begin to get ideas that you can use in your essay. You might get additional ideas by asking other questions, ones that begin with "what," "when," "where," and "how." Let's look at an example.

Suppose you were writing an essay describing a personal experience that changed or influenced you in a significant way. Questions to help generate information you could use in your essay would include these:

- For whom am I writing this essay?
- What is my purpose in writing this essay?
- What experience will I describe?
- When did it happen?
- Where did it happen?
- Why did it happen?
- Who were the people involved?
- What effect did this experience have on me?
- How did it change me?
- How did it make me grow as a person?
- How did it influence my values, attitudes, ideals?

Not all of the information that you would generate through such an exercise would necessarily find its way into your finished paper. Some would, and your ideas would be developed more thoroughly as a result.

ASSIGNMENT 1-3

Select one of the three essay topics you designed in Assignment 1-2 above. Make up a list of ten to fifteen questions that would help you generate ideas that you might be able to use in your essay.

FREEWRITE

Freewriting: brainstorming on paper to help a writer come up with ideas.

Another way of getting started and of generating ideas that you can use in a writing assignment is a strategy called **freewriting**.

Freewriting is brainstorming on paper. It is based on the premise that the physical act of writing stimulates thinking. To freewrite, simply begin with a subject you want to explore and write for a brief but uninterrupted period, usually about ten minutes. Write about anything that comes to mind, without concerning yourself with spelling, grammar, paragraphing, or any of the other conventional elements of good writing. Much of what you write will be of little value, but something should emerge from a freewriting session that you can eventually incorporate into your assignment.

The author of this example of freewriting was asked to write an essay on what influence television had upon his life:

> I have to write an essay on how television influences my life. Does it have a positive influence or a negative influence on me. I like watching comedies. Seinfeld was hilarious the other night. Jerry had to wear this ridiculous shirt during a tv interview with Bryant Gumbel because he and Elaine were out for dinner with Kramer's girlfriend who talked so quietly no one could hear her. They were tired or too polite to tell her to speak louder they pretty much agreed to everything she said, and after dinner Kramer told Jerry how pleased he was that he had agreed to appear on national television in a shirt designed by Kramer's girl. The George plot was about a talent scout discovering what beautiful hands George has and how he could make a fortune as a hand model. He gets one job, is well paid, thinks he will be able to move away from his parents again, but, of course, he burns his hands at the end of the show. TV makes us laugh and laughter reduces stress. I think tv has a good effect on me. It is also informative. I do enjoy wathching news and social issue type programs, and I think these keep me informed. I have probably been wathcing too much lately though. May be its effective my homework time. Some programs I could do without. I watch too much sports. A football game is a three hour commitment. Maybe I'll do a pro and con essay. Benefits of tv verses disadvantages. That might make it too long. Most people will be knocking tv. Maybe I'll write just a pro essay. That will be easier too. TV is good as long as you don't watch too much. That's a thesis probably, but maybe too self-evident. Maybe I want something a little more original.

Looping: second round of freewriting, focusing on key point emerging from original freewriting.

In a refinement of freewriting, called **looping**, you circle (loop) the useful information that your freewriting generated and, using that information as your focal point, freewrite again. Looping resulted in this refinement of the above example of freewriting:

> ok something more original. Maybe I could go with advantages and argue that the more tv you watch the more informed you will be. I don't want to alienate my readers though by going overboard on anything. There's the violence issue too. A lot of people will be knocking television for being too violent. I should mention that even if I go with the benefits of moderate tv watching. I will need three points:
>
> 1.   tv entertains us, makes us laugh and this reduces stress, making us healthier and better able to function in other tasks. All work and no play...
>
> 2.   tv informs. There are even all news channels now. There are dozens of talk shows some of the National Enquirer variety but still some that interview important leaders, entertainers, artists, etc. Those can be informative.
>
> 3.   i could say something about children's tv but that's not quite on topic. again, some tv is good for kids but some parents use it as an electronic baby sitter. i need a third point. About three minutes to go in this exercise. Maybe after

HELPFUL HINTS

Writer's block can usually be treated with freewriting.

I write about the first two a third will emerge miraculously. Entertains, informs...what about something about humanizing us, making us wiser, better citizens of a democracy..all that. What about interactive tv? What about a point about the future of tv. How it's far from perfect now but will improve as new uses are found for it.

Looping and freewriting can be repeated until you feel you have found those extra details, those examples, those comparisons, contrasts, causes, and effects that are going to develop your ideas thoroughly and satisfy the needs and demands of your readers.

ASSIGNMENT 1-4

Try freewriting to access ideas for an essay that has been assigned to you or that you are currently working on. Select a topic of interest to you if one has not been assigned. Bring the results of the freewriting or questioning to class, and be prepared to discuss the success, or lack thereof, of the method you used.

KEEP A JOURNAL

Journal: daily written inventory of a writer's ideas, thoughts, questions, observations.

You can improve the content of your written work by keeping a **journal**. A journal is a daily account (the word comes from the French word *jour*, meaning "day") of those activities and thoughts that you think will be worth rereading and reflecting upon in the future. If you have ever had a great idea or insight, meant to write it down but didn't, and then realized a few days later that you have forgotten it, you should know the value of a journal. The palest ink, goes an old Chinese proverb, is better than the most retentive memory.

Your English teacher might ask you to write about a personal experience or to express your opinion on a current social issue. In this case, a journal really comes in handy. Your personal experiences and your intellectual and emotional responses to those experiences should be recorded in your journal. You might be able to use that material in at least one, or perhaps more, of your assignments.

You might also, of course, record your reactions to a poem from your literature class, to a marketing strategy from a business class, or to a historical incident from a history class. This work could pay dividends when you have an assignment to complete later in the term. Many teachers recommend that their students keep an IQ Journal in which ideas (I) and questions (Q) are recorded.

Keep a journal and your writing will improve because of the daily practice you are getting. In your journal you will find insights and ideas that you should be able to use in future writing assignments.

ASSIGNMENT 1-5

Today, begin to keep a journal in which you record daily observations, thoughts, and feelings that you think are significant enough to put into writing. Try to write in your journal each day. Remember to consult early journal entries every once in a while, especially for observations related to your classes.

MAKE UP ANALOGIES

Analogy: a comparison a writer makes with the subject of her essay to develop ideas to be used in that essay.

A fourth method of discovering what you already know about a topic but may not be aware of is to draw an **analogy** comparing your subject with something else. If there is an abstract dimension to your topic, an analogy is especially useful because it can simplify or make concrete a vague or abstract term or concept.

Try, for example, to complete this sentence: Writing an essay is like _____. Writing an essay, you might decide, is like building a house. A house needs a foundation, which might be the equivalent of the main idea of an essay. The frame of the house might correspond to the outline of an essay. A builder adds wood and bricks and mortar to the frame to build a house; a writer adds words and sentences to an outline to form an essay.

But wait. A writer might start to write and discover her main idea in the process; an outline might emerge only after some writing has been done. A builder could not start to build a house, then lay the foundation and build the frame. In reality, writing an essay is nothing like building a house. Writing an essay is rarely an orderly or step-by-step process. A writer often starts to write, abandons what he has written, starts all over, stops again, makes up an outline, changes his topic, starts all over again, and continues in a similar manner until the paper is complete. A builder working in this way would soon be out of business. Building a house is a careful, step-by-step process. Writing is much more of a **recursive process**. The analogy has broken down but, in the process of constructing it, you have discovered a useful insight into the process of essay writing.

Recursive process: method of writing whereby the writer refines, reshapes, and revises his topic, structure, style, and content during and throughout the entire writing process.

ASSIGNMENT 1-6

1. Fill in the blanks of these sentences to compose analogies:

   a. Reading books by _____ is like _____.
   b. Listening to _____ sing is like _____.
   c. Meeting your fiance's parents for the first time is like _____.
   d. Spending an hour in my _____ class is like _____.

2. Create five analogies of your own.

TALK IT OVER

Just as freewriting about a subject gives you insight into that subject, so too does talking about it. Composition teachers often divide their students into small groups and encourage them to talk about essays they are working on. If a common topic is assigned, the teacher might get a class discussion going. Small group and class discussions are valuable prewriting exercises, in that they allow students to benefit from the knowledge of their peers.

Also, other friends and family members might have interesting and useful ideas related to the subject of your essay. Engage them in conversation; tell them about the assignment; ask them if they have any ideas about the topic, or any books or articles they can recommend.

Be aware, as well, that most teachers do not mind if you come to see them during their office hours to discuss the form and content of your paper. Indeed, some teachers insist on at least some one-to-one conferencing time, especially while you are in the process of writing a major paper.

ASSIGNMENT 1-7

There are always, on college and university campuses, controversial issues related to campus politics and internal policies: limited parking, activity fees, the high costs of texts, walk-safe programs, controversial speakers, etc. Ask another student or a faculty member what he or she thinks about one such issue. Describe, in a single paragraph, what you learned about the issue by discussing it with this person.

Draft: version of an essay before the essay is revised and submitted for grading.

You can use the idea-getting strategies described in this lesson at any stage of work on an essay or a report. These strategies will certainly help you get started, but you can also use them after you have completed a **draft** and are beginning to revise your work. Perhaps you will find it effective to profile your reader when you are revising a draft in order to give focus to the changes in content and style that you might decide to make. Perhaps you will want to reassess your purpose after your first draft has been completed. Perhaps you will start to write quickly and confidently, then stall, and have to use some freewriting to get going again. A discussion with a peer or a teacher might give you additional ideas to use in your paper.

The strategies described in this lesson will help you achieve a writing process that is flexible enough to take advantage of any opportunity to make your work more interesting and informative. And that is a good place to start!

SUMMARY

- Before you begin to write, compose and answer pointed, relevant questions about your topic.

- Use freewriting. It can help you get started, and it can also pick you up and carry you along if you stumble on the way.

- Try to write every day. Keep a journal or a diary. The information you store there might come in handy some time.

- To discover hidden, subtle dimensions to the subject of your essay, compare it with something quite different.

- Ask your friends and family members whether they have any ideas or insights that might help you get ideas for a paper you are working on.

QUESTIONS FOR STUDY AND DISCUSSION

1. What are the benefits of asking "the reporter's questions"—who, why, when, what, where, how—as a prewriting exercise?

2. Define the terms "freewriting" and "looping." Explain why you might try freewriting and looping and what benefits they provide.

3. Define the three rhetorical modes and give an example of an essay topic that would be written in each mode.

4. Under what circumstances might more than one rhetorical mode be combined in a single essay?

5. List three benefits of keeping a journal.

6. How might you generate a discussion with a friend or family member to help you get some information for an essay you are working on?

SUPPLEMENTARY EXERCISES

1. Compose a list of questions that would help you discover and develop ideas that could be used in the following:

   a. Essay about a person who has influenced you

   _____

   _____

   _____

   b. Review of a novel you have read in the last year

   _____

   _____

   _____

   c. Review of a work of nonfiction you have read in the last year

   _____

   _____

   _____

   d. Letter to a potential employer for whom you would like to work

   _____

   _____

   _____

   e. Biology lab report

   _____

   _____

   _____

f. Review of a restaurant where you have eaten recently

_____

_____

_____

g. Letter to your bank manager explaining why you cannot make your car payment this month

_____

_____

_____

2. Identify the dominant rhetorical mode of the following essay topics. Place an "I" in the blank to indicate informative mode, a "P" to indicate persuasive mode, and an "E" to indicate expressive mode.

a. Describe how the Trudeau government responded to the FLQ Crisis.

_____

b. Do you think the Trudeau government's response to the FLQ Crisis was reasonable, too soft, or unnecessarily harsh? Support your answer.

_____

c. Compare and contrast the personalities and political ideologies of Marx and Engels.

_____

d. The fur traders of New France exploited the Native population. Discuss.

_____

e. Where do you go to "get away from it all" and think about issues important to you? Describe the landscape and the surroundings of your "getaway" spot.

_____

f. Compare and contrast cubism and post-impressionism.

_____

g. Describe and explain the effects on a child's personality of three methods of parenting.

_____

h. Was Dutch colonialism beneficial to Indonesians?

_____

i. Describe three characteristics often found within dysfunctional families.

_____

j. Windows '95 is not any better than the Mac software developed in the late 80s. Discuss.

_____

3. Practise your freewriting using the following topics. Devote five to ten minutes to each topic.

   a. Macdonald's restaurants

   _____

   _____

   _____

   _____

   _____

   b. School uniforms

   _____

   _____

   _____

   _____

   _____

   c. Strikes by professional athletes

   _____

   _____

   _____

   _____

   _____

   d. Sexual harassment

   _____

   _____

   _____

   _____

   _____

   e. Chemistry professors

   _____

   _____

   _____

   _____

   _____

4. Complete the following journal entries:

   a. I don't know why _____ is such a popular book.

   b. I think _____ is going to turn out to be my favourite course this semester.

   c. My roommate is beginning to get on my nerves.

d. I had a long talk with my mother today.

e. Either I get a part-time job or a student loan.

5. Rewrite your journal entries in Question 4 for any one of the readers listed below. Select different readers for each entry.

   a. Your mother

   b. Your English teacher

   c. A close friend

   d. A counsellor

   e. Your father

6. Develop the following analogies:

   a. My dog is like _____

   b. My desk is like _____

   c. My car is like _____

   d. My study habits are _____

   e. My high-school English teacher was _____

Lesson Two

Doing Research

Where Knowledge Is Stored

Class Notes and Textbooks
Books
Periodicals

Databases
The Internet
Library Services

Lesson One, in part, discussed ways of accessing information you already possess but may not be aware of. But these methods have limitations—you can't "get at" what you don't know, no matter how much freewriting you do or how profound your journal entries are.

Usually, some of the information you need to complete a writing assignment adequately has to come from **secondary sources**. Sometimes you already know about the assigned topic, but more often than not a lot of research is necessary to complete an assignment successfully. Even a personal narrative essay about, say, your trip to Mexico, can benefit from some research. Perhaps you did not learn on your trip to Mexico the total population figure for the country, or the form of government in power, or the annual per capita income, but it is possible that this information would help you write a more effective essay. This, and of course volumes and volumes of other information, is available at a library.

CLASS NOTES AND TEXTBOOKS

The library is not the place to begin your research. When an essay or a report has been assigned, your research should start with a careful review of the lecture notes and textbook chapters relevant to your topic. Some of the information you need should be available there. Lecture notes and texts should at least tell you who the authorities are in the field about which you are writing, so that when you go to the library, you will have a name to look up in the card catalogue or computer. Most textbooks include, at the end of each chapter or at the end of the book, lists of sources—called **bibliographies**, **references**, or *works cited*—which tell you where you can find more information.

Secondary sources: books, journals, magazines, and databases that contain information you might use in a research paper.

HELPFUL HINTS

Check your textbooks and reference books for source lists.

Bibliographies: a list at the end of an essay of all sources a writer has consulted.

References: a list at the end of an essay of all sources a writer has cited within an essay.

Read your course outlines carefully as well. Teachers often include, in their course outlines, a supplementary reading list, which might contain sources that you could use for a research paper.

BOOKS

Reference book: books such as encyclopedias or dictionaries that contain general information about a wide variety of topics.

If you need an overview of the assigned topic, consult a **reference book**. Reference books are located in a special section of the library, usually on the main floor, and include encyclopedias, biographical dictionaries, yearbooks, and almanacs.

A good place to begin searching for information is in a general encyclopedia, such as *The New Encyclopaedia Britannica*. This encyclopedia has a *Propaedia* that lists all of the subjects covered. It also has a *Micropaedia*, a twelve-volume set of books containing brief articles on subjects listed in the *Propaedia*. The *Macropaedia* is a nineteen-volume series containing detailed discussions of key topics briefly discussed in the *Micropaedia*. In the *Micropaedia*, for example, the article on William Shakespeare takes up about one-and-a-half columns on a three-column page. In the *Macropaedia*, the entry for Shakespeare is twenty pages long.

To find the reference book that will provide you with the information you require, consult Eugene P. Sheehy's *Guide to Reference Books*, which should be at the reference desk of your library.

ASSIGNMENT 2-1

List five reference books that your library owns that you think could be useful to you as a student. Select reference books related to your major or program of study. Explain why you think each book could be useful. How can these reference books help you pursue your education and, ultimately, your career?

Card catalogue: a list of all books contained in a library.

Since reference books cannot be taken out of the library and because they might not contain the information you need, you should start by looking in the **card catalogue** or in a computer data bank. Either of these will provide you with a list of the books, held by or available through your library, that are of use to you. The card catalogue or computer also provides the book's call number so you can find the book in the "stacks," the rooms where the books are shelved. The call number of the Library of Congress system, which most colleges and universities use, consists of two letters followed by a number, possibly followed by another letter and another number. The call number of this book, *Lessons in Essay Writing*, for example, is PE1471.S65 1997.

The public library, which also contains information useful to you, probably uses the Dewey Decimal System. This is a system of numbering used to classify books by subject. The sciences, for example, are numbered in the 500s, while history is numbered in the 900s. Books about Canadian history are numbered 971. The three numbers are followed by a decimal point, then by more numbers that pinpoint the exact location of the book in the stacks. A book about the history of

British Columbia, for example, might be numbered 971.1134. The last three letters of the author's name follow the number. The call number of *Lessons in Essay Writing* under the DDS is 808′.042.

If you know the author and the title of a book that you want to use, look up the author's name or the book title in the card catalogue or type the author's name or book title into the computer in order to find the book's call number. Instructions for using the computer to access the information you need should be posted close to the terminal you are using. Encyclopedia articles often end with bibliographies that list the books that have been consulted by the encyclopedia editors; you might start your card catalogue or **on-line search** by checking for some of these books.

If you do not know the name of any authors who have written books about the subject you are researching, look up the name of your subject in the card catalogue or on screen. The librarian can help you find key words related to your topic, which will help lead you to useful books.

On-line search: a search, done on a computer, for research material.

ASSIGNMENT 2-2

Look up information on a subject of interest to you in a reference book that includes bibliographies for its entries. Then look up and record the call number of one of the books mentioned in the bibliography. Find the book in the stacks. Read the first chapter of that book and write a brief (a hundred words or so) summary of its contents.

PERIODICALS

Periodicals include popular magazines, specialized magazines, and academic journals that are published on a regular basis: weekly, monthly, bimonthly, quarterly, or yearly. Articles in periodicals can be very useful sources of information; indeed, if your essay is on a topic that requires current knowledge in a fast-changing field, they are essential. The information in some fields is nearly obsolete by the time a book is published. Periodicals are published more frequently and contain more up-to-date information.

Your library has a catalogue that lists the titles of periodicals it carries, the issues it owns, and where they are located in the library. If you know which issue of a journal you want, you can check the periodical holdings catalogue to see whether your library owns it. The catalogue listing tells you where the periodical is located and whether or not the contents of the periodical are available on **microfilm**.

If you need help finding specific articles on your topic, you should consult a **periodical index**—a list of articles in magazines, newspapers, or journals—on particular areas of interest. Periodical indexes are published monthly, quarterly, or annually and are available in print and often electronically.

Periodicals: weekly, monthly, bimonthly, or quarterly publications including popular magazines, specialized magazines, and academic journals.

Microfilm: information such as back issues of magazines and newspapers stored on spools of film.

Periodical index: long alphabetical list in print or electronic form of articles available in magazines and journals.

The Reader's Guide to Periodical Literature, for example, lists by author and subject all of the articles that are published in more than 150 popular magazines. If you were writing an essay about choosing a good backpack, for example, you would find, in the August '94 issue alone, these three relevant articles ("v" stands for "volume"; "il" for "illustrated"):

No stress backpacking. il *Outdoor Life* v193 p86 F '94

Picking a pack. T.E. Huggler. il *Outdoor Life* v193 p16+ Mr '94

Today designers are adding a glamorous edge to the once purely practical backpack—with everything from exotic skins to intricate beading. C.P. Price. il *Vogue* v184 p440 Mr '94

HELPFUL HINTS

Use periodicals and computer networks for topics that require the most up-to-date information.

Other periodical indexes that list articles of interest to the general public include *Magazine Index* and *The New York Times Index*.

General periodical indexes are not always useful to college students, who usually write essays related to specific academic disciplines. Fortunately, specialized indexes are published for virtually every academic discipline as well. Often they list not only journal articles but also books that have been published in the field they are targeting. Educators can consult *The Education Index*; English teachers can check the *CCCC Bibliography of Composition and Rhetoric*; businesspeople have the *Business Periodicals Index*; engineers have the *Engineering Index*; social scientists, musicians, artists, and so on can consult specialized periodical indexes. To find the periodical index that is most useful for your purposes, ask your college librarian to assist you, and consult Sheehy's *Guide to Reference Books*.

ASSIGNMENT 2-3

Name two periodical indexes that your library subscribes to that you think will be useful to you in the next few years. In one paragraph, explain why you think they will be useful to you. Are these indexes available electronically or in print form only? If they are available on database, is a summary of the article provided?

DATABASES

Database: information stored on a computer or computer system or network.

You can also gather the research materials you need by checking a **database**, an electronic index accessed through a computer. Like a periodical index, a database lists books and articles written on an innumerable variety of topics. Some databases also provide summaries of the books and articles, so the researcher can check whether the material is relevant before taking the time to search for the entire text. There are two types of databases: computer services, which offer information germane to a specific field, and networks, which consist of many computer services linked together, and which always seem to be replacing or at least incorporating computer services.

The Educational Resources Information Center, ERIC for short, is an example of a computer service. Suppose you want information about the punctuation skills of college students. If you tap into this well-known database, you will find twenty-six articles in thirteen different journals on this subject. There is, for example, an article on the apostrophe in the Fall 1988 issue of *The Journal of Basic Writing*. In the September 1972 issue of *The English Journal*, there is an article about teaching the use of the comma and the semicolon. The May 1972 issue of *College Composition and Communication* also has an article on the use of the comma.

THE INTERNET

Internet or 'Net: 50,000 computer databases linked together.

The **Internet** is an example of a computer network. It consists of some 50,000 computer services in about ninety countries joined together. The Internet is widely used in business and industry to promote sales and communicate with customers. It has also become an important research tool. Some Internet advocates claim that by the turn of the century 80 percent of the world's knowledge will be stored on the 'Net. All research might eventually be done via computer.

HELPFUL HINTS

Use reliable sources written by experts in the field.

There is also a lot of useless information on the Internet, because anyone who knows how to use the system can publish anything on it. You must always look for reliable sources written by experts in the field when you are doing research, but you must take extra care that information you take from the Internet is valid and reliable.

Until recently, the Internet was the preserve of computer experts. Now, more and more user-friendly software is being produced that makes the 'Net available to anyone with access to a computer that can tap into the system, as most library computers can do. Software programs known as "spiders" are currently being developed to help researchers sift, track, and retrieve the best information available.

HELPFUL HINTS

Do not get tangled in the Internet. Retrieve the information you need and get on with your essay.

It is essential that you have a specific, focused topic before you begin a database search. You might need help from your librarian, and you do not want to waste her time by arriving with only a vague idea of the topic of your essay. The librarian needs key words or descriptors to type into the computer, another reason why a focused topic is essential. If your topic is too broad, you will likely be overwhelmed by the number of sources the database will give you. Moreover, database searches can cost you a lot of money; it pays to know exactly what you are trying to find.

Because databases have such vast stores of information, it is impossible to use all of the information on your topic that is stored on the database you choose. Combine the database information with the information available to you in regular texts, reference books, and periodicals and you might begin to suffer from that modern affliction known as "information overload." Relax: you can't read everything about your topic; you have to be selective. Try to get the best sources available, but limit yourself to those you can realistically read and understand in the time you have to complete your assignment. You can write a better essay if you know a few sources thoroughly than if you know many sources superficially.

ASSIGNMENT 2-4

Select a subject of interest to you, perhaps a subject related to an assignment. Find two articles about that subject on a computer service or network. In one or two paragraphs, explain the process you went through to find this information.

LIBRARY SERVICES

One of the main duties of college and university librarians is to orient students to the services the library offers. Most libraries offer tours and orientation sessions. Your composition instructor might arrange such a tour for your entire class. If he does not, you are well advised to sign up for the tour yourself.

Another important duty of librarians is to help students with their research projects. You should not hesitate to ask your librarian for help. He or she can help you uncover valuable research materials for your writing assignments—information you might not otherwise have known was available.

ASSIGNMENT 2-5

Select a subject of interest to you. In an essay of approximately 500 words, describe and explain the process you would go through to collect information on that subject.

SUMMARY

- Begin your research after you have exhausted the methods for getting ideas covered in Lesson One (ask questions, freewrite, keep a journal, make up analogies, talk it over).

- Review your lecture notes and relevant portions of your textbooks. These sources will contain useful information for many writing assignments.

- For an overview of a topic, consult a reference book such as an encyclopedia. Consult Sheehy's *Guide to Reference Books*.

- A call number identifies the location of a book in the stacks. Find a book's call number in the card catalogue.

- Consult periodical indexes, either in print or electronic form. These indexes are essential to research topics that require the most up-to-date information.

- Find out which computer services and networks can be accessed from your library. Learn how to use them.

QUESTIONS FOR STUDY AND DISCUSSION

1. Where can you look for bibliographies that list sources you might be able to use for a writing assignment?
2. What is a call number? How can you find a call number?
3. When might you use a periodical index?
4. What are the differences between reference books and the books you will find in the stacks?
5. What exactly does a librarian do?
6. What is the difference between a computer service and a computer network?
7. What are the advantages and disadvantages of using the Internet as a research tool?

SUPPLEMENTARY EXERCISES

1. Provide the call numbers, according to your college or university library's card catalogue, for the following books:
   a. *The Canadian Encyclopedia*, published in Edmonton by Hurtig _____
   b. *The Apprenticeship of Duddy Kravitz* by Mordecai Richler _____
   c. *The Wealthy Barber* by David Chilton _____
   d. *Revolution from Within* by Gloria Steinem _____
   e. *The Stone Diaries* by Carol Shields _____
   f. *Post-Capitalist Society* by Peter Drucker _____
   g. *The Oxford English Dictionary* _____
   h. *Romeo and Juliet* by William Shakespeare _____
   i. *Mary, Queen of Scots* by Antonia Fraser _____
   j. *Mary, Queen of Scotland and Isle* by Margaret George _____
   k. *The Wealth of Nations* by Adam Smith. _____
   l. *Handbook of Modern Nursing* _____
   m. *Dictionary of the Bible* _____
   n. *International Television Almanac* _____
2. Provide the call numbers, according to your college or university library's card catalogue, for the following magazines:
   a. *Maclean's* _____
   b. *Sports Illustrated* _____
   c. *Runner's World* _____

     d. *Scientific American* _____

     e. *Psychology Today* _____

     f. *Redbook* _____

     g. *Computer World* _____

     h. *Atlantic Monthly* _____

     i. *Chatelaine* _____

     j. *National Geographic* _____

3. Provide the call numbers, according to your college or university library's card catalogue, for the following journals:

     a. *New England Journal of Medicine* _____

     b. *Harvard Business Review* _____

     c. *Modern Fiction Studies* _____

     d. *Cinema Journal* _____

     e. *Canadian Journal of Public Health* _____

     f. *Corrections Today* _____

     g. *Restaurant Business* _____

     h. *Journal of Psychology* _____

     i. *Critical Inquiry* _____

     j. *Journal of Management* _____

4. Put a checkmark beside the computerized indexes in the following list to which your college or university library has access:

     a. ABI/Inform _____

     b. Newsbank _____

     c. ERIC _____

     d. PsychLit _____

     e. Social Sciences Citation Index _____

     f. SciTech Reference Plus _____

     g. PAIS _____

     h. InfoTrac _____

     i. MLA International Bibliography _____

     j. MEDLINE _____

5. Try to find, in your college or university library, the following information:

     a. The front-page headline in *The Globe and Mail* or *The New York Times* on the day you were born

     _____

     b. The title of a book about growing mushrooms

     _____

c. An article about space travel from a magazine that is at least five years old

    _____

d. A biographical dictionary that includes an entry on Stephen Hawking

    _____

e. A recipe from a newspaper that is at least five years old

    _____

Citing Sources, MLA Method

Acknowledge All of Your Sources

Books
Journal Articles
Magazine Articles
Encyclopedias

Literary Works
Videotapes
The Internet
Other Sources

If you have acquired information from books, journals, magazines, or videotapes to use in a writing assignment, you must acknowledge the source of that information. If you don't acknowledge sources properly, you could be guilty of **plagiarism**, a serious offence at colleges and universities. You must acknowledge not only direct quotes but also ideas you have borrowed from a secondary source. The **acknowledgement** is usually given in parentheses just after the quote or the idea you are using. At the end of the essay, more information about the source is provided in a list of references or works cited. What actually appears in parentheses and in the source list depends upon the citation method your professor requests.

The **MLA (Modern Language Association)** and **APA (American Psychological Association)** methods are two of the most commonly used systems for acknowledging ideas and information in written work. In this lesson, the MLA method for acknowledging secondary sources is explained. Lesson Four outlines the APA method.

BOOKS

If you are using the MLA method, your citation will come after you have quoted from or used an idea from a secondary source. You must give the author's name and the page number of the author's work on which the quote or idea appears. Here is an example of a book used as a secondary source and cited using the MLA method:

Plagiarism: failure to give credit to the author of a quote or idea, implying instead that quote or idea is your own original work.

Acknowledgement: credit given to the author of a quote or idea you have used in your essay.

MLA method: a method designed by an association of English educators of giving credit to original authors of quotes and ideas used in a research paper.

APA method: a method designed by an association of psychologists of giving credit to original authors of quotes and ideas used in a research paper.

As a group, these studies indicated rather clearly that engaging young writers actively in the use of criteria, applied to their own or to others' writing, results not only in more effective revisions but in superior first drafts (Hillocks 160).

HELPFUL HINTS

Not included in MLA parenthetical citation: (1) date of publication; (2) abbreviation for page number.

The parenthetical citation above tells us that the information in the passage comes from page 160 of a book or article written by Hillocks. Note that there is no comma between the name and the page number and no abbreviation for the word "page." Including commas and abbreviations is a very common error students make when using the MLA system.

If you have already mentioned the author's name, only the page number need appear:

Hillocks claims that, as a group, these studies indicated rather clearly that engaging young writers actively in the use of criteria, applied to their own or to others' writing, results not only in more effective revisions but in superior first drafts (160).

At the end of the essay, the complete information about the source is provided in a list called **Works Cited**, arranged alphabetically by the authors' last names:

Works Cited: the MLA-method list of sources used by a writer and mentioned in the text of his or her essay.

Hillocks, George, Jr. <u>Research in Written Composition: New Directions for Teaching</u>. Urbana Illinois: ERIC Clearinghouse on Reading and Communication Skills, 1986.

Note the punctuation, the indentation, and the use of underlining. Although, in published work, such as this text, italic type is always used to indicate the name of a title, in your essays underlining can be used for the same purpose (as shown in all the examples in this text). Italics can be used instead of underlining if your word processor can change type styles. If you decide to list not only the works you cite in your essay but all the works you consulted while researching the essay, that list is called "Works Consulted."

ASSIGNMENT 3-1

1. The following excerpt from a research paper contains a quote from page 303 of Robert Gittings's book, *John Keats,* published in 1968 in Boston by Little, Brown, and Company. Provide, in MLA format, a parenthetical citation and a Works Cited entry for the excerpt.

   Gittings has this to say about the sources of "La Belle Dame Sans Merci":

   Wordsworth for the cadence of the poem, Coleridge for its nightmare quality, Spencer for its medieval setting, Burton for the melancholy of its hero, all contribute to, but none account for the intensity and underlying depth of a poem which brought Keats's darkest and most fundamental experiences to the surface.

2. The following excerpt from a research paper contains a quote from page 97 of the second edition of Eliot Wasserman's book *The Steroid Conspiracy*, published in 1993 by Paw Books of Vancouver. Provide, in MLA format, a parenthetical citation and a Works Cited entry for the excerpt.

> As more and more athletes from what was once East Germany come forward with their confessions, the Olympic Committee "will be under increased pressure to review world records in several events."

JOURNAL ARTICLES

The information needed to complete a writing assignment successfully often comes from scholarly or academic journals. The type of parenthetical citation used for such journals is the same as that used for a book. But the entry in the source list (Works Cited) is quite different. Here is an excerpt from an essay in which an idea borrowed from an article in an academic journal is acknowledged using the MLA method.

> Special interest groups distort, sometimes ignore, the truth to advance their own political ends. Walker has shown how both pro-environment groups and lobbyists who represent the forest industry have taken out of context sections of the same government report in order to support action each group has taken (413).

Here is how this source would be acknowledged in the list of Works Cited at the end of the essay:

> Walker, Morris. "The War Against Truth: How Political Lobby Groups Function." North American Journal of Media and Communication 87 (1994): 411-428.

The number 87 refers to the volume number, found on the cover of the journal. The numbers 411-428 refer to the page numbers on which the article appears.

Pagination: the numbering of each page of a written document.

Journals (like the one cited above) tend to be **paginated** continuously by calendar year. If a year's first issue ended on page 112, the next issue would begin on page 113. The first issue of that journal in the following year would begin back on page 1.

HELPFUL HINTS

You will need to know if the journals you use are paginated by issue or by volume.

Some journals are paginated by issue: each issue begins on page 1. When you cite journals that always begin on page 1, you need to include the issue number of that journal along with the volume number. If the journal cited above, *North American Journal of Media and Communication*, were paginated by each issue, the Works Cited entry would be as follows:

> Walker, Morris. "The War Against Truth: How Political Lobby Groups Function." North American Journal of Media and Communication 87.3 (1994):11-28.

Note that the issue number, 3, is inserted after the volume number and preceded by a period.

ASSIGNMENT 3-2

1. The following excerpt from a research paper contains a quotation from an article by Min-Zhan Lu, published in the journal *College English*, volume 54, issue 8, 1992. The article is called "Conflict and Struggle: The Enemies or Preconditions of Basic Writing." *College English* uses continuous pagination, so the first page in the issue used here is page 887. Lu's article begins on page 887 and ends on page 913. The quote in the excerpt is on page 910. Provide, in MLA format, the parenthetical citation and the Works Cited entry for the excerpt:

   > Lu also believes that more research "which critiques portrayals of Basic Writers as belonging to an abnormal-traumatized or underdeveloped state" is urgently needed.

2. The following excerpt from a research paper contains information from page 18 of an article by Samual Kono published in the *Journal of the World Health Society*, volume 2, issue 2, 1991. The article is called "AIDS in Africa." The journal is paginated by issue. The article begins on page 3 and ends on page 21. Provide, in MLA format, the parenthetical citation and the Works Cited entry for the following excerpt from a research paper:

   > Authorities in most African countries are reluctant to reveal accurate information, but there can be little doubt the infection rate is now higher than in any other continent.

MAGAZINE ARTICLES

Here is an excerpt, using the MLA citation method, from an essay that has borrowed information from a magazine published each month:

> Trevor King, IBEX's capable young CEO, claims that the notebook computer his company is producing will be even smaller than its Apple counterpart (Ashton 14).

Here is how this source would be acknowledged in the Works Cited section of the essay:

> Ashton, Lisa. "Upstart IBEX Ready to Challenge Apple and IBM." <u>Computer World</u> May 1994: 96-103.

ASSIGNMENT 3-3

The information in the following excerpt from a research paper comes from an article called "Dodger Blues" written by Ron Fimrite. The article appears in the September 28, 1992, issue of *Sports Illustrated*. The article begins on page 18 and ends on page 21. The information in the above excerpt appears on page 20. Provide, in MLA format, the correct parenthetical citation and Works Cited entry for this excerpt:

Davis and Strawberry wanted to be teammates ever since they played ball together as children on the playgrounds of Los Angeles.

ENCYCLOPEDIAS

Here is an excerpt from an essay that acknowledges information, using the MLA method, taken from an encyclopedia:

> In the last twenty years, however, the figure has been almost entirely removed from figure skating. Now it is athletic ability, especially the ability to jump, which judges look for and they are unlikely to be satisfied with anything less than triple jumps ("Figure Skating").

Here is how this source would be cited in the Works Cited list:

> "Figure Skating." <u>The Encyclopedia of Sport</u>. 1994 ed.

HELPFUL HINTS

Unsigned articles are alphabetized by title.

Because this article is unsigned, it would be alphabetized by its title. Some encyclopedias do include authors' names, and if the article were signed, the author's name and the page number would be in the parenthetical citation and would precede the title in the Works Cited list.

ASSIGNMENT 3-4

Provide the correct parenthetical citation and Works Cited entry in the MLA method for the following essay excerpt:

> The <u>Encyclopaedia of Religion and Ethics</u> defines confirmation as "an act, closely connected with baptism, in which prayer for the Holy Spirit is joined with some ceremony, through which the gift of the Spirit is believed to be conferred."

The information comes from The *Encyclopaedia of Religion and Ethics*, volume 4, page 1. The encyclopedia is edited by James Hastings and was published in New York in 1971 by Scribners.

LITERARY WORKS

Anthologized: refers to a poem, story, or essay that is printed in an "anthology," a book that contains related works.

In the essays you write in your literature classes, you almost always quote passages from poems, stories, and/or plays to support the points you are making. Essays about literature use the MLA method of parenthetical citation. But literary works are not cited like other secondary sources because they are often published in many editions or are **anthologized** in many different books. Here is a summary of how you should cite quotations from poem, stories, and plays.

Poems

If you quote from a poem, you need only cite the line numbers you have quoted:

> Again, in Sonnet 18, Shakespeare suggests that his own work will guarantee immortality to his beloved friend:
>
> > So long as man can breathe or eyes can see,
> > So long lives this, and this gives life to thee.
> > (13-14)

This poem is printed in so many different anthologies that a person reading the essay in which the quote appears can go to any number of sources to check the accuracy of the quote or to see the whole text of the poem. This, primarily, is why it is necessary to include only line numbers in the parenthetical citation.

You must, however, include in your list of Works Cited the bibliographical information for the anthology that was your source for the poem. The citation for the Shakespearean sonnet quoted above would be as follows:

> Shakespeare, William. "Sonnet 18." <u>Elements of Literature: Fiction, Poetry, Drama</u>. Ed. Robert Scholes et al. Toronto: Oxford University Press, 1990. 441.

Note the Latin abbreviation, et al., that follows the name of the editor, Robert Scholes. The anthology *Elements of Literature* has four editors. If a book has more than three authors or editors, only the first name listed on the book's title page is necessary in the citation, followed by et al. Et al. is the Latin abbreviation for "and others." The number 441 following the date of publication refers to the page number in the anthology on which "Sonnet 18" can be found.

If the poem you have quoted from is very long and is divided into books, as the epic poems of Homer and Milton are, include in your citation the book number, followed by a period, followed by the line numbers. For example:

> Satan, at last, sees the planet upon which he will be begin to extract his revenge:
>
> > And, fast by, hanging in a golden chain,
> > This pendant world, in bigness as a star
> > Of smallest magnitude close by the moon.
> > (2. 1051-1053)

In the list of Works Cited, this source would be cited as follows:

> Milton, John. "Paradise Lost." <u>The Norton Anthology of English Literature</u>. 6th ed. 2 vols. Ed. M.H. Abrams et al. New York: W.W. Norton, 1993. Vol. 1, 1474-1610.

Novels and Short Stories

If you quote from a novel, include the page number and then the chapter number, separated from each other by a semicolon:

> Austen's insights into human nature and her incomparably concise style are both illustrated after the jealous Miss Bingley maneuvers Darcy into revealing his feelings for Elizabeth:
>
> > He went away, and Miss Bingley was left to all the satisfaction of having forced him to say what gave no one any pain but herself (304; ch. 45).

The Works Cited entry for the above quote would be:

> Austen, Jane. <u>Pride and Prejudice</u>. Cleveland: Fine Editions Press, 1946.

If you quote from a short story, put the page number on which the quote appears in parentheses after the quote:

> Even Miss Emily's house, decorated as it is "with cupolas and spires, and scrolled balconies" (139), tells of an owner trapped in the past.

The Works Cited entry for the above quote would be:

> Faulkner, William. "A Rose for Emily." <u>The Heath Introduction to Literature</u>. 4th ed. Ed. Alice S. Landy. Toronto: D.C. Heath, 1992. 139-147.

Plays

If you quote from a play written in verse, list the act, the scene, and the line numbers, separated from each other by periods. (Line numbers would not be included in plays not written in verse). For example:

> It is no accident, of course, that Hamlet admires in Horatio those very qualities he lacks:
>
> > ...and blest are those
> > Whose blood and judgment are so well commeddled
> > That they are not a pipe for Fortune's finger
> > To sound what stop she please.
> > (3.2.68-71)

The Works Cited entry for the above quote would be:

> Shakespeare, William. "The Tragical History of Hamlet, Prince of Denmark." <u>The Complete Signet Classic Shakespeare</u>. Ed. Sylvan Barnet. New York: Harcourt Brace Jovanovich, 1972. 910-961.

ASSIGNMENT 3-5

Provide the parenthetical citation and the Works Cited entry for the following essay excerpt:

Plath is uncompromising, explicitly comparing her father to a Nazi:

> Every woman adores a Fascist,
> The boot in the face, the brute
> Brute heart of a brute like you.

These are lines 48-50 from Sylvia Plath's poem "Daddy." The poem begins on page 620 and ends on page 623 in *The HBJ Anthology of Literature*. This anthology is edited by Jon C. Stott, Raymond E. Jones, and Rick Bowers. It was published in 1993 in Toronto by Harcourt Brace Jovanovich.

VIDEOTAPES

Today we are almost as likely to get information from films and videotapes as we are from books. Here is an excerpt from an essay that has borrowed information from a videotape:

> Any aerobic activity done while the back is arched can lead to injury (Tai Chi for Beginners).

Note that the title is underlined, not in quotation marks.

In the Works Cited list, this videotape would be acknowledged as follows:

> Tai Chi for Beginners. Videocassette. Fitness World Media Inc., 1993, 45 min.

ASSIGNMENT 3-6

Provide, in MLA format, the correct parenthetical citation and Works Cited entry for the following essay excerpt:

> Interestingly, director Tomas Pune sees Galileo not as a victim but as the architect of his own downfall.

The author is referring to a videocassette called *Heavenly Bodies*. The film was made in 1985 by Skywalker Productions of Vancouver.

Internet access number: number that helps Internet user retrieve desired document.
Date of access: the date, included in Works Cited entry for an Internet document, on which the writer accessed that Internet document.

THE INTERNET

A parenthetical citation for information taken from the Internet is called the **Internet access number** and is not different from parenthetical citations for other sources. However, in your Works Cited entry, you must include not only the date of publication, but also the **date of access**; that is, the date you accessed the information from the Internet. This is necessary because an article taken from a journal on the Internet can be constantly changed and updated. If your reader searches for the source, she might find information different from what you cited. You must also include whatever access numbers, access letters or other access codes are available to make it easy for your reader to retrieve the document you have cited.

Here is an excerpt from an essay that uses information from an article on the Internet:

> Censorship cases are rarely successful in court because it is so difficult for judges and juries to agree on a definition of pornography (Alston 5).

Here is how this article would be acknowledged in the list of Works Cited:

> Alston, Robin. "The Battle of the Books." <u>Humanist Review</u> 7.0176 (10 Sept. 1993): pp. 1-10. On-line. Internet. 10 Oct. 1993.

The number after the title of the journal is the Internet access number. The second date is the date of access.

ASSIGNMENT 3-7

The following information is taken from page 65 of an article called "New Events for the Atlanta Olympics" by Ralph Alcock. The information comes from a magazine called *Onsport*, available on the Internet. The access number is 2395.01. The article begins on page 65 and ends on page 89. The article was published on Feb. 28, 1994. The author of the paper using this article accessed the article on June 10, 1994. Provide, in MLA format, a parenthetical citation and a Works Cited entry for this information.

> Alcock makes a valid point when he notes that "if beach volleyball and the modern pentathlon can be olympic sports, why should ballroom dancing be excluded?"

OTHER SOURCES

The preceding examples show you how to acknowledge some but not all of your secondary sources. There always seems to be one source, at least, that presents a challenge. Perhaps it is a translation; perhaps it is the third edition of a book of articles, that is edited by four different people; perhaps you are using a government publication, a dissertation, or a daily newspaper.

If you are using the MLA method and you are not sure how to acknowledge a source, consult *The MLA Handbook for Writers of Research Papers*, written by Joseph Gibaldi and Walter S. Achtert.

A RESEARCH PAPER USING MLA DOCUMENTATION METHOD

Here is an example of a complete research paper, with sources acknowledged using the MLA method of parenthetical citation. Note the parenthetical citations used throughout the paper and the format of the list of Works Cited at the end. Research papers in excess of 2000 words begin the Works Cited on a separate page. For a paper of fewer than 2000 words, start the Works Cited on the last page of your paper if there is adequate space.

English: The First One Thousand Years

Ravi W.
English 101
February, 19XX

A thousand years ago, an English poet wrote a poem about the Battle of Maldon, a heroic attempt by English forces to defeat a Viking attack against the town of Maldon in Essex. Facing defeat, the old warrior Byrhtwold, the leader of the English forces, tries to rally his troops with these words:

> Hige sceal þe heardre, heorte þe cenre
> mod sceal þe mare, þe ure maegen lytlad. (311-312)

Byrhtwold was speaking English and his English soldiers would, of course, have understood him. To modern speakers of English, this is a foreign language requiring translation:

> Courage must be the firmer, heart the bolder, spirit the greater,
> the more our strength wanes. (Crossley-Holland and Mitchell 14)

Only the word "heorte" (heart) is recognizable in the original.

Old English is a Germanic language, born in the wake of the invasion of England by German tribes, most notably the Angles and the Saxons, during the fifth century. Their language was a branch of Indo-European, which dates back to about 5000 B.C. and from which modern European and some Asian languages sprang. Indo-European might, in turn, be a branch of another language, possibly a literal mother tongue, from which all other human languages might have emerged (Wright).

When the Germans (the Angles and the Saxons) landed on the English shores, they were met by an even earlier group of Indo-Europeans, the Celts, whom they forced north and west, where today live Celtic descendants: the Welsh, Scots, and Irish. The Celts were not strangers to invaders, having been victims of Roman imperialism beginning in 55 B.C. and ending early in the fifth century, when the mighty Roman Empire began to collapse. Some English place names, Manchester and Winchester, for example, are derived from the Roman word "castra," meaning "camp" (McCrum, Cran, and MacNeil 52).

The Celts fought hard against the German invaders, and, under one King, Artorius—probably the legendary King Arthur—had some success. But the Anglo-Saxons were determined to mine the rich minerals and settle the fertile soil of this beautiful island, and soon routed the Celts, adding insult to injury by calling them "wealas," which means foreigners and is the Anglo-Saxon root word for Wales and Welsh (McCrum, Cran, and MacNeil 56).

Old English literature, especially poems like <u>Beowulf</u> and <u>The Battle of Maldon</u>, quoted above, show how much the Anglo-Saxons admired courage, honour, and strength. But they were farmers as well as warriors, and modern words that relate to the land—words like "shepherd," "earth," "plow," "swine," "wood," and "field"—are Anglo-Saxon in origin. Other words of Anglo-Saxon origin—such as "glee," "laughter," and "mirth"—reveal yet another aspect of their culture (McCrum, Cran, and MacNeil 58).

In 597, Christian missionaries came to England, bringing with them hundreds of Latin words that gradually became anglicized. Words related to Christianity—"angel," "disciple," "priest," "litany," "shrine"—entered the language. Words already in the language—"God," "heaven," "hell"—originally pagan, acquired Christian connotations (McCrum, Cran, and MacNeil 63).

Late in the eighth century Scandinavian invaders—the notorious Vikings—began to arrive. By the middle of the ninth century, they had conquered half of the country, the South saved thanks largely to the leadership of King Alfred the Great. As time went by, the two cultures blended, a process that was eased by the similarity in language. Old English and Old Norse, the language spoken by the Vikings, are so similar in fact that it is not always easy to tell which words have Viking origins. Place names ending in "by" and "wick," such as Derby and Chiswick, are probably Old Norse, as are words beginning in "sk": sky, skin, skirt. Old Norse also enriched English with words that were nearly the same as existing English words but with subtle distinctions in meaning. The Old English had "craft;" the Vikings gave them "skill." An Old English farmer might "want" a new horse; after the Vikings had settled, the farmer could also "wish" for a new horse (McCrum, Cran, and MacNeil 71).

After the Vikings came the Normans from the north of France, who, under William the Conqueror, defeated the English King Harold at the Battle of Hastings in 1066. The Normans established French and Latin as the languages of law and government. As a result, words with French and Latin roots—"perjury," "attorney," "nobility," "royal," and "sovereign," for example—entered the language (McCrum, Cran, and MacNeil 73-

74). Thirteenth-century English is still a puzzle to modern speakers, but is easier to decode than the English in which <u>Beowulf</u> and <u>The Battle of Maldon</u> were written. In <u>Kyng Alisaunder</u>, written 300 years after <u>The Battle of Maldon</u>, one of Alexander's enemies taunts the Greek King, complaining that Alexander has "brent myne tounes, myne men ys-lawe." The modern translation, "burned my towns, slain my men," (Burnley 127) is markedly closer to the original than is the modern translation of the passage from <u>The Battle of Maldon</u>, quoted above.

Norman French influenced English but posed no threat to its survival. For 300 years the language of the court, it still did not trickle down to the common people who, too busy to worry too much about the goings on at court, calmly continued to speak their mother tongue in day-to-day life. In time, young Norman men began to marry young English women and young Norman women began to marry young English men; their children and their children's children learned English as their first language. In time, hostility developed between France and England and the new generations of Normans declared their allegiance to their new homeland and fought in its defence. English re-asserted itself in legal and government circles. By the middle of the fourteenth century, English farmers, judges, bishops, and Kings were again conversing, praying, and conducting the affairs of state in English.

All that was needed to entrench English permanently was a great poet of the people, one who would write in English and immortalize the array of colourful English men and women of all social classes and occupations. Geoffrey Chaucer was born in 1340 and wrote <u>The Canterbury Tales</u>, probably around 1390. The opening lines remain the most famous example of Middle English writing:

> Whan that April with his showres soote
> The droughte of Marche hath perced to the roote,
> And bathed every veine in swich licour
> Of which vertu engendred is the flowr;
> Whan Zephyrus eek with his sweete breeth
> Inspired hath in every holt and heeth
> The tendre croppes, and the yonge sonne
> Hath in the Ram his halve cours y-ronne;
> And smale fowles maken melodye,
> That sleepen al the night with open ye—
> So priketh hem Nature in hir corages—
> Than longen folk to goon on pilgrimages,
> And palmeres for to seken struange strondes,
> To ferne halwes, couthe in sondry londes;
> And specially, from every shires ende
> Of Engelond to Caunterbury they wende,
> The holy blisful martyr for to seeke,

That hem hath holpen, whan that they were seke.
(1-18)

Chaucer's English, as the opening lines to <u>The Canterbury Tales</u> illustrate, is easier to decode than Old English but is still a challenge to modern English speakers. Students who must read Chaucer's work require texts that are heavily annotated. In one recent edition, for example, every line of the above excerpt, except lines 15-16, is annotated (Kolve and Olson 3). A full translation is not required, however, as it is for Old English texts.

Many letters that are silent in today's spoken English were pronounced by Chaucer and his fellow English speakers. The final "e" in words like "ride" and "hope" would usually have been pronounced, as would the "k" in "knife" and the "gh" in "thought." Verbs often ended in "en," the verb "to seek," for example, being "to seken." Past participles were often prefixed by "y," as in "hadde y-ronne" (Kolve and Olson xvi).

Around 1477, William Caxton brought a new European invention, the printing press, to England (Bolton 17). He printed his books in the English used in London, Chaucer's English. The printing press revolutionized literacy, making books readily available to all segments of society. London English became and remains the standard because of Caxton's decision to print his books in the English used in London. As Bolton notes:

> We can...say that spelling was by and large stabilized by the time Shakespeare was born, and that the standard of stability was the literary dialect of London English exemplified by and descended from Chaucer. (18)

Shakespeare was born in 1564, and wrote his plays and poems in the 1590s and early 1600s, before his death in 1616. His influence on the language was enormous. Scores of words never in print before, appear, for the first time, in Shakespeare's work: "accommodation," "assassination," "dexterously," "indistinguishable," "obscene," "pedant." This is a minuscule list of words coined by or put into print for the first time by Shakespeare (McCrum, Cran, and MacNeil 98).

Shakespeare, moreso even than Chaucer, shows us how versatile and flexible the English language is, how well it lends itself to the expression of a thought that is at once concise, metaphorical, and profound. He remains the most quoted of all English authors. If your lost property has "vanished into thin air," notes Levin "you are quoting Shakespeare." You are quoting Shakespeare, he continues, if

> you have ever refused to budge an inch or suffered from green-eyed jealousy, if you have played fast and loose, if you have been

> tongue-tied, a tower of strength, hoodwinked or in a pickle, if you
> have knitted your brows, [or] insisted on fair play. . . (qtd. in
> McCrum, Cran, and MacNeil 98)

Perhaps you make "a virtue of necessity"; perhaps you can't sleep "a
wink" some nights; maybe you "stand on ceremony" occasionally, or get
"too much of a good thing," or live in "a fool's paradise." All of
these everyday expressions have their origins in Shakespeare's work.

In 1611, when Shakespeare's career as a writer was coming to a
close, the King James version of the Bible was published. Beautifully
written in simple and straightforward English, the King James Bible can
easily be read today by anyone who can read English. The printing press
allowed for wide distribution at home and abroad of the King James
Bible. The English language as we know it now was already firmly entrenched.

The English of the 1690s, then, is easily read by readers in the
1990s. But even after 1700, the language continued to grow and change,
as it continues to do so now. The changes are minor compared to the
change from the English of The Battle of Maldon to the English of
Shakespeare, but significant nevertheless.

Since the early seventeenth century, for example, English has continued to borrow and adapt hundreds of words from other languages.
While the King James Bible was being written and published, explorers
were meeting the Native people of North America. From their languages
came words like "hickory," "chipmunk," "moose," "tomahawk," and "kayak"
(McCrum, Cran, and MacNeil 123). As years passed, European immigrants
began to arrive, bringing with them many words from many languages—
words that were soon incorporated into English. Gefvert provides a
small list of examples:

> From French we borrowed "brochure" and "chaperone;" from
> Portuguese, "veranda;" from Spanish, "cafeteria" and "marijuana;"
> from Italian, "serenade" and "umbrella;" from Swedish, "ski;" from
> Dutch, "cookie;" from German, "hamburger" and "kindergarden;" from
> Arabic, "algebra;" from Persian, "paradise." (344)

Asian languages have enriched English with words like "tea" and "silk."
From African languages, words like "banana" and "jazz" have come into
English (Gefvert 344). Today, of course, the process continues. English-
speaking countries welcome immigrants whose many gifts include new words
that soon find their way into English dictionaries.

Scientific and technological inventions and discoveries also bring
new words into the language. When the telephone and telegraph were invented, for example, they needed names. The word-makers of the day took
the Greek root "tele," meaning "far or distant," and added to it other
Greek roots like "phone," meaning "sound," and "graph," meaning "write

or mark" (Francis 319). Scores of other words have entered the language this way. New English words entering the language in the wake of the computer revolution could fill a small dictionary. Our fathers' dictionaries did not include "on-line," "software," "computer hacker," or "interface."

Even in the last forty years, then, English has changed. Its flexibility and adaptability are perhaps the outstanding characteristic of English—the reason why it has, at about 500 000 words, the largest vocabulary of any language, and the reason why it is the closest thing we have to an international language, spoken by a billion people scattered throughout every country in the world (McCrum, Cran, and MacNeil 10). This flexibility and adaptability is also the reason why English has changed so much over its first thousand years of use and why it continues to change and develop. When the history of the next thousand years of English is written, it will be written in a language that will have an even larger vocabulary than the one we have now and with a grammar that has changed to reflect the changes in the society that uses it.

Works Cited

Bolton, W.F. <u>A Short History of Literary English</u>. London: Edward Arnold, 1967.

Burnley, David. <u>The History of the English Language: A Source Book</u>. New York: Longman, 1992.

Chaucer, Geoffrey. <u>The Canterbury Tales: Nine Tales and the General Prologue</u>. Ed. V.A. Kolve and Glending Olson. New York: W.W. Norton, 1989.

Crossley-Holland, Kevin., trans. and Bruce Mitchell, ed. <u>The Battle of Maldon and Other Old English Poems</u>. New York: St. Martins, 1967.

Francis, W. Nelson. "Word Making: Some Sources of New Words." <u>Language: Introductory Readings</u>, 3rd. ed. Eds. Virginia P. Clark, Paul A. Eschholz, and Alfred F. Rosa. New York: St. Martins, 1981. 316-328.

Gefvert, Constance J. <u>The Confident Writer: A Norton Handbook</u>. New York: Norton, 1985.

Kolve, V.A. and Glening Olson, eds. <u>The Canterbury Tales: Nine Tales and the General Prologue</u>, by Geoffrey Chaucer. New York: W.W. Norton, 1989.

McCrum, Robert, William Cran, and Robert MacNeil. <u>The Story of English</u>. Rev. ed. London: Faber and Faber, 1992.

Roberts, Paul. "A Brief History of English." In <u>Language: Introductory Readings</u>, 3rd. ed. Eds. Virginia P. Clark, Paul A. Eschholz, and Alfred F. Rosa. New York: St. Martins, 1981. 585-595.

Wright, Robert. "Quest for the Mother Tongue." <u>The Atlantic</u> April 1991: 39-68.

SUMMARY

- Cite all sources carefully and accurately to avoid plagiarism.
- Acknowledge sources quoted directly or paraphrased.
- Acknowledge sources twice—first, within the essay; second, at the end of the essay.
- Within the text, place the author and the page number of the source within parentheses.
- At the end of the text, list sources in the Works Cited. Authors, titles, date of publication, volume number, and place of publication are included in Works Cited.
- Double-check the punctuation of your Works Cited entries to ensure that they are correct.

QUESTIONS FOR STUDY AND DISCUSSION

1. What is plagiarism and how can it be avoided?
2. When does the name of an author *not* have to be included in a parenthetical citation?
3. How does the Works Cited entry for a journal with continuous pagination differ from one paginated by issue?
4. How does the citation for a journal article differ from the citation for a magazine article?
5. How does the Works Cited entry for a reference book differ from an entry for a non-reference book?
6. How does the citation for a literary work differ from one for a "regular" source?
7. When would you include the title of a source in a parenthetical citation?
8. How does the Works Cited entry for an article from the Internet differ from the entry for an article in print?

SUPPLEMENTARY EXERCISES

1. Correct and list any errors you spot in the MLA parenthetical citations for the following excerpts from research papers:
    a. In an early article about Mahler's work, Cook (1975) argued that the composer's music was seriously flawed by "the unfortunate debt he owes to banal songs sung in Vienese beer halls" (Cook, "Gustave Mahler's Popular Appeal," p. 46). But in his recent biography of Mahler, Cook (1995) has toned down the criticism and claims that

Mahler "deserves credit for trying to write music which would have widespread appeal" (Cook, <u>The Life of Gustav Mahler</u>, 1995, p. 321).

_____

_____

_____

b. There are, however, some educators who continue to insist that IQ tests are "accurate predictors of academic success." (Levin, 81)

_____

_____

_____

c. The complex interrelationship among the proteins, carbohydrates, and fats the body ingests is not yet completely understood, but it is clear that they do not function independently. Low-fat complex carbohydrates are the current darling of nutrition fanatics, but

"if the body ingests more carbohydrates than it needs, the excess will be stored as fat. Similarly, if the body ingests too much protein, but not enough carbohydrate, some of the amino acids that protein has produced will be converted into carbohydrate (Davis 1986 79)."

_____

_____

_____

2. For a research paper about how to get motivated to begin and sustain an excercise program, you have used the sources described below. Arrange these sources into an MLA list of Works Cited.

a. Two articles from the Encyclopedia of Sport, published in London by Perval Press. One article is called "Aerobics," the other is called "Motivation." They are unsigned. The Encyclopedia was published in 1994.

_____

_____

_____

b. An article by Mary Norbert from the February 1994 issue (volume 5) of the magazine Fitness World. The article begins on page 35 and ends on page 46. The title of the article is "Vitamin Z."

_____

_____

_____

c. A book of essays edited by J.W. Atkinson and John Raynor. The book is called Motivation and Achievement. It was published in New York by Halstead in 1994.

_____

_____

_____

d. A journal article by D.C. Anderson, C.R. Crowell, Martin Donan, and G.S. Howard called Performance Posting, Goal Setting, and Activity-Contingent Praise as Applied to a University Hockey Team. The article appears in volume 73 of the Journal of Applied Psychology, 1988. The journal is continuously paginated. The article begins on page 87 and ends on page 95.

_____

_____

_____

e. A journal article by M. Bar-Eli, N. Levy-Kolker, G. Tenenbaum, and Robert Weinberg called Effects of Goal Difficulty on Performance of Aerobic, Anaerobic and Power Tasks in Laboratory and Field Settings. The article is in the continuously paginated Journal of Sport Behaviour, volume 16, 1993, pages 17-32.

_____

_____

_____

f. The third edition of a book by R.M. Cox called Sport Psychology: Concepts and Applications, published in Madison, WI by Brown and Benchmark in 1994.

_____

_____

_____

g. A collection of articles edited by R.N. Singer, M. Murphey, and L. Tennant and published in a book called Handbook of Research on Sport Psychology, published in New York by Macmillan, in 1994.

_____

_____

_____

h. An article by C. Pemberton and P.J. McSwegin. The article is called
    Goal Setting and Motivation. It appears in the Journal of Physical
    Education, Recreation, and Dance, volume 60, issue 1, 1989. The jour-
    nal is paginated by issue. The article begins on page 39 and ends on
    page 41.

    _____

    _____

    _____

i. An article by S. Weinberg called Motivating Athletes Through Goal
    Setting. The article appeared in the paginated-by-issue Journal of
    Physical Education, Recreation, and Dance, volume 53, issue 9, 1982,
    pages 46-48.

    _____

    _____

    _____

j. A 1993 article by D. Gould called Goal Setting for Peak Performance.
    The article is in the second edition of a book edited by J.M. Williams.
    The book is called Applied Sport Psychology: Personal Growth to
    Peak Performance. It was published by Mayfield publishers of
    Mountain View, CA. The article begins on page 158 and ends on page
    169.

    _____

    _____

    _____

k. A book by R. Martens called Coaches Guide to Sport Psychology, pub-
    lished in 1987 in Champagne, IL, by Human Kinetics.

    _____

    _____

    _____

Citing Sources, APA Method

Acknowledge All of Your Sources

Books
Journal Articles
Magazine Articles

Encyclopedias
Videotapes
The Internet
Other Sources

HELPFUL HINTS

Do not use the APA method for essays for your literature class; use the MLA method.

In Lesson Three, you learned how to acknowledge secondary sources by using the method prescribed and recommended by the Modern Language Association. If you are writing a paper in education or the social sciences, however, you are expected to cite your sources using the method prescribed and recommended by the American Psychological Association. The APA method is explained in this lesson.

BOOKS

HELPFUL HINTS

Remember to include publication date and abbreviation for page number in parenthetical citations.

To acknowledge a book from which you have borrowed information, an APA parenthetical citation is similar to an MLA citation, the main difference being the APA method also includes the year the source was published:

> As a group, these studies indicated rather clearly that engaging young writers actively in the use of criteria, applied to their own or to others' writing, results not only in more effective revisions but in superior first drafts (Hillocks, 1986, p. 160).

Note, also, that there are commas between the name and the date, and that the word "page" is abbreviated to "p." before the page number.

If the name appears in the text, the date follows the name while the page number follows the quote or the idea borrowed from the source:

> Hillocks (1986) claims that, as a group, these studies indicated rather clearly that engaging young writers actively in the use of criteria, applied to their own or to others' writing, results not only in more effective revisions but in superior first drafts (p. 160).

At the end of the essay, the complete information about the source appears in a list called "References" (the counterpart of the MLA's "Works Cited"), arranged alphabetically by the authors' last names. The References entry for the source used above would be:

Hillocks, G. Jr. (1986) <u>Research in written composition: New directions for teaching</u>. Urbana, Illinois: ERIC Clearinghouse on Reading and Communication Skills.

Note carefully the differences between the MLA's Works Cited format and the APA's References format. In the APA method, the first line is indented but the others are not (the reverse of the indentation style used in the MLA method). This is a recent change to the APA system. In the APA method, only the initial of the first name is given and the date of publication comes (in parentheses) right after the name. And in the APA method, words in the book title are not capitalized, unless they are the first word in the title, the first word in the subtitle, or words that would normally be capitalized.

If you list not only the works you cite in your paper but all the works you consulted while researching your paper, and if you are using the APA method, that list is referred to as a "Bibliography." If you are using the MLA method, that list is referred to as "Works Consulted."

ASSIGNMENT 4-1

1. The quote from the following excerpt comes from a book by Harvey Kirby and Margaret Ridge called *Young Offenders*. The book was published in 1993 in Vancouver by Pever Press. The quote appears on page 201. Provide, in APA format, a parenthetical citation and a References entry for the following excerpt from a research paper.

   Kirby and Ridge also believe that violence on television programs and films does influence teenage behaviour. Studies that indicate otherwise, they claim, are flawed because "studies of teen violence will refuse to make a connection between watching violence and committing violence unless 95% or more violent acts can be shown to be influenced by a violent film or TV program."

2. The information from the following excerpt comes from the second edition of a book called *Attic Treasures* by Mary Watson. The book was published in 1993 in London by Leisure Books. The information appears on page 137. Provide, in APA format, a parenthetical citation and a References entry for the following excerpt from a research paper.

   Needlecraft designs or "samplers" are very collectible now, ones made in the eighteenth century fetching prices at auction up to $600.

JOURNAL ARTICLES

Here is an excerpt from an essay that uses the APA format to acknowledge a journal article:

> Special interest groups distort, sometimes ignore, the truth to advance their own political ends. Walker (1994) has shown how both pro-environment groups and lobbyists who represent the forest industry have taken out of context sections of the same government report in order to support action each group has taken (p. 413).

Note the inclusion of the date after the author's name, and the inclusion of the abbreviation for page (p.) at the end of the excerpt.

Here is how this source would be acknowledged in the list of References at the end of the essay:

> Walker, M. (1994). The war against truth: How political lobby groups function. North American Journal of Media and Communication, 87, 411-428.

Unsigned articles are alphabetized by title.

Note that only the first initial of the author's first name is used and that the date comes after the name. Words in the article title are not capitalized, except for the first word, the first word of a subtitle, and words that would normally be capitalized. The journal title, however, *is* capitalized and underlined; the volume number is also underlined.

You will note, perhaps, that the page numbers (411-428) in the above entry seem high for an issue of a journal that you might not think would contain so many pages. You are right. The journal cited above, like many other academic journals, is paginated not by issue but by year. In other words, the first volume of the issue in any given year begins on page 1, and the next issue begins where the first ended: if the first issue of the year ended on page 114, the next issue would begin on page 115.

You will need to know if journals you use are paginated by issue or by volume.

Some journals are paginated not continuously but by issue; that is, all issues begin on page 1. If the journal cited above were paginated by issue, then the issue number would be added to the References entry, in parentheses next to the volume number:

> Walker, M. (1994). The war against truth: How political lobby groups function. North American Journal of Media and Communication, 87(4), 11-28.

Again, note that the first line of a reference *is* indented and that the issue number is in parentheses, not underlined, immediately following the volume number.

ASSIGNMENT 4-2

1. Provide, in APA format, the parenthetical citation and the References entry for the following excerpt from a research paper:

   > Lu also believes that more research "which critiques portrayals of Basic Writers as belonging to an abnormal-traumatized or underdeveloped state" is urgently needed.

The quotation in this passage is from an article by Min-Zhan Lu, published in the journal College English, volume 54, issue number 8, 1992. The article is called "Conflict and Struggle: The Enemies or Preconditions of Basic Writing." College English uses continuous pagination, so the first page in the issue used here is page 887. Lu's article begins on page 887 and ends on page 913. The quote in the above excerpt is on page 910.

2. Provide, in APA format, the parenthetical citation and the References entry for the following excerpt from a research paper:

> Tobin and Tamsin argue that Kennedy's intervention will backfire, and that public opinion will be against an American outsider criticizing Canadian logging practices.

The information in this passage is from an article by R. Tobin and B. Tamsin, published in volume 7, issue 3, of the *Friends of the Earth Review*. The article is called "The Fight for the Carmanah Valley." The journal is paginated by issue. The article begins on page 87 and ends on page 91. The quote in the above excerpt is on page 91.

MAGAZINE ARTICLES

Here is an excerpt from an essay that uses the APA format to acknowledge a magazine article:

> Trevor King, IBEX's capable young CEO, claims that the notebook computer his company is producing will be even smaller than its Apple counterpart (Ashton, 1994, p. 14)

Here is how this source would be acknowledged in the References section of the essay:

> Ashton, L. (1994, May). Upstart IBEX ready to challenge Apple and IBM. Computer World, pp. 96-103.

Note that the words in the title of the article are not capitalized unless they would always be capitalized: the words "ready" and "challenge" are not capitalized as they would be in the MLA method. The name of the magazine is underlined and capitalized. Note that "pages" is abbreviated to "pp."

ASSIGNMENT 4-3 The information in the following excerpt comes from a magazine article called "Dodger Blues" written by Ron Fimrite. The article appears in the September 28, 1992, issue of *Sports Illustrated*. The article begins on page 18 and ends on page 21. The information in the excerpt appears on page 20. Provide, in APA format, the correct parenthetical citation and References entry for the excerpt.

Davis and Strawberry wanted to be teammates ever since they played ball together as children on the playgrounds of Los Angeles.

ENCYCLOPEDIAS

Here is an excerpt from an essay that uses the APA format to acknowledge information from an encyclopedia:

In the last twenty years, however, the figure has been almost entirely re-
moved from figure skating. Now it is athletic ability, especially the ability to
jump, which judges look for, and they are unlikely to be satisfied with anything less than triple jumps (Figure Skating, 1994).

In the References list, the source would be acknowledged as follows:

Figure skating (1994). In The Encyclopedia of Sport.

If there were an author's name at the end of the encyclopedia entry, the
name would appear, followed by the date, followed by the title. Page numbers
are not needed because encyclopedias are organized alphabetically.

ASSIGNMENT 4-4

Using the APA method, provide the correct parenthetical citation and References
entry for the following essay excerpt:

The Encyclopaedia of Religion and Ethics defines confirmation as "an act,
closely connected with baptism, in which prayer for the Holy Spirit is joined
with some ceremony, through which the gift of the Spirit is believed to be
conferred."

The information comes from the *Encyclopaedia of Religion and Ethics*, volume 4,
page 1. The encyclopedia is edited by James Hastings and was published in
New York in 1971 by Scribners.

VIDEOTAPES

Here is an example of how information taken from a videotape would be cited
using the APA method:

Any aerobic activity done while the back is arched can lead to injury. (Tai Chi
for beginners, 1993)

And in the References list:

Tai Chi for beginners. (1993) [Videocassette]. Fitness World Media.

ASSIGNMENT 4-5

Provide, in APA format, the correct parenthetical citation and References entry for the following essay excerpt:

> Interestingly, director Tomas Pune sees Galileo not as a victim but as the architect of his own downfall.

The author is referring to the film version, on videocassette, of *Heavenly Bodies*. The film was made in 1985 by Sky Walker Productions of Vancouver.

THE INTERNET

According to the 1994 edition of the *Publication Manual of the American Psychological Association*, a standard method of acknowledging on-line information has not yet been developed. References for on-line sources must certainly contain the same information they would if they were print sources, but references for on-line sources also require additional information such as access codes, numbers, and letters.

At this time, then, it would be acceptable to cite the source as if it were a print source but to add the name of the network or computer service, an indication that the material was obtained on-line, and the access code. Here is an example:

> Battista (1994) notes that Stone first revealed "the menacing sexuality which would become her trademark" (p. 23) when she played opposite Arnold Schwarzenegger in Total Recall.

The References entry for this source from the Internet would be

> Battista, L. (1994, August 7). The films of Sharon Stone. [on-line] Reelworld, 173, 34-47. Internet. ISSN: 7614-9928.

OTHER SOURCES

The preceding examples show you how to acknowledge some but not all of your secondary sources. But there always seems to be one source, at least, that presents a challenge. Perhaps it is a translation; perhaps it is the third edition of a book of articles that is edited by four different people; perhaps you are using a government publication, a dissertation, or a daily newspaper.

If you are using the APA method and you are not sure how to acknowledge a source, consult *The Publication Manual of the American Psychological Association*, Fourth Edition. You should be able to find this manual and others by other academic agencies in the reference section of your college library.

A RESEARCH PAPER USING APA DOCUMENTATION METHOD

Here is a complete research paper with secondary sources acknowledged using the APA method. Note that a research paper in excess of 2000 words begins the Works Cited on a separate page. For a paper of fewer than 2000 words, start the Works Cited on the last page if there is adequate space.

The Drawbacks and Benefits of Writing with a Computer

Author's Name
Course Name, Number, and Section
Date

While technology makes a process more efficient, it does not necessarily make the product better. A baked potato cooked in minutes in a microwave tastes no better than one baked for an hour in an oven or buried for an hour in the embers of a barbecue. A salesperson with a pager, cellular phone, and fax machine might be able to keep in touch with her customers more efficiently, but this efficiency will not necessarily lead to an increase in sales. And a writer working on a computer will write quickly and edit with ease, but will not necessarily produce a better essay than will her friend who prefers a pencil and note pad.

<u>The Drawbacks</u>
Indeed, some researchers have identified significant writing problems that are the direct result of the use of a computer. Grow (1988) has found that because word processors make editing so easy, writers working at computers tend to over-edit at the sentence level and so have less time and energy to revise to improve overall content:

> Drawn in by the word processor's ability to facilitate small changes, such writers neglect the larger steps in writing. They compose when they need to be planning, edit when they need to revise. (p. 217)

Grow also notes that because the word processor makes it so easy to copy blocks of text from previous work, writers are tempted to pad their work with material from another paper, stored in a file so easily accessed by the computer. Blocks of text are piled onto other blocks of text with scant concern for transition and coherence. And even when they don't borrow text from other files, writers, encouraged by the freedom the computer gives them, write too much. "Instead of saying it well one time, unfocused writers devise dozens of ways of coming close to saying what they mean" (p. 219).

Cogdill (1995) agrees, claiming that writing on a computer can adversely affect style. Inexperienced writers working on a word processor tend to do a "mind dump" (p. 47), to write reams of words and sentences because the computer makes it so easy to do so. When these writers try to go back to edit and revise, they are overwhelmed with the sheer volume of work they have produced and are intimidated by the prospect of refining it. Inexperienced writers working on a computer also become too concerned about the appearance of the text on the page. Like the proverbial kids in candy stores, they become so fascinated with the different type sizes, with headers and footers, decorative icons, and all of the other bells and whistles the modern word-processing software has to offer, that they spend too much time beautifying their manuscripts and not enough time revising and polishing the actual text (p. 48).

A third problem that can adversely affect writing performance, though this problem does decrease each year as more and more schools teach computing skills, is computer anxiety. Reed (1990) found that students who felt intimidated by computers did not write as well as students who had more computer experience. Students less familiar with computer-generated writing must be given time to become as much at ease with the computer as they are with their pencils.

<u>The Benefits</u>
Although writers and writing teachers recognize the pitfalls, described above, of writing on a computer, almost all of them still recommend that students word process their college writing assignments, provided that students learn how to make effective use of the technology. The professional literature is full of advice on how students can use computers to improve their writing (for a summary see Hobson and Gee, 1994).

Most experts in the field strongly recommend that writers compose on screen but revise, at least once, on hard copy. On screen, revising and editing is done piecemeal, because writers can only revise what they see. Piecemeal revision is useful but, unless writers can see the whole text, global revisions might not be done (Hawisher, 1987, p. 157). The result can be an essay with weak overall unity and unclear transitions between and among blocks of related text.

Writing teachers and researchers also recommend that students use the specialized software that comes with most word-processing programs, but do so judiciously. Spell checkers cannot distinguish homonyms; a sentence that reads "There work is done" will pass through the spell check, even though the first word should read "Their." Grammar checks have some usefulness but they won't catch, among other errors, dangling modifiers (Rosen & Behrens, 1994, p. 783). Marius and Wiener (1994) recommend the use of the search function as a way of avoiding redundancy (p. 631). If a writer thinks she has used a word too frequently, she can, with a push of a key, find out exactly how many times in an essay she has used a particular word and, with a push of another button, access the thesaurus to find a suitable synonym.

What excites writing teachers most about computer-generated writing are the possibilities offered by a network, a system that connects the computers in a writing class and allows students to peer edit and work collaboratively. Rosen & Behrens (1994) suggest students send each other letters in which they describe the approach they will be taking in their assignments and ask for written feedback (p. 780). Rada (1994) found that students who made written comments, via a network, about other students' written work improved the writing quality of not just their peers' essays but their own as well. Fey (1994) found that student writing improves when students carry on a dialogue, in writing, in which they offer suggestions to improve each other's work.

With networks, writers can revise and edit work collaboratively much more efficiently than they could passing hard copy around a room. With spell checks, writers can correct a word in a fraction of the time it takes to look a word up in an old-fashioned paper dictionary. But computers cannot think for themselves or develop a weak idea or make style more graceful. The computer makes writing, as it makes so many of the tasks of life, easier, but it needs the guidance of a human mind to make writing more interesting and intelligent.

References

Cogdill, S. (1995). Computers and writing. In W.H. Roberts & G. Turgeon (Eds.), About language: A reader for writers (4th ed.) (pp. 46-51). Boston: Houghton Mifflin.

Fey, M.H. (1994). Finding voice through computer communication: A new venue for collaboration. Journal of Advanced Composition, 14, 221-238.

Grow, G. (1988). Lessons from the computer writing problems of professionals. College Composition and Communication, 39, 217-220.

Hawisher, G.E. (1987). The effect of word processing on the revision strategies of college freshmen. Research in the Teaching of English, 39, 154-161.

Hobson, E.H. & Gee, K.R. (1994). Ten commandments for computer-assisted composition instructors. Teaching English in the Two-Year College, 21, 224-230.

Marius, R. & Weiner, H.S. (1994). The McGraw-Hill college handbook (4th ed.). New York: McGraw Hill.

Rada, R. (1994). Collaborative hypermedia in a classroom setting. [on-line]. Journal of Educational Multimedia and Hypermedia, 3(1), 21-36. Abstract from Telnet. ISSN: 1055-8896.

Reed, W.M. (1990). The effects of computer-based writing instruction and mode of discourse on writing performance and writer anxieties. [on-line]. Computers in Human Behaviour, 6, 211-221. Abstract from Telnet. ISSN: 0747-5632.

Rosen, L.J. & Behrens, L. (1994). The Allyn & Bacon handbook (2nd ed.) (Instructors ed.). Needham Heights, MA: Allyn and Bacon.

SUMMARY

- Acknowledge all of your sources carefully and accurately to avoid plagiarism.

- Include the year of publication in APA parenthetical citations.

- Do *not* use quotation marks in APA citations or in the list of References.

- Do *not* capitalize article titles and book titles except for first words in titles and subtitles and words that would normally be capitalized.

- Underline the names of books, journals, and magazines.

- If you use information from the Internet, include in your citations enough information so that your readers can find the sources on-line.

QUESTIONS FOR STUDY AND DISCUSSION

1. Describe the differences between the MLA and the APA methods for citing sources parenthetically within the body of a research paper.

2. Describe the differences between the MLA Works Cited and the APA References for:

    a. books

    b. articles from journals

    c. articles from magazines

3. When does the name of an author *not* have to be included in a parenthetical citation?

4. How does the References entry for a journal with continuous pagination differ from one paginated by issue?

5. How does the citation for a journal article differ from the citation for a magazine article?

6. How does the References entry for a reference book differ from an entry for a non-reference book?

7. When would you include the title of a source in a parenthetical citation?

SUPPLEMENTARY EXERCISES

1. Correct any errors you spot in the APA parenthetical citations for the following excerpts from research papers:

a. In an early article about Mahler's work, Cook (1975) argued that the composer's music was seriously flawed by "the unfortunate debt he owes to banal songs sung in Vienese beer halls" (Cook, 1975, "Gustave Mahler's Popular Appeal," p. 46). But in his recent biography of Mahler, Cook (1992) has toned down the criticism and claims that Mahler "deserves credit for trying to write music which would have widepsread appeal" (Cook, 1992, The Life of Gustav Mahler, 1992, p. 321).

_____

_____

_____

b. There are, however, some educators who continue to insist that IQ tests are "accurate predictors of academic success." (Levin, 81, 1993)

_____

_____

_____

c. The complex interrelationship among the proteins, carbohydrates, and fats the body ingests is not yet completely understood, but it is clear that they do not function independently. Low-fat complex carbohydrates are the current darling of nutrition fanatics, but

> "if the body ingests more carbohydrates than it needs, the excess will be stored as fat. Similarly, if the body ingests too much protein, but not enough carbohydrate, some of the amino acids that protein has produced will be converted into carbohydrate (Davis 1993 79)."

_____

_____

_____

2. For a research paper about how to get motivated to begin and sustain an excercise program, you have used the sources described below. Arrange these sources into an APA list of References. (Note that the sources are the same as those for Question 2 in Lesson Three's Supplementary Exercises.) After you have completed the exercise below, compare your responses with your responses to the Lesson Three question. Note carefully the differences between the MLA and APA methods.

a. Two articles from the Encyclopedia of Sport, published in London by Perval Press. One article is called "Aerobics," the other is called "Motivation." They are unsigned. The Encyclopedia was published in 1994.

_____

_____

_____

b. An article by Mary Norbert from the February 1994 issue (volume 5) of the magazine, Fitness World. The article begins on page 35 and ends on page 46.

_____

_____

_____

c. A book of essays edited by J.W. Atkinson and John Raynor. The book is called Motivation and Achievement. It was published in New York by Halstead.

_____

_____

_____

d. A journal article by D.C. Anderson, C.R. Crowell, Martin Donan, and G.S. Howard called Performance Posting, Goal Setting, and Activity-Contingent Praise as Applied to a University Hockey Team. The article appears in volume 73 of the Journal of Applied Psychology, 1988. The journal is continuously paginated. The article begins on page 87 and ends on page 95.

_____

_____

_____

e. A journal article by M. Bar-Eli, N. Levy-Kolker, G. Tenenbaum, and Robert Weinberg called Effects of Goal Difficulty on Performance of Aerobic, Anaerobic and Power Tasks in Laboratory and Field Settings. The article is in the continuously paginated Journal of Sport Behaviour, volume 16, 1993, pages 17-32.

_____

_____

_____

f. The third edition of a book by R.M. Cox called Sport Psychology: Concepts and Applications, published in Madison, WI, by Brown and Benchmark in 1994.

_____

_____

_____

g. A collection of articles edited by R.N. Singer, M. Murphey, and L. Tennant and published in a book called Handbook of Research on Sport Psychology, published in New York by Macmillan, in 1994.

_____

_____

_____

h. An article by C. Pemberton and P.J. McSwegin. The article is called Goal Setting and Motivation. It appears in the Journal of Physical Education, Recreation, and Dance, volume 60, issue 1, 1989. The journal is paginated by issue. The article begins on page 39 and ends on page 41.

_____

_____

_____

i. An article by S. Weinberg called Motivating Athletes Through Goal Setting. The article appeared in the paginated-by-issue Journal of Physical Education, Recreation, and Dance, volume 53, issue 9, 1982, pages 46-48.

_____

_____

_____

j. An 1993 article by D. Gould called Goal Setting for Peak Performance. The article is in the second edition of a book edited by J.M. Williams. The book is called Applied Sport Psychology: Personal Growth to Peak Performance. It was published by Mayfield publishers of Mountain View, CA. The article begins on page 158 and ends on page 169.

_____

_____

_____

k. A book by R. Martens called Coaches Guide to Sport Psychology, published in 1987 in Champagne, IL, by Human Kinetics.

_____

_____

_____

PLANNING AND OUTLINING

A Solid Structure
The Main Parts of an Essay
Organizing a Compare/Contrast Essay
Organizing a Persuasive Essay
Formal Outlines

Organizational structure: the order in which the paragraph components of an essay are arranged.

Any essay or report you write for a college or university class must have a clear **organizational structure**. In its most basic form, an essay has a main idea followed by several points that support, develop, and augment it. The main idea, presented in the essay's introduction, is usually found within the first few paragraphs. The points in support of the main idea are stated and developed in paragraphs that constitute the body of the essay. As a rule, each point is developed in a separate paragraph. The essay ends with a concluding paragraph that summarizes the body paragraphs and reiterates the essay's main idea. To produce a well-organized essay, as the old saying goes, you simply tell them what you're going to tell them, then tell them, then tell them what you've told them.

THE MAIN PARTS OF AN ESSAY

Let's look at a complete essay, paying particular attention to its organizational structure. Paul was asked to write an essay of approximately 500 words about a hobby he enjoyed; his hobby is photography. Photography is too broad a topic to be covered in 500 words, so after considering a number of possibilities, Paul decided to explain how even a novice photographer could take effective pictures. He jotted down the three points he wanted to communicate to his readers:

1. find out where the light is

2. compose your picture

3. find a good point of view

Since the assignment called for a short essay, Paul planned to devote one paragraph to each point. With one introductory and one concluding paragraph, Paul would produce a basic five-paragraph essay. He planned, he wrote, he revised, and he ultimately produced this essay.

The Art of Taking Good Pictures

Paul H.
English 100-21
December, 19XX

It takes considerable training, study, and experience to become an accomplished professional photographer. An amateur, on vacation, celebrating her child's birthday, or attending her sister's wedding, can not hope to take photographs matching the quality of a professional's. But amateur photographers can still take excellent pictures if they remember a few basic principles of good photography. To take good pictures, a photographer must pay attention to composition, lighting, and point of view.

Photography is an art form. The art of making art, the old saying goes, is "putting it together." Photographers should not just aim and shoot; they should take a few moments to compose the pictures they take. The amateur's natural inclination is to frame her subject in the centre of the picture, but this is often not the best thing to do. Action shots, for example, should place the centre of the action at one edge of the picture. A galloping horse or an Olympic sprinter looks best away from the centre, running towards some open space. An interesting building—a cathedral, for example—can look quite dramatic photographed from the side of a tree, with a branch with a bit of foliage hanging into the picture to provide a sense of space and distance. A good amateur photographer looks for natural lines and patterns—a fence, a staircase, a mountain, or a river—to include in a picture to guide her viewer's eye toward the primary focus of a photograph.

Some photographers believe they don't take pictures of objects at all; they take pictures of light, and the objects are there to give light something to reflect off. If this overstates the case somewhat, it still underscores the importance of lighting in picture-taking. Light can be hard or soft, blue or golden; it can come from the sun or the moon or candles or light bulbs; it can be behind a photographer or to his side or in front of him. A good photographer will stand with the light behind her when she wants to highlight bright colours and fine detail in the picture she is taking. She will stand with the light to one side when she wants strong shadows that will add shape, texture, and volume to her picture. She will stand with the light source in front of her to exaggerate depth or to produce a translucent glow around her subject or, perhaps, to silhouette her subject.

Finally, a good, even if amateur photographer, will find an interesting point of view from which to take a picture. The photographer who is going to get a really interesting shot of the parade is the one who has climbed up the tree. The best picture of the swimming party will come from the photographer lying on her stomach at poolside, capturing the splashing and the laughter of the children (while, of course, managing to protect her lens). Good photographers shoot lengthwise and widthwise shots and might even hold their camera at an angle to capture life being lived a little bit off kilter. Insects and flowers can look stunning photographed extremely close up; distant, wide-angle shots are good for sunsets and landscapes.

Photography is one of those activities in which many participate but few do well. Yet anyone can take pictures they would be proud to show off

> to their friends. A good photographer must compose a shot and consider
> the angle, distance, and height that will bring out the best in her
> subject. And a good photographer must, perhaps above all else, really
> see the light.

Introductory paragraph: paragraph (in longer essays, more than one) that introduces an essay, usually stating the essay's topic and main idea.

Body paragraphs: paragraphs that follow the introductory paragraph and that develop the essay's main idea.

Concluding paragraph: paragraph that follows body paragraphs and that lets readers know that what was promised in the introductory paragraph has been delivered.

Notice, again, the organizational structure Paul has used. He has a five-paragraph essay, beginning with an **introductory paragraph**, which expresses his main idea; moving to three **body paragraphs**, each of which develops a point relevant to his main idea; and ending with a **concluding paragraph**, which reiterates his main idea.

Planning an essay, such as Paul's essay on photography, is not difficult. The topic lends itself to a clearly defined plan: suggest three ways in which a novice photographer can take better pictures. Fortunately, many of the essay topics assigned to you will have, inherent in them, an obvious organizational structure. Essay topics that require you to explain a process or describe the causes of a certain event or discuss how a particular event has affected society are usually not hard to plan. There are, however, two types of essay, commonly assigned in college and university classes, for which the organizational structure is not so immediately apparent. These are the compare/contrast essay and the argumentative or persuasive essay.

ASSIGNMENT 5-1

In a magazine you enjoy reading, find an example of an informative (expository) essay that you think is well written. Identify the main idea of the essay and the points the author makes to support or develop her thesis. Does the author use one paragraph for each main point or does she use more than one paragraph to develop any of her ideas?

ORGANIZING A COMPARE/CONTRAST ESSAY

Compare/contrast essay: a kind of informative essay that describes similarities and differences between two related objects or people.

Professors in nearly all academic disciplines assign **compare/contrast essays**: essays that compare and contrast two poems, two psychological theories, two systems of government, two tragic heroes, two advertising campaigns, two treatments for an illness, or two cures for a social problem. By assigning a compare/contrast essay, professors can evaluate their students' knowledge of two aspects of a subject and their students' ability to discuss a subject analytically.

One English teacher, for example, gave this assignment to his students.

Read carefully the following story:

> Tanzan and Ekido were once travelling together down a muddy road. A heavy rain was still falling.
>
> Coming around a bend, they met a lovely girl in a silk kimono and sash, unable to cross the intersection.
>
> "Come on, girl," said Tanzan at once. Lifting her in his arms, he carried her over the mud.
>
> Ekido did not speak again until that night when they reached a lodging temple. Then he could no longer restrain himself. "We monks don't go near females," he told Tanzan, "especially not young and lovely ones. It is dangerous. Why did you do that?"
>
> "I left the girl there," said Tanzan. "Are you still carrying her?"

In an essay of approximately 500 words, compare and contrast the characters of Tanzan and Ekido.

How would you structure the essay that this assignment would generate? There are two possibilities.

You might identify certain general characteristics the two characters share, then discuss the similarities and differences between the two characters in terms of those general characteristics. You might decide to discuss similarities and differences in the occupations, the personalities, and the values of the two characters.

A second possibility would be to begin by discussing how the two characters are similar, then discuss how the two characters are different. One student who chose this type of organizational structure produced the following compare/contrast essay:

HELPFUL HINTS

An effective compare/contrast essay requires careful planning.

Tanzan and Ekido: A Comparison and Contrast

Madelaine R.
English 100, Section 18
December, 19XX

The story of Tanzan and Ekido is very short, consisting of five brief paragraphs, three characters, some dialogue, and the barest possible descriptions of setting. The story seems to be set in Japan. The story is insightful, in spite of its brevity. Its theme comes across most clearly by comparing and contrasting the two main characters, Tanzan and Ekido.

The men share the same occupation. They are both monks and they are travelling together, to what destination and for what purpose we are never told. Although they belong to the same strict religious order, they have very different personalities.

The differences come across, first, when they meet a lovely young girl, unable to cross a very muddy road. Ekido does nothing, aware that the rules of his monastery strictly forbid any kind of contact with women. Tanzan sees a fellow traveller in distress and immediately carries her across the road, his vow to avoid all contact with women overridden by his desire to do a good deed. Kindness and compassion, Tanzan apparently reasons, must also be exercised by men of God.

Ekido falls silent and seems to become sullen. He does not speak for a long time. When he does, at the lodging temple, it is to upbraid Tanzan for breaking the rules of their religious order. "I left the girl there," said Tanzan. "Are you still carrying her?"

Tanzan's reply highlights another difference between the two men. Ekido is not completely comfortable with his faith, not completely convinced, at least subconsciously, that he followed the correct career path. Women still intrigue him, still tempt him.

Tanzan, on the other hand, is secure in his faith. He can help another person, oblivious to that person's physical attractiveness. His faith is strong enough that not only does he resist temptation, he is unaware there is anything to be tempted by.

Both monks, then, have taken the same vows but each interprets those vows in a different way. Ekido thinks the vow of chastity means that a monk should, under all circumstances, stay away from beautiful young women. Tanzan thinks beautiful young women are ordinary people, not sex objects, and just as deserving of help as anyone else. Tanzan is a true monk, a true man of God. Ekido thinks his devotion surpasses Tanzan's because he doesn't go near women, but, in reality, he is less of a monk than Tanzan because he is afraid—afraid if he carries in his arms a beautiful young girl, he will fall from grace. Grace, to Tanzan, is gender-neutral.

Notice, again, the organizational structure Madelaine has used. The similarities between the two monks are obvious and not as important as the differences, so they are discussed first, in the paragraph immediately following the introductory paragraph. In the next four paragraphs, the differences between the two monks are discussed. The differences between the men are the key to the meaning of the story, so they are discussed in more detail than are the similarities. The organizational structure of the essay is complete with the concluding paragraph, which summarizes the story's main point.

ASSIGNMENT 5-2 In an essay of approximately 750 words, compare and contrast one of the following:

1. two TV sitcoms

2. two talk-show hosts

3. two musical groups

4. two methods of getting fit

5. two diets

6. two clothing designers

7. the work of two film directors

8. Or, in consultation with your instructor, choose your own topic.

ORGANIZING A PERSUASIVE ESSAY

Persuasive essay: essay that tries to convince the reader that the writer's position on a controversial issue is valid.

HELPFUL HINTS

An effective persuasive essay acknowledges opposing points of view.

Many of your professors will ask for papers that present an argument on an issue related to the course content. Your purpose in writing a **persuasive essay**, you will remember from Lesson One, is to convince your readers that your position on a controversial subject is the correct and reasonable position to take.

Insofar as an argumentative essay takes a position on a certain subject and then presents evidence in support of that position, it is similar to an informative essay. What really distinguishes it from an informative essay, and what makes a persuasive essay more of a challenge to plan, is the *opposing* argument, which must in the course of the essay be acknowledged and refuted.

Let's look at an example. Charlotte chose to write a persuasive essay explaining her conviction that angels really do exist and influence human lives. Here is her essay, which uses the MLA method to cite secondary sources.

Earth's Angels

Earth's Angels
Charlotte W.
May, 19XX

Angels exist and, under certain circumstances, will intervene in our lives, usually to provide us with help or support during critical times. Make this claim while sitting at a table in your college cafeteria and some of your table-mates, wide-eyed with disbelief, will find a way of excusing themselves. Yet the evidence in support of the existence of angels is compelling.

Christians will find angels in over half of the books of their Bible. An angel begged Abraham not to sacrifice his son; another angel saved Daniel from the lion's den; the archangel Gabriel visited a young woman named Mary and told her she would bear a son and name him Jesus (Gibbs 58). Many other religions, eastern and western, also include angels in a prominent place in their belief systems. Jews and Muslims, Buddhists and Hindus, all believe in angels (Gibbs 58).

In popular culture, angels are, quite literally, everywhere. Five million copies of books about angels have been sold in North America. There are angel newsletters, angel fan clubs, angel posters and greeting cards (Woodward 53). Angels dance (don't ask how many) on the head of a pin. There are angels in the outfield, there are places where angels fear to tread, there are angels of the morning, there is a whole city of Angels.

More compelling proof that angels exist comes from reports of personal encounters some fortunate people have had. In July 1977, Gary Cannady, a retired American Air Force master sergeant, answered his door and stood face to face with a very tall, black-skinned, blue-eyed man who identified himself as Thomas. Thomas explained he was sent by God to cure Gary's wife, Ann, of her terminal cancer. Ann described how the angel moved his right hand toward her, palm outward, but did not touch her. She felt an incredible heat emanating from Thomas's hand, and she fainted. "As I lay there," she explained,

> a strong white light, like one of those search lights, traveled through my body. It started at my feet and worked its way up. I knew then, with every part of me—my body, my mind, my heart—that something supernatural had happened." (Gibbs 60)

Ann's amazed doctor told her later that there was no longer any sign of cancer in her body, and admitted he had witnessed a medical miracle. In Sophy Burnham's *A Book of Angels*, in Billy Graham's book, *Angels: God's Secret Agents*, and in the many other books and newsletters about angels, many similar, well-documented stories are told (Woodward 54). Skeptics, of course, scoff at and patronize believers, arguing that there is not a shred of scientific proof in support of the existence of angels. The current fad, they say, is really a sad commentary on the state of modern society. We are threatened and oppressed by horrible diseases like AIDS, by the threat of terrorism, by violence, and as a way of coping with our fear and insecurity, we hope for and search for a guardian angel. The belief in angels is nothing more than a New Age con game. It is comforting to imagine fluffy teddy bears with wings who fly around rescuing and giving spiritual hugs to weak and needy people, but these people, unfortunately, are deluding themselves.

In fact, angels are not really fluffy and cherubic at all. The evidence suggests they are complex, multi-faceted supernatural beings, who can be warriors as well as nurturers. One of the most famous angel sightings took place in August 1914, during the battle of Mons. Allied soldiers reported the presence of warrior angels on the battlefield, helping to hold the allied position against a German attack. After the war, German soldiers confirmed the angelic presence, claiming that "the allied position was held by thousands of troops—though in fact there were only two regiments there" (Gibbs 61). One of the allied soldiers who witnessed the presence of angels at the Battle of Mons was my own great-grandfather.

Moreover, to argue that something does not exist because science has not proved its existence is to take an unimaginative, limited, and narrow-minded view of the world. Angels always have, and always will, belong to the realm of faith, not science. Lack of "scientific" proof of the existence of angels is quite irrelevant, as irrelevant to believers as the lack of scientific proof of the existence of God. Certainly there are New Age hucksters who are trying to profit from the recent resurgence of interest in angels, who are selling how-to books and seminars on how to become an angel, how to find your "inner angel."

In fact, nowhere in classical theology do humans ever metamorphose in any way into angels (Levine 59). Angels cannot be laughed out of existence because some unscrupulous New Ager holds ridiculous seminars on how to unleash "the angel within." Angels have been around forever, and many people have seen them, interacted with them, and been rescued by them. Nothing could ever challenge the certainty of those of us who believe in angels, because we are united by the unbreakable bond of faith.

Works Cited

Gibbs, Nancy. "Angels Among Us." *Time* Dec. 27, 1993: 56-65.
Levine, Laura. "Cherubs of Love." *Time* Dec. 27, 1993: 59-60.
Woodward, Kenneth L. "Angels: Hark! America's Latest Search for Spiritual Meaning Has a Halo Effect." *Newsweek* Dec. 27, 1993: 52-57.

HELPFUL HINTS

Do not let your emotions get the better of your reason when you are writing a persuasive essay.

Charlotte has written a clear and forceful essay, its clarity and force the result, in part, of its strong organizational structure. In the first paragraph, Charlotte announces her belief in angels, admits many people are skeptical, and promises to present evidence to support her belief. In the next three paragraphs, she presents her evidence. In the fifth paragraph, she acknowledges and summarizes opposing arguments. In the next two paragraphs, she pokes holes in arguments that angels cannot really exist. In her eighth and last paragraph, she completes her refutation and reiterates the points in support of her argument.

ASSIGNMENT 5-3 Write a persuasive essay of approximately 750 words in which you argue either for or against one of the following propositions:

1.   The tactics of some environmental groups are counter-productive.

2.   Smoking should be prohibited in all public places.

3.   We would all be healthier if we didn't eat meat.

4.   Mothers of children under five should not work outside the home.

5.   Running (cycling, swimming, etc.) is the best exercise for overall fitness.

6.   Or, in consultation with your teacher, select a topic of interest to you.

FORMAL OUTLINES

Scratch outline: point-form list of ideas to be developed in an essay.

Formal outline: point-form list of ideas, arranged in a logical system of headings and sub-headings, which will be developed in an essay.

The authors of the model essays in this lesson began with a **scratch outline**, similar to the one Paul jotted down after he had decided to write about how to take good photographs. A rough scratch outline is a good place to begin a writing assignment.

Occasionally, your teachers will ask you to hand in, along with your essay, a **formal outline**, complete with a set of headings and subheadings. The formal outline for Charlotte's essay on angels, for example, would look like this:

Title: Earth's Angels

I.   Introduction: present main idea that angels exist and influence human life

II. Evidence in support

    A.   Angels and world religions
    B.   Angels and popular culture
    C.   Reports of encounters with angels

III. Opposing arguments

    A.   Lack of scientific proof
    B.   Product of fear and insecurity
    C.   New Age nonsense

IV. Refute opposition

    A.   Faith not science
    B.   Nature of angels
    C.   Encounters with angels

V.   Conclusion: Believers share the bond of faith

HELPFUL HINTS

Let your outline guide but not prescribe your writing process.

Recursive process: strategy of writing an essay whereby author does *not* work from an outline but develops content, shapes, revises, and refines essay while writing drafts.

Linear process: logical and deliberate step-by-step strategy by which an author composes an essay.

If your teacher asks you to hand in a formal outline of your essay, along with the essay itself, the outline will likely be the last thing you write. Usually, you give final shape to your essay *while*, not before, you write and revise it.

Remember that writing is rarely a clear, step-by-step process, and that you are doing nothing wrong if you struggle, start and stop, change the order of your paragraphs, then halfway through abandon some ideas and incorporate others. You might get an idea for a better introductory paragraph while you are writing your concluding paragraph. Or a new but important point might come to you at the end of one of your drafts, forcing you to go back and change your original outline. Writing is, to use the term favoured by experts in the field, a **recursive** and not a **linear process**. You must end up with a clear, well-organized product, but if the process you go through to end up with this product is some form of organized chaos, you are working the way most writers work.

ASSIGNMENT 5-4   Construct a formal outline for the essay you used in response to Assignment 5-1.

SUMMARY

- Write a clear beginning, middle, and end for your essay.
- Organize a compare/contrast essay by first discussing similarities, then discussing differences.
- In a persuasive essay, present evidence in support of its thesis *and* acknowledge and refute opposing arguments.

QUESTIONS FOR STUDY AND DISCUSSION

1. Explain this maxim as it applies to essay writing: First tell them what you're going to tell them, then tell them, then tell them what you've told them.

2. Why is a compare/contrast essay more difficult to organize than other kinds of informative essays?

3. What elements does a persuasive essay need that informative essays usually do not need?

SUPPLEMENTARY EXERCISES

1. Turn the following passages of freewriting into clear essay outlines. Feel free to add to or subtract from the information provided.

    a. The violin, the cello, and the bass are the main stringed instruments in a orchestra—an orchestra needs a wide range of instrument—flexibilty—to play the complex, powerful, wide-ranging music demanded of it. brass instruments—the trumpet—brilliant tone which makes it a popular instrument for solos—as early as Bach. the violin is also a solo instrument—Scheherezade by Rimsky-Korsacoff—the violin like a person—a character in that drama. The cello—Yo Yo Mah—also a solo instrument—bigger than the violin—rich, noble sound. the bass—more of a "support" instrument (the violin often carries the melody)—sometimes used as a rhythm instrument—bass "riffs"—back to brass instruments—trombone—bigger than trumpet—more solemn tone—very precise tuning—slide rather than valves as in trumpet to change notes—beautiful French horn—tiny mouthpiece—difficult to play but very distinct, celebratory sound—stretched out its tube would be 12 feet long! several concertos have been written for French horn. Woodwind Instruments—holes which open and close to produce right sounds—flute—made of metal unlike other woodwinds which are made of wood. blow sideways to produce "feminine" (?!) sound—piccolo smaller and an octave higher—clarinet—a single reed instrument because a single cane reed is attached to the mouthpiece—like violin and trumpet in carrying melody—capable of greater range of noise from loud to soft of any other woodwind instrument—little used before Mozart—now an orchestra staple—oboe—double reed instrument like its cousin the bassoon—two cane reeds slightly apart around a small metal tube in turn surrounded by cork—requires very little breath—Bach and Handel loved the oboe—reedy, penetrating tone—Saxophone—alto sax Kenny G—invented by A. Sax in 1846—single reed—not always associated with orchestras—modern instrument. Percussion—kettle drum or timapani most important orchestra drum—large copper bowl covered with calf skin—can change notes but difficult while a piece is being played—notes can be changed with foot pedal—bass drum—triangle—cymbals. Keyboard instruments—piano—solo instrument—dramatic because more physical movement required from player—many concertos, etc. written for piano—pedals can make notes more sustained—grand piano strings are horizontal as opposed to vertical in upright piano—organ—air blown through pipes (today electronically) when a note is pressed the air is released—does not play louder when key is pressed harder unlike piano—stops control air flow hence sound hence an organ can sound sometimes like a flute, sometimes like a clarinet—versatile instrument—has several keyboards unlike piano—also pedals which play very low notes—

_____

_____

_____

_____

_____

_____

_____

_____

_____

_____

_____

_____

_____

_____

_____

_____

b. should the lyrics of popular music—rap and hip hop and heavy metal especially be banned, censored? Dr. Dre—music advocates or seems to advocate violence against women, against whites, especially against white cops. is it legitimate social protest—note blacks experiences with white police in Los Angeles—note that newspapers, even when they run anti-censorship editorials, will not reprint the lyrics some of which are very brutal—bestiality—younger teenagers can't buy liquor or see certain films but they can buy obscene cds and tapes—2 live crew—to prosecute for obscenity, the material must be without artistic merit and pander to prurient interests. Is 2 live crew without artistic merit? Their record sold close to 2 million copies. X-rated material readily available—where do you draw the line? Are teenagers who listen to obscene rap lyrics more likely to commmit crimes?—it seems every innovative form of musical expression has had to battle censorship—on the Ed Sullivan Show, Elvis could not be photographed from the waist down—Tipper Gore wants warning labels put on cds, similar to ratings for movies—is this a good idea? is this a possible compromise solution? what do the studies of the relationship between watching violent movies or hearing violent lyrics and committing acts of violence have to say? Studies done by sociologists tend to discount the theory that teenagers who like violent films and music are more prone to commit violence themselves. yet society seems to be becoming more violent. almost everyday it seems, we can read in the paper about some teenager who has acted violently after seeing or hearing violence or after playing violent games like Dungeons and Dragons— provide examples of "obscene" lyrics.

_____

_____

_____

_____

_____

_____

_____

_____

_____

_____

_____

_____

_____

_____

_____

_____

_____

_____

c. the assignment is to compare and contrast some aspect of the behaviour of men and women. maybe compare and contrast the ways in which men and women communicate in conversation—women tend to want to discuss things like a major purchase—men are more likely to go out and make the purchase without discussing it with their partner—men are more silent than women, usually. Similarities? both men and women want to communicate effectively to each other and believe they are doing so when the other thinks they are not. When women complain about something, other women tend to offer sympathy and empathy. Men tend to suggest solutions, thinking this is what the women want. See Deborah Tannen's two books "That's Not What I Meant" and "You Just Don't Understand" for more examples. men see human relationships in terms of competition and their conversation reflects this. women are more inclined to see human relationships in terms of cooperation and their conversation reflects their world view. Listen to men and women talk about their work, about their bosses. men seek independence and enjoy "one-upping" their bosses; women are usually better team players—if the boss succeeds, they succeed—women are more willing to talk about their feelings—men tend to think this is "unmanly"—Asking for directions or other information—women are usually more willing to do so—men feel this puts them in an inferior position and so will drive around aimlessly for hours hoping to find the street they are looking for—why don't you just stop and ask someone, the woman will ask, frustrated—praise—women give it more than men?—women who speak forcefully, aggressively, who give orders are put down as "nags" but men who do the same are considered dynamic, leaders—who talks more? women have the reputation for doing so but studies don't support this—women talk more within the home, men outside of the home—other people will often be surprised to hear a woman say her husband is not very communicative because they know him as a man who has a lot to say. gossip. men tend not to like it when their partners discuss personal problems with other women—it shows weakness, failure—men prefer to solve problems alone, women seek help and communicate their need for help—favourite subjects for discussion: men tend to talk about politics, sports, news—women tend to talk about personal, health, family matters. telling jokes—who tells them more? are the subjects of the jokes different? Arguments—men tend to be more aggressive? want to "win" —women tend to want to compromise—solve the problem the argument generated.

_____

_____

_____

_____

_____

_____

_____

_____

_____

_____

_____

_____

_____

_____

_____

_____

_____

_____

_____

Writing an Effective Introduction

Make a Good First Impression
The Blueprint Thesis
The Short Thesis
Tone

If you have ever taken a bus tour, you know that you get a good idea about how interesting and enjoyable the tour will be when the guide first stands up and addresses your group. If she is confident, intelligent, personable, articulate and witty, and if she tells you where you are going and what to look for when you get there, you know you are likely to have a good experience.

A teacher knows the extent to which she will enjoy your paper—and will begin to evaluate the quality of your paper—after she has read the introductory paragraph (or paragraphs, if it is a major assignment). She will have expectations similar to those you have when you first listen to your tour guide. An effective introduction is strong and confident; it sets the stage for the rest of your essay; and, most important, it tells your readers where you are taking them. In other words, an effective introduction captures your readers' interest, sets the tone and style of your essay, and presents the essay's thesis, or central idea.

Consider this introduction to an essay about the characteristics of good writing:

College students are often apprehensive about writing essays. The list of the characteristics of good writing seems formidable and intimidating. Professors want written work to be informative, well-organized, clear, and concise. They want correct grammar, spelling, and punctuation. They want to read essays that have unity and coherence, and some variety in diction and sentence structure. They look for originality and creativity, style and substance. How much there is to keep in mind, students lament, in order to write well. Can not the rules for good writing be made less daunting, more accessible? Fortunately, they can. All of the characteristics of good writing can be synthesized and reduced to four fundamental rules. To write well, students must explore their topic, develop their ideas, express themselves clearly, and develop an effective style.

Expository essay: (same as *Informative essay*) informs readers about a subject using examples, details, definitions, comparisons, contrasts, causes, and effects.

Thesis: central or controlling idea of an informative or persuasive essay.

HELPFUL HINTS

An introductory paragraph *should* get your readers' attention; it *must* present your thesis.

This is a typical, standard, and effective introductory paragraph for an **informative** or **expository essay**. It begins with a general statement about the topic of the essay: the challenge of writing essays in college. Then it continues, still in fairly general terms, to discuss the many qualities of good writing. After that, it asks if these many qualities can be "synthesized and reduced." Then it answers the question with a direct and specific statement: To write well, students must explore their topic, develop their ideas, express themselves clearly, and develop an effective style.

The last sentence of the above opening paragraph is the **thesis**. It tells the reader the central idea of the essay and provides an overview of the points the essay will cover. After reading the last sentence of the opening paragraph, the reader knows the writer will cover four points. If it is a basic informative or expository essay, each point is likely to be developed in a separate paragraph. In other words, this thesis tells its readers that the essay they are reading consists of six paragraphs: the introductory paragraph, four body paragraphs (one for each of the four points touched on in the thesis), and a concluding paragraph.

ASSIGNMENT 6-1

Find an example in a magazine, a textbook chapter, or in one of your own essays of an introduction that contains a thesis that appears at the end of the introduction and that summarizes the points that the body paragraphs will develop.

THE BLUEPRINT THESIS

Thesis statements that announce the central idea of the essay and then branch out into three or four phrases that synopsize the body of the essay are common in college writing. In fact, they are revered by most teachers, and for good reason. A thesis statement that summarizes the three or four points that will be fully developed in the essay's body provides a clear blueprint for the rest of the essay. A reader knows exactly where the essay is going and, therefore, his ability to follow along and to understand is enhanced.

Consider this opening paragraph from an essay that presents an interpretation of John Keats's famous poem "Ode to a Nightingale":

At the time he wrote "Ode to a Nightingale," in the spring of 1819, Keats had been diagnosed with tuberculosis, and knew he had not long to live. This news came soon after Keats, who had trained as a doctor, had cared for his brother, Tom, as he died slowly and painfully of the same fatal illness. In "Ode to a Nightingale," Keats gives voice to his despair. In this poem, he describes his anguish and his suffering; he expresses his desire to escape from his world of pain and sorrow with the help of the nightingale's beautiful song; and he describes the initial success but ultimate failure of his attempt to escape his reality.

Anecdote: brief story used to add interest to an informative or persuasive essay.

This introductory paragraph captures the reader's interest with an interesting and relevant biographical anecdote. Then it moves smoothly from the **anecdote** to the thesis, which cues the reader on the three points that will be discussed in the body of the essay.

ASSIGNMENT 6-2   Compose two thesis statements that summarize the three points that the writer will develop in the body of the essay.

The introductory paragraph with the three-part thesis also works well for a letter of application:

Dear Mr. Shaw:

Today I met with City College's employment counsellor who told me your Resort is looking for a qualified ski instructor. I am writing to apply for this position. I believe I have the training, the experience, and the personal qualities you are looking for.

The training, the experience, the personal qualities—busy potential employers have to appreciate such a specific thesis, which will make it easier for them to know what the letter contains and where in the letter they can find the information they need.

ASSIGNMENT 6-3   Write an introductory paragraph for a letter of application.

For a film or a book review, you can also use the three-part thesis at the end of the introductory paragraph effectively:

It has been some years since I have seen a film that forced me to revise my list of my top ten all-time favourite movies. But this week, I saw a film that will be added to my list. The movie is *Forrest Gump*. *Forrest Gump* tells a sweeping, humorous, and inspiring story; it contains fascinating characters brought alive so effectively by the actors who portray them; and it is, technically, one of the most innovative films made in the last few years.

This is an effective introductory paragraph because it begins with a broad statement about the student's all-time favourite films; then it narrows the discussion to one film; and finally it presents the thesis, complete with the reasons (to be developed fully in the body of the review) why the author admires the film he is reviewing.

ASSIGNMENT 6-4   Write an opening paragraph for a film review.

Blueprint thesis statements are usually at the end of introductory paragraphs, but they do not have to be. Here is an example of an opening paragraph from a famous essay by Bertrand Russell called "What I Have Lived For." Note that the thesis statement is the first sentence of the paragraph:

> Three passions ... have governed my life: the longing for love, the search for knowledge, and unbearable pity for the suffering of mankind. These passions, like great winds, have blown me hither and thither, in a wayward course, over a deep ocean of anguish, reaching to the very verge of despair.

Here is one more example of an introductory paragraph that ends with a thesis summarizing the points that the body of the essay will develop:

> "First impressions," according to one old adage, "are lasting impressions." We often form opinions of other people quickly, based on brief, initial encounters. We form our opinions of an article or an essay we are reading in much the same way. To be taken seriously, to be admired and appreciated, an essay must give a good first impression—it must have an effective opening paragraph. An effective opening paragraph will present the central idea of an essay, engage the reader's interest, and set the tone of the essay.

Note, also, that this paragraph begins with a quotation, a common technique writers use in their introductions to capture their readers' interest.

Review once more the blueprint thesis statements in the introductory paragraphs presented in this lesson:

> All of the characteristics of good writing can be synthesized and reduced to four fundamental rules. To write well, students must explore their topic, develop their ideas, express themselves clearly, and develop an effective style.

> In this poem, he describes his anguish and his suffering; he expresses his desire to escape from his world of pain and sorrow with the help of the nightingale's beautiful song; and he describes the initial success but ultimate failure of his attempt to escape his reality.

> I believe I have the training, the experience, and the personal qualities you are looking for.

> *Forrest Gump* tells a sweeping, humorous, and inspiring story; it contains fascinating characters brought alive so effectively by the actors who portray them; and it is, technically, one of the most innovative films made in the last few years.

> Three passions, simple but overwhelmingly strong, have governed my life: the longing for love, the search for knowledge, and unbearable pity for the suffering of mankind.

An effective opening paragraph will present the central idea of an essay, engage the readers' interest, and set the tone of the essay.

Notice again how the blueprint thesis cues the reader about the points that will be discussed in detail in the body paragraphs. The blueprint thesis helps the writer structure the essay and enhances the reader's ability to follow along and understand the writer's work.

ASSIGNMENT 6-5

Find an example of an introductory paragraph that uses a quotation to help engage the reader's interest. Bring your example to class and be prepared to discuss it with your classmates.

THE SHORT THESIS

As effective as the blueprint thesis is, a writer might choose not to summarize the points that the essay will contain. Perhaps the points are too complex to be summarized in phrases or clauses; perhaps the writer wants to keep the reader in suspense about the evolution of an argument he is developing. For these or other reasons, a writer might choose to use a short thesis in the introductory paragraph. Here is an example:

> Literary interpretation is transitory; it changes as times change. John Donne's poem "The Flea," for example, used to be read as a description of a harmless, typical young man who, in a playful and witty manner, tries to talk the young woman he is with into having sex with him. Contemporary readers, women especially, are less likely to be amused by this eloquent young man and are more likely to find his behaviour offensive. The narrator of "The Flea" could, in fact, be charged with sexual harassment.

HELPFUL HINTS

Your thesis statement does not always have to be the last sentence of your introductory paragraph.

The last sentence of the opening paragraph is still the thesis, but this thesis does not summarize the reasons to be used in support of the writer's position. The writer decided that the paper would be more effective if the arguments used to support the main point were withheld until the body of the essay.

Here is another example of an opening paragraph that uses a short thesis. The thesis statement is the second sentence of the paragraph:

> In early February, 40 Innu from Davis Inlet rode snowmobiles north to the drill camp on Labrador's east coast and issued an eviction notice to the miners. The Innu Nation, an Indian band with a land claim on the area that includes the massive mineral strike at Voisey Bay, demanded an end to the project that will soon be one of the richest nickel mines in the world. Aside from forcing a suspension of drilling operations, the protesters burned and vandalized equipment and building materials, doing about $15,000 worth of damage. The standoff—at one point more than 75 Innu faced off with 57 RCMP officers—lasted 12 days before ending peacefully.

Tim Falconer

This opening paragraph commands the reader's attention through the use of an anecdote, a common and effective opening paragraph technique. The thesis is effective in that it is a part of the narrative, but, at the same time, goes beyond the narrative to indicate the essay's controlling idea.

Let us look at one more example of an introductory paragraph that uses a short thesis. In fact, in this paragraph the thesis, the second sentence, is only six words long:

> Hardly a May has gone by in the last 15 years that hasn't seen me ski. I love to ski in May. Or rather, I love the fact that in May, the skiing is deteriorating at even the best-covered ski areas in Canada, Sunshine Village and Blackcomb. The magic interlude of good corn snow, wedged between an ever-weakening night-time freeze and an ominously intensifying sun, shrinks by day. More and more hours are taken up surfing ankle-deep slop. It's basically skiing for the sake of, well, saying you skied. That makes it fairly easy to bid the closing season adieu, reflect on the great skiing the season granted and look forward to the summer excitement that beckons; mountain biking, sailing, white-water hiking, climbing, whatever. It makes a nice, natural and easy transition from winter to summer.
>
> George Koch

ASSIGNMENT 6-6

Find an example of an introductory paragraph that contains a thesis that does *not* summarize the points to be developed in the body of the essay. Bring your example to class and be prepared to discuss it with your classmates.

TONE

Tone: refers to attitude, ranging from light to formal, a piece of writing conveys.

The introductory paragraph sets the tone of the essay. The **tone** is the personality, the attitude a piece of writing conveys to its readers. A research paper in the sciences or social sciences usually has a formal tone:

> The purpose of this paper is to report the results of a study on the spread of the acquired immune deficiency syndrome among the indigenous people of northern Zaire. The study was conducted over a three-year period, from June, 1991 to June, 1994. During this time, 171 new cases of AIDS were reported within the three tribes who participated in this study.

Note that the author uses a short thesis, and that the thesis is the first sentence of the paragraph. This is a common technique for introducing scientific papers.

A personal narrative essay about, say, an embarrassing moment, is going to convey a much different tone. What is the tone of this opening paragraph?

> Kids have a way of saying the wrong thing, at the wrong time, in the wrong place. My most embarrassing moment came last weekend when I took my four-year-old niece in to our local video store.

Obviously, this essay is going to have a much less formal tone than the tone used in the essay about the spread of AIDS. The subject is less serious, the purpose is more to entertain than to inform, and the audience is more general.

Falling between the formal tone of the first essay and the informal tone of the second is the essay that adopts a moderate tone, not too serious, not too light. The following paragraph introduces an essay about a serious subject, but it is written for a general audience, so the tone is moderate:

> It is ten years since the Conservative government first tentatively broached the subject of free trade with the United States, beginning a voyage that was to end three years later in the signing of the Canada-U.S. Free Trade Agreement (FTA). The deal was a path-breaker in many ways. It transformed Canada from one of the most protected economies in the developed world to one of the most open. It also ignited an extraordinary export boom in this country, the historic dimensions of which are only beginning to become clear.
>
> Andrew Coyne

Note, as well, the short thesis statement, which is the second sentence of the paragraph.

Tone, then, is determined by the subject, the purpose, and the audience. A serious subject with a serious purpose, written for a specialized audience, uses a formal tone. For a general reader, a writer uses a light or informal tone for an amusing subject and purpose, and a moderate tone for a more serious subject.

ASSIGNMENT 6-7 Find an example of an introductory paragraph that suggests that the tone of the essay will be formal. Find an introductory paragraph that suggests that the tone will be informal. Bring your examples to class and be prepared to discuss them with your classmates.

SUMMARY

- An effective essay has a clear and strong introduction.
- The essay introduction must present the central idea of the essay called *the thesis*.
- The blueprint thesis summarizes the points that the body of the essay will develop.
- The short thesis, also commonly used, does not summarize the essay's main ideas.
- An effective introduction engages the reader's interest.
- An effective introduction establishes the tone (the attitude or "personality") of the essay.

QUESTIONS FOR STUDY AND DISCUSSION

1. What is the thesis statement of Lesson Six?

2. What is the thesis statement of Lesson One?

3. List three techniques that writers often use to capture their readers' interest.

4. Define the term *tone* as it applies to essay writing. Make up a title for an essay that would have a formal tone and one for an essay that would have an informal tone.

SUPPLEMENTARY EXERCISES

1. Add a thesis statement to the following introductory paragraphs. Change, add to, or delete from the paragraphs as you see fit in order to incorporate the thesis statements effectively. Reverse the arguments expressed in persuasive thesis statements if you disagree with them. The thesis statements do not necessarily have to be the last sentence of the paragraph.

   a. In a certain television commercial, a teacher takes his fine arts class to a gallery to give them a lesson on abstract art—a form, the teacher explains, that means different things to different people. "What does this painting say to you, John?" the teacher asks one of his students. "I see a hamburger," the student responds, then begins to explain what he means in mouth-watering detail. "Does anyone see anything different"? the teacher asks. The other students are silent, obviously still transfixed by their classmate's description, which has clearly caused an epidemic of hunger pangs. "That's what it is all right," the teacher says, "let's eat!"

      _____

      _____

      _____

   b. I did not hesitate to lend Jeff the money because while he is forever borrowing money from me, he always pays me back. I did, however, make the usual plea: "Wait two months and it will be out on video; we can *both* see it, we can see it with half a dozen friends at half the cost." The expression on Jeff's face told me my attempt to reason with him was doomed to fail.

      _____

      _____

      _____

c. It is the most vicious of all vicious circles. A nation starves, unable to feed its burgeoning population. Philanthropic organizations, rock musicians, churches—their hearts in exactly the right places—rally around to raise millions of dollars to buy food to feed the children whose sorrowful faces appear before us each night on the national news. For a time, conditions improve; the children are fed.

    _____

    _____

    _____

d. Film producers argue that by making violent movies, they are simply giving the public what it wants. Their opponents argue that they are manufacturing a need, then fulfilling that need, and in the process abandoning all sense of social and artistic responsibility in the interest of power and profit.

    _____

    _____

    _____

e. They are not all young men or old women. They don't all drive "hot" cars nor do they necessarily drive "clunkers." But bad drivers do share certain common characteristics.

    _____

    _____

    _____

2. Write effective introductory paragraphs that incorporate the following thesis statements. Alter the thesis statements if you wish.

a. But if imitation is the sincerest form of flattery, then Ralph Klein's political future, perhaps even at the federal level, will be guaranteed.

    _____

    _____

    _____

    _____

    _____

b. We need only look at recent hostilities at Oka, Gustafson Lake, and Ipperwash Park to realize how serious Native-Canadian discontent has become.

_____

_____

_____

_____

_____

c. Although in theory an enlightened and democratic concept, in practice collaborative management will not work: a camel, the old expression goes, is a horse designed by a committee.

_____

_____

_____

_____

_____

d. Young women with eating disorders tend to crave attention, have low self-esteem, and adopt as role models movie stars and fashion models.

_____

_____

_____

_____

_____

e. Despite widespread skepticism, there is, at least, enough circumstantial evidence to prove that UFOs really exist.

_____

_____

_____

_____

_____

f. Soon cities with fewer than three million people will not be able to support professional sports, businesses will not be able to afford to advertise during major sporting events, and fans will not be able to pay the ticket prices that owners will have to charge to support such exorbitant salary demands.

_____

_____

_____

_____

_____

g. Most students attend college to train for a rewarding career, to broaden their social circles, and to expand their intellectual horizons.

_____

_____

_____

_____

_____

h. Education will help but if date rape is really to end, women must be more willing to charge offenders, and the courts must recognize date rape as a serious crime.

_____

_____

_____

_____

_____

i. Tennis ace Michael Chang, hockey star Theoren Fleury, and basketball phenom Mugsy Bogues prove that small in size does not mean small in prowess.

_____

_____

_____

_____

_____

j. With a test-tube pregnancy, career women will not have to take time off work; they will not have to go through the pain, discomfort, and trauma of childbirth; and they will have the pleasure of watching their child grow and develop not just from birth, but from conception.

_____

_____

_____

_____

_____

k. Grisham's novels are so successful because his plots always concern ordinary people struggling against big business or government, his characters are easy and fun to identify with, and his writing style is clear and engaging.

_____

_____

_____

_____

_____

Writing Effective Body Paragraphs

Check Paragraphs for...

Unity
Development

The main idea or ideas, introduced or implied in the essay's introduction, are developed in the body of the essay. Depending upon the assignment, the topic, the purpose, and the audience of an essay, there might be any number of paragraphs in the body. Effective body paragraphs have two main characteristics: they are unified and well developed.

UNITY

Unity: quality of a paragraph in which all sentences relate to one topic.

Topic sentence: sentence that contains the paragraph's main idea.

Transitional sentence: usually first sentence of a paragraph; establishes connection with last sentence of previous paragraph.

Unity is established when a paragraph contains a **topic sentence** and the other sentences in the paragraph clearly relate to it. The topic sentence contains the main idea of the paragraph; it is, to the paragraph, what the thesis (Lesson Six) is to the whole essay.

The topic sentence is often the first sentence of a paragraph. If the first sentence is **transitional**—that is, if it signals a change in focus from the preceding paragraph—the topic sentence is often the second sentence. It is possible, however, that a writer might choose to delay the topic sentence until the end of the paragraph in order to add emphasis or perhaps an element of surprise. Often the topic of a paragraph is not stated explicitly in a single sentence, but, instead, is implied in two or more sentences.

Other sentences in the paragraph should relate to the topic sentence or the paragraph tends to be confusing and disjointed. Lack of unity will effectively confuse a reader.

Let's look at an example of a well-written, unified paragraph. Alain wrote an essay describing his dream car, the Acura NSX-T. His first body paragraph described the car's physical appearance. This is his second body paragraph:

Complementing the NSX-T's exquisite design is its equally exquisite engine. A three-litre V6 with four valves per cylinder operated by dual overhead camshafts, the engine delivers 270 horsepower at 7100 r.p.m.'s. The engine is located in the middle of the car just behind and beneath the driver, but it is so quiet that, with the CD player at its lowest volume, it can barely be heard. It is fed through an efficient electronic fuel system, which delivers a respectable 100 highway kilometres for nine litres of fuel. The engine is torque rated at 252 lbs-ft at 6600 r.p.m. It can propel the car from zero to sixty in a heartbeat.

Note how unity is established in this paragraph. The topic sentence is the first sentence, which tells the reader that discussion is moving from the design of the NSX-T to its engine. All of the other sentences relate to the key phrase in the topic sentence, "exquisite engine."

Here is another example of a unified paragraph:

The Canadian Centre for Drug-free Sport published a study in August 1993 that reports on a survey of more than 16,000 Canadian students between the ages of 11 and 18. The survey results are disturbing. Only 4 per cent of students surveyed, and only 2.4 per cent of those 16 and older, said they had never heard of anabolic steroids. Two-thirds of male students and one-half of female students surveyed believed that—as Ben Johnson showed the world—steroids would help improve an athlete's performance. One in five of the students reported knowing someone who had used steroids, and among students 16 and older, almost one in three knew someone who had used steroids.

British Columbia Medical Association

The second sentence is the topic sentence. The four other sentences all relate to the topic sentence. The first describes the survey the topic sentence is referring to. The other three explain the contention made in the topic sentence that the survey results are disturbing.

ASSIGNMENT 7-1

Explain in writing how unity is established in the following paragraph.

Another episode from ancient Greek history led to the creation of an event in the Summer Olympics and gave a running shoe company its name. In 490 B.C., the Athenian army defeated a Persian attack at the Battle of the Plains of Marathon. The victorious generals dispatched a young soldier back to Athens to announce the outcome. The messenger was so elated by the victory and so honoured to be the one chosen to bear the news that he ran the twenty-six miles back to Athens, and so established the distance of the Olympic race named after the Battle of Marathon. Unfortunately, the young soldier was so emotionally and physically exhausted from the whole ordeal that he dropped dead just as he was shouting the Greek word for victory—"nike."

DEVELOPMENT

There are various ways of expanding upon a topic sentence in order to create a well-developed paragraph. You might provide specific examples or details relevant to your topic sentence. You might tell a story or an anecdote that sheds light on the topic. You might define a key term around which your topic sentence is built, or compare and/or contrast the subject of your topic sentence with something else. You might explain the causes of what you are writing about or you might explain its effects.

Let's look at and discuss an example of each method of paragraph development.

Examples

Here, from the sample research paper in Lesson Three, is a paragraph developed through the use of examples:

> Since the early seventeenth century, for example, English has continued to borrow and adapt hundreds of words from other languages. While the King James Bible was being written and published, explorers were meeting the Native people of North America. From their languages came words like "hickory," "chipmunk," "moose," "tomahawk," and "kayak" (McCrum, et al., 1992, p. 123). As years passed, European immigrants began to arrive, bringing with them many words from many languages—words that were soon incorporated into English. Gefvert (1985) provides a small list of examples:
>
>> From French we borrowed "brochure" and "chaperone;" from Portuguese, "veranda;" from Spanish, "cafeteria" and "marijuana;" from Italian, "serenade" and "umbrella;" from Swedish, "ski;" from Dutch, "cookie;" from German, "hamburger" and "kindergarten;" from Arabic, "algebra;" from Persian, "paradise." (344)
>
> Asian languages have enriched English with words like "tea" and "silk." From African languages, words like "banana" and "jazz" have come into English (Gefvert 344). Today, of course, the process continues. English-speaking countries welcome immigrants whose many gifts include new words that soon find their way into English dictionaries.

The structure of this body paragraph is simple and straightforward. The topic sentence, the first sentence in the paragraph, announces the subject; the other sentences provide examples of English words borrowed from other languages.

ASSIGNMENT 7-2 Write a paragraph on a topic of your choice, developed by the use of examples.

Details

Here is an example of a paragraph developed through the use of details:

> Another quality of good writing is clarity. Several elements must be present in an essay for writing to be clear. Writing is clear when it is well-organized, concise and cohesive; when the links among sentences in a paragraph and paragraphs in the whole work are explicit. Grammatically correct sentences are clearer than sentences that contain grammatical errors, and properly punctuated sentences are clearer than sentences punctuated incorrectly. Even the smallest unit of writing—the word—is important to clarity. Words used correctly and spelled correctly are clearer than ambiguous and misspelled words.

Note that, in this paragraph, the first sentence provides the reader with a transition from the previous paragraph. Clearly, the essay is about the characteristics of good writing; the previous paragraph discussed one quality of good writing, and this paragraph discusses another. In this paragraph, the topic sentence is not the first but the second sentence. The other sentences provide details, elucidating the topic sentence.

ASSIGNMENT 7-3

Find, in a magazine or journal article or in one of your textbooks, an example of a paragraph developed using details. Identify the topic sentence. Be prepared to read this paragraph to other students in your class.

Anecdote

We usually associate anecdotes with expressive writing, but a paragraph containing an illustrative story can be effective in an informative or persuasive essay as well. Here is an example, from Jeremy's essay, about the characteristics of obsessive runners:

> A second characteristic of obsessive runners is their refusal to miss a race, to take a day off even if their health is threatened, or to drop out of a race they have started to run, even if they feel very sick. Colds, sore throats, the flu—none of these are excuses for rest. The most dramatic example of a runner who refused to quit has to be twenty-six-year-old Eliot Abraham who, a third of the way into the 1993 Sundance Marathon, felt a slight jolt to his head. For the rest of the race, he later explained, he was aware of an unfamiliar sensation in his head that may have affected his time but that would not affect his determination to complete the race. When he did complete the race, he sought medical attention. "Mr. Abraham," the doctor told him, "you have been shot."

The first sentence of this paragraph is the topic sentence. To illustrate his topic sentence, Jeremy tells a dramatic story. He even includes some dialogue, a nice touch in an informative essay.

ASSIGNMENT 7-4   Write a paragraph, on a topic of your choice, developed by the use of anecdote.

Definition

In the course of writing an essay, you often need to define certain terms you are using. Complex terms sometimes need a complete paragraph for an adequately developed definition. Here is a paragraph from an essay about newer methods of analyzing and interpreting literature:

> Another approach to the analysis and interpretation of literature is <u>deconstruction</u>. Deconstruction critics believe that a literary work cannot have a single, recoverable meaning because language is, by nature, an imperfect signifier that means different things to different people. Reading is not an objective but a subjective activity. Each reader interprets a text in light of that reader's gender, political orientation, socio-economic status, ethnic origin. And the same reader will read the same texts in different ways at different times, depending upon the forces and influences in the reader's life at the time the text is being processed. Meaning, therefore, is always breaking down; it is always deconstructing.

The first sentence is the topic sentence, which simply names the term that is to be defined. Notice how, in the last sentence, the term being defined is mentioned again.

ASSIGNMENT 7-5   Find, in a magazine or journal article or in one of your textbooks, an example of a paragraph developed by definition. Identify the topic sentence. Be prepared to read this paragraph to other students in your class.

Comparison and Contrast

Here is a body paragraph from Amy's essay about rising stars in the world of women's figure skating. This paragraph is developed using comparison and contrast.

> They are both figure skaters, both Americans, both among the best in the world. The similarities, however, end there. Tania is powerful, athletic, and aggressive. Her programs are full of jumps, most of them triples, doubles coming only after a triple has been executed. Artistically, she remains somewhat unrefined, her arms and hands sometimes seeming especially stiff and artificial. Nicki, on the other hand, is poised and graceful, a ballerina on skates. She lacks the strength Tania has to propel herself high enough into the air for a perfect triple-double combination. But where she loses marks for technical merit, she gains them for artistic expression.

Note that this paragraph does not contain a single topic sentence. Instead, the topic is implied within the paragraph's first two sentences. The other sentences provide examples and details that develop the implicit topic.

ASSIGNMENT 7-6

Write a paragraph on a topic of your choice, developed by the use of comparison/contrast.

Causes

Paragraphs developed by causes begin with a "why" question, directly or indirectly stated. Here is a paragraph from Jill's interpretation of Bobbie Ann Mason's short story "Shiloh":

> Why does Norma Jean decide to leave Leroy? She decides to leave partly because Leroy annoys her. She admits she was happier when he was driving his truck and was away from home much of the time. Now he is always at home, underfoot, smoking marijuana and dreaming of building a log cabin, in which Norma Jean has little interest. But the real cause of her discontent is her new-found identity. Norma Jean has grown up. She is a different person than the eighteen-year-old girl who, pregnant with a child who would die in infancy of sudden infant death syndrome, had to get married. She is working out, attending college classes, even thinking about standing up, at last, to her overbearing mother. Leroy is not as far off the mark as Norma Jean says he is when he asks her whether this is some "women's lib thing."

Note that the topic sentence, the first sentence of the paragraph, is in the form of a question. The other sentences in the paragraph contribute to the answer to that question.

ASSIGNMENT 7-7

Find, in a magazine or journal article or in one of your textbooks, an example of a paragraph developed by causes. Identify the topic sentence. Be prepared to read this paragraph to other students in your class.

Effects

Effects: paragraph that describes the consequences or results of the subject of the topic sentence.

Janine's essay is about the joys of owning a pet. Her essay contains this example of a paragraph developed using **effects**:

> Certainly my own dog, a border collie named Leo, has this effect on me. It is impossible to stay depressed around Leo. This semester, I have a Wednesday from

hell: calculus in the morning, sociology <u>and</u> a biology lab in the afternoon, European history in the evening. But when I come home, dragged out and depressed, Leo is there, panting, tail wagging, overjoyed to see me. In seconds I feel better. In the morning, it is the same. I hate getting up in the morning; Leo loves getting up, fetching his leash, and dropping it on my sleeping head. His enthusiasm rubs off. When it comes to maintaining a positive outlook on life, Leo is my role model.

The first two sentences provide the topic of the paragraph: my dog has positive effects on my outlook on life. The other sentences explain what Janine means.

ASSIGNMENT 7-8 Write a paragraph on a topic of your choice, developed by the use of effects.

Combining Methods of Paragraph Development

You will notice, in the preceding sample paragraph, that Janine is describing the effects her dog has on her, but that, in the course of the paragraph, she uses an anecdote to develop her topic. She has, in effect, used two methods of paragraph development. Writers often combine two or more methods of paragraph development in order to adequately develop their topic sentences.

In the process of completing the assignments for this chapter, you will have noticed that many paragraphs do not fit neatly into one of the developmental pigeonholes. Many paragraphs combine developmental methods. A definition might be followed, in the same paragraph, by details or examples. In the course of comparing two objects, a writer might use an anecdote without necessarily beginning a new paragraph. As long as paragraph unity is maintained, there is nothing wrong with combining methods of paragraph development—a combination of methods is more the rule than the exception. Method of development is less important than adequate development, and less important than paragraph unity.

Here is an example of a paragraph that uses examples, details, and an anecdote to develop its topic sentence:

Prenger (1993) urges parents to stop worrying about being an embarrassment to their teenage children. Parents must understand, she says, that their very existence is an embarrassment that they can do nothing about. The teenage children of the Rolling Stones are embarrassed by their parents, even if their friends might think rocker parents must be cool. Prenger describes her friend Dale, a musicologist who never spoke when driving his teenage daughter and her friends to the movies or the mall, fearing anything he said would embarrass Jenny. When she explained to Dale that he was an embarrassment whether or not he spoke, he felt liberated, "like a killer popping off another victim, oblivious to whether he would have to serve seventy-five or 150 years in prison" (90). Now

> Dale happily plays his classical music in the car and explains it to his mortified daughter and her dumbfounded friends.

The first sentence is the topic sentence; the second adds detail; the third provides an example in support of the topic sentence; the last half of the paragraph tells an anecdote related to the topic sentence.

Here is another example of a paragraph that uses a combination of methods to develop its topic sentence:

> The chemotherapy room has a circle of large and adjustable chairs, padded to comfort the patient who must sit there for up to three hours being hydrated, and poisoned by a needle that bites into the boney back of the hand—left hand this week, right hand next. A variety of personalities and cancers occupied the recliners during my therapy. One patient in the circle munched on candies as he propped up his severely swollen ankles, another tossed off her scarf to share her newly bald scalp and the stray hairs that still protruded from it, another joked away her hysteria with her husband after they had made the long drive from a city up-island, another sat stern and silent in her tailored smile, and yet another talked of his coming trip to England. Nurses who administer chemotherapy have the daunting task of making patients relax. They are masters of diplomacy, quick to bring a heating pad to cover hand and needle, to offer sedatives to those nauseated with fear, and lunch to those with an appetite. I spent my time reading short stories and convincing myself that I looked forward to lunch. Eating is a constant challenge for patients as their scales dip and their bodies wither with an acute sensitivity to the smells of food. I almost swooned at the smell of basmati rice, a food I had never been conscious of smelling before. But I could indulge with abandon in extravagant ice creams. Peanut butter and banana sandwiches were no longer the enemy. Unfortunately, my fantasy foods often seemed better in the abstract than in the on-your-plate reality. When I did not lose my hair or need hospitalization, I worried that the chemotherapy was not working. The oncologist assured me that the degree to which patients react externally is not a measure of whether the chemotherapy is honing in on the cancer cells, distinguishing them from the healthy cells that grow at a slower rate.
>
> Elizabeth Simpson

This paragraph describes the writer's experience undergoing chemotherapy. It is a descriptive, anecdotal paragraph from a narrative essay, but it is filled with interesting examples and details. It also includes the compare/contrast developmental method, as the responses of several patients to their ordeal are effectively described.

ASSIGNMENT 7-9

Find, in a magazine or journal article or in one of your textbooks, an example of a paragraph developed by a combination of methods. Identify the topic sentence. Be prepared to read this paragraph to other students in your class.

Short Paragraphs

HELPFUL HINTS

Body paragraphs usually require 100-150 words for adequate development.

While adequate paragraph development is, generally speaking, crucial to the success of a piece of writing, a short paragraph, even a one-sentence paragraph, can be used effectively on occasion. A short paragraph can be used in a long piece of writing to establish transition between two main points or arguments that the essay or report is presenting. Sometimes a writer uses a short paragraph if she has a startling or pivotal point to make. The brevity of the paragraph heightens the effect the writer is trying to achieve. For this reason, opening paragraphs, which should do something to grab the reader's attention, sometimes consist of only one or two sentences.

Here, for example, is a paragraph from an essay about the pros and cons of renting rather than owning a house. The paragraph comes between the two main sections (the pros and the cons) of the essay:

> There are, then, significant short-term advantages to renting over owning a house. In the long term, however, ownership is the better choice.
> One reason why owning...

A short paragraph can also be used effectively for an essay's introductory paragraph. Here is an example from William Zinsser's essay "Simplicity" about the quality of writing he values most:

> Clutter is the disease of American writing. We are a society strangling in unnecessary words, circular construction, pompous frills and meaningless jargon.

This paragraph begins with a short, simple sentence introducing the essay's topic, then ends with a blueprint thesis.

ASSIGNMENT 7-10

Find, in a magazine or journal article or in one of your textbooks, an example of a short paragraph used as a transition between two main sections of an essay, and a short paragraph used as an introduction.

SUMMARY

- An effective body paragraph has a topic sentence that expresses the main idea of the paragraph.
- Other sentences in the paragraph should develop the topic sentence in sufficient detail.
- A paragraph has unity when its sentences relate to and develop the topic sentence.
- There are various methods of paragraph development. Methods can be combined within a single paragraph.
- Used occasionally, short paragraphs can be effective.

QUESTIONS FOR STUDY AND DISCUSSION

1. What is the difference between a topic sentence and a thesis statement?
2. What is unity and how do you establish unity in a paragraph?
3. What is an anecdote? When might you use an anecdote to develop a body paragraph?
4. When could a single-sentence paragraph be used in an essay?

SUPPLEMENTARY EXERCISES

1. Develop each of the following units of information into well-written, unified paragraphs. Change, add to, or delete from the information as you see fit. To maintain paragraph unity, you might have to delete some information. Underline the topic sentence of each of your completed paragraphs.

    a. Grisham's plots are one factor that helps account for his popularity—People love to read about the underdog fighting against powerful organizations—*The Client*—a child and his inexperienced woman lawyer fight organized crime and the FBI—*The Pelican Brief* a young, female law student is up against big business that will stop at nothing to protect its profits—*The Chamber*—an old man wastes away on death row while his lawyer grandson fights an impersonal justice system and politicians more concerned with getting elected than doing what is right. Most recent book—*The Rainmaker*—a poor boy who just scraped through law school fights a huge insurance company whose criminal refusal to pay for a life-saving operation cost his client's child his life.

    _____

    _____

    _____

    _____

    _____

    _____

    b. Mugsey Bogues—guard for the Charlotte Hornets—Five feet four inches—looks like a child who came down from the stands onto the basketball court—a foot shorter than the *average* professional basketball player—averages ten points in the games he plays—uses his height to his advantage—does not try to check opposing players—concentrates on getting open for shots—also can dribble around opposing forwards who must bend impossibly low to check him.

    _____

    _____

_____

_____

_____

_____

_____

c. TV comedy, *Friends*—David Schwimmer plays Ross—a paleontolo-
gist—in love with Rachel, another one of the six friends who make up
the cast—brother to Monica, another cast member—Ross seems per-
petually gloomy and vulnerable—insecure—his wife, pregnant with
Ross's child, left him for another woman—he has a pet monkey,
Marcel, but had to give him up to a zoo when he (Marcel) reached sexual maturity ("Hey, he beat you," Joey says to Chandler)—Ross tall
and dark though more lovable than good-looking. Critics predict
Schwimmer will be the one who emerges as a real star. Fans wait and
hope Rachel will start to pay attention to Ross and get together with
him—she sees him as a good friend—Ross wants more.

_____

_____

_____

_____

_____

_____

d. Today cellular telephones are small enough to fit in a shirt pocket—
soon they will be small enough to be worn like a watch on user's writ,
and as many people who have watches will soon have cell tels. AT&T
Bell Laboratories has created a "wristphone." It beeps and vibrates
when someone calls—just like Dick Tracy, the user holds the phone to
his ear to listen and talks into it to respond. Anyone with a cellular
phone will be instantly accessible any time any place. Many more
satellites would have to be launched to accommodate increased number and use of cell tels.

_____

_____

_____

_____

_____

_____

_____

e.   The Internet—a worldwide network of computers made up of many
     small regional networks around the world—a "network of net-
     works"—currently links approximately 30 million users worldwide—
     approximately three million in Canada. Becoming the most important
     means of storing and exchanging information for government, busi-
     ness, educational institutions. Experts say Internet will connect a bil-
     lion users by year 2000—not, at present, user-friendly. Companies
     such as Novell are developing software that will make it easier to re-
     trieve documents from Internet and to publish on the Internet. Costs
     between $20 and $40 per month.

_____

_____

_____

_____

_____

_____

f.   When interest rates are raised even a half of 1 percent, the repercus-
     sions are enormous—everything will cost more—houses because
     mortgage rates go up—cars because car loans are more expensive—
     people will have less disposable income so fewer goods and services
     will be bought and sold. On the other hand, inflation will be held in
     check because prices would stabilize with less money circulating
     within the system—also interest rates for people investing in govern-
     ment bonds and GICs would rise. Raise in interest rate good for
     savers, bad for spenders.

_____

_____

_____

_____

_____

_____

g. Taking cue from behavioural psychology—linguists believed young children learned language by imitating older children and adults, parents—parent names an object, child repeats name and is rewarded with praise, hence child remembers name of object—noted linguist Noam Chomsky realized that children learning language said things parents would never say: "I bringed it back," "We singed it at church." i.e. children learning language tend to regularize irregular verbs. Language learning more complex than previously believed—children learn words but also learn *rules* and internalize and apply those rules—when language deviates from normal rules, children make mistakes they gradually correct as the process continues.

_____

_____

_____

_____

_____

_____

_____

h. Personnel manager associated with hiring new staff—job of personnel manager in modern organization much more complex—responsible for tracking and administering benefits to which employees are entitled—training new staff—complex process in today's high-tech offices—writing job descriptions for each employee—crucial in present times—equal pay for work of equal value—senior personnel executive in modern organization often has rank of vice-president, so important has the job become.

_____

_____

_____

_____

_____

_____

_____

i. Current popularity of independent schools surprising—parents pay local taxes to support public education system but still send children to private school—often major financial sacrifice—fees exceed fees at universities—$7000 a year not uncommon and much more for boarders—governments do usually contribute but to a maximum of 50%

and usually closer to 33% of cost of running independent schools—
church-run schools—e.g. Catholic schools—less expensive—loss of
faith in the public education system—belief that children will get a
better academic and social education in a safer environment.

_____

_____

_____

_____

_____

_____

_____

j. Lou Gehrig's "iron man" record of playing in 2130 consecutive base-
    ball games was believed to be unassailable. But early in September
    1995, Cal Ripkin—shortstop for Baltimore Orioles—number 8—
    played in his 2123st consecutive game. Streak began May 1982.
    Amazing that he has never missed a game though he has been in-
    jured—nothing serious enough so that at least he could not appear as
    a pinch hitter. Not just a durable player, also an accomplished one—
    lifetime batting average of .271. Lifetime fielding percentage of .979.

_____

_____

_____

_____

_____

_____

_____

Writing an Effective Conclusion

The End
Summarize the Body
Reiterate the Thesis

Imagine a hockey game without the third period or a football game without the fourth quarter, and you will begin to realize the importance of a strong conclusion in writing. Games that go undecided, business that is unfinished, and issues that go unresolved are annoying and frustrating. To avoid frustrating your readers, you must give them a strong and effective conclusion that gives them the sense that the business of the paper is finished, the issues have been resolved, the game is over and a winner has been declared.

An effective concluding paragraph (or paragraphs for a longer essay) should summarize the body of an essay and reiterate the thesis. Sometimes the conclusion will address further implications of the topic. Experienced writers will often use an interesting anecdote or an effective quotation to heighten the impact of their conclusion.

In no type of writing is an effective conclusion more important than in a detective story. Readers even cheat sometimes and read the end first, so desperate are they to find out "who done it." In the video profile at the end of this lesson, three detective-story writers talk about their work.

SUMMARIZE THE BODY

A good concluding paragraph briefly summarizes the essay's body paragraphs. One student, for example, wrote a persuasive essay in which she challenged the claims of the cosmetics industry that skin creams could rejuvenate skin and smooth out wrinkles. In her essay, Brenda criticized the misleading advertising of cosmetics companies and revealed the flaws in the studies they cited in support of the beneficial effects of their products. Here is part of her concluding paragraph:

> In summary, there is no independent scientific evidence to support any claim by any cosmetics company that one of their "miracle creams" performs anything close to miracles. Studies that cosmetics companies refer to in their advertisements are clearly suspect, conducted as they were by dermatologists employed by those same companies and undertaken without the controls that scientific studies must have to be considered valid.

Notice how, in two sentences, Brenda presents a synopsis of the detailed discussion contained in the body of her essay.

REITERATE THE THESIS

Reiterate: restate using different words.

An effective concluding paragraph also **reiterates** the essay's central idea, reminding the reader one last time of the importance of the essay's thesis. Brenda's thesis was that cosmetics companies exploit the public's obsession with eternal youth by claiming their products have beneficial effects, even though scientific evidence refutes those benefits. Here now is her entire concluding paragraph:

> In summary, there is no independent scientific evidence to support any claim by any cosmetics company that one of their "miracle creams" performs anything close to miracles. Studies that cosmetics companies refer to in their advertisements are clearly suspect, conducted as they were by dermatologists employed by those same companies and undertaken without the controls that scientific studies must have to be considered valid. Why do millions of women believe the companies' claims? They believe because they want to believe their youthful beauty can be recaptured. The billion-dollar North American cosmetics industry is a monument to the triumph of vanity and fantasy over science.

Notice how, in the final sentence, the writer reiterates her thesis in a clear and pointed manner.

EXAMPLES OF SUCCESSFUL CONCLUSIONS

Let's examine six more examples of effective concluding paragraphs, and discuss why these paragraphs work.

Henri chose to write an essay in which he explained how he thought the Vancouver Canucks could win the Stanley Cup. His title was "The Impossible Dream." His thesis was that Vancouver could win the Cup if the team could get the best efforts from its star players, if the young defencemen could keep opponents' goals down, and if the coaching staff could make consistently intelligent decisions. Here is his concluding paragraph:

> The impossible dream could come true. In spite of a mediocre regular season, Vancouver could win it all if the right factors fall into place. At least two of their

star players, preferably Bure and McLean, must be at the very top of their games. Young defencemen must play with the skill and confidence of veterans. And Rick Ley must match the cunning and the strategy of some formidable opposing coaches. If all of this happens, the Vancouver Canucks will have their turn to sip champagne from Lord Stanley's Cup.

HELPFUL HINTS

Establish a connection between your concluding and your introductory paragraphs.

Notice how, in the first sentence of his concluding paragraph, Henri reiterates the title of his essay. Then he summarizes the points he made in the body of his paper. Finally, in his last sentence, he restates his thesis, but he does so in a way that distinguishes it from the way he stated it in the opening paragraph. In the opening paragraph, state your thesis in a direct and businesslike way; in the concluding paragraph, restate your thesis with a little bit of flair, in a memorable and more imaginative way.

ASSIGNMENT 8-1

Write an introductory paragraph for the sample concluding paragraph above.

Vicki wrote a paper that presented an interpretation of John Keats's poem "Ode to a Nightingale." Her thesis was this: "In this poem, Keats describes his anguish and his suffering, he expresses his desire to escape from his world of pain and sorrow with the help of the nightingale's beautiful song, and he describes the initial success but ultimate failure of his attempt to escape his reality."

Here is the concluding paragraph of Vicki's essay:

Eventually, though, Keats would resolve the anguish and torment that comes through so powerfully in "Ode to a Nightingale." He would resign himself to the reality of his illness and accept the fact that his illness meant his life would be so very brief. He would come to learn that the truth cannot be ignored, but that, even though the truth does hurt, it does not have to diminish the beauty of life. He would learn, and write in his next poem, "Ode on a Grecian Urn," that "Beauty is truth, truth beauty."

HELPFUL HINTS

Address future implications in a concluding paragraph but do not introduce a whole new topic.

In the first sentence of her concluding paragraph, Vicki reiterates her thesis. Then, she uses a strategy common in concluding paragraphs—she touches upon a future dimension or a further implication of her topic. She mentions the next poem Keats wrote and how, in that poem, he continued to deal with, and resolve, the issues that went unresolved in "Ode to a Nightingale." She ends with a key quote from that later ode.

ASSIGNMENT 8-2

Find an example of a concluding paragraph that makes effective use of a quotation. Try looking in magazines or journals, or even in one of your textbook chapters, for your example. Or, if possible, use a concluding paragraph from one of your own essays. Bring your paragraph to class and be prepared to share it with your classmates and to discuss why you think it is an effective concluding paragraph.

For one writing assignment in his English composition course, Sean wrote about lions, specifically about those qualities the lion possesses that give it the reputation as king of the jungle. In his essay, Sean described the lion's majestic physical appearance, its skill and efficiency as a hunter, and its ability to provide leadership for members of its pride. Here is Sean's concluding paragraph:

> But the lion's reputation as king of the beasts is not new. The great fable writer Aesop wrote a story that illustrates that, for well over 2000 years, the lion has been celebrated for its courage, pride, and intelligence:
>
> > A vixen sneered at a lioness because she could only bear one cub at time. "Only one," the lioness replied, "but a lion."

In his last paragraph, Sean reiterates the main ideas of his essay and the points in support of his main ideas. Then he includes a brief anecdote, a fable by Aesop, which gives further support to his thesis and provides a pointed and memorable conclusion to his essay.

ASSIGNMENT 8-3

Write a concluding paragraph on a topic of your own choice that uses an anecdote.

Here, again, is the concluding paragraph from the research paper in Lesson Four:

> With networks, writers can revise and edit work collaboratively much more efficiently than they could passing hard copy around a room. With spell checks, writers can correct a word in a fraction of the time it takes to look a word up in an old-fashioned paper dictionary. But computers can't think for themselves or develop a weak idea or make style more graceful. The computer makes writing, as it makes so many of the tasks of life, easier, but it needs the guidance of a human mind to make writing more interesting and intelligent.

This paragraph summarizes both sections of the body of the essay: the benefits and the drawbacks of writing with a computer. In the process, it reiterates the thesis of the essay and hints at broader implications.

ASSIGNMENT 8-4

Reread the concluding paragraph that you wrote for your compare/contrast essay from Assignment 5-2. Explain why you think that concluding paragraph is effective or explain how you might change it in light of what you have learned in Lesson Eight.

Here is the concluding paragraph from an article written by a woman who has just learned how to use the Internet. Throughout the article, she compares the process to the first time she engaged in another activity. She concludes:

> A mere nine hours after being digitally deflowered, I was exhausted but also strangely exhilarated. As I wiped the sweat from my brow, I took a moment to survey all that I had accomplished. With fingers still trembling from the experience, there was only one thing left to do. I celebrated my first time the only way a non-smoker and true net aficionado would—I reached for my keyboard and ordered pizza (URL http://pizza. indirect.com) via the Web.
>
> Elvira Kurt

Her concluding paragraph continues and completes the comparison (or metaphor—see Lesson Eighteen) used throughout the article. She reiterates her thesis that learning to use the Internet is an exhilarating and useful experience, and leaves her readers with a smile on their faces as she rejects the cigarette that traditionally follows "the first time" and, instead, goes back to her computer and orders a pizza.

Concluding paragraphs can be short and can still communicate that sense of completion the reader demands. Indeed, short concluding paragraphs can be effective and emphatic by virtue of their brevity. Here is the concluding paragraph to Nancy Masterson Sakamoto's essay "Conversational Ballgames" about the different manner in which westerners and Japanese carry on a conversation. In Japan, everyone waits their turn before speaking, and the order of speaking is determined largely by social status. When it is a Japanese person's turn to speak, the speaker usually talks for a long time, saying all he or she wants to say, before falling silent until the next turn comes around. Sakamoto concludes:

> Maybe that's why polite conversation at the dinner table has never been a traditional part of Japanese etiquette. Your turn to talk would last so long without interuption that you'd never get a chance to eat.

As the six preceding sample paragraphs illustrate, a good concluding paragraph completes an essay by summarizing the body and reiterating the essay's main idea, but does so in such a way—through a quote or an anecdote, for example—that the readers don't feel they are getting simply a rehash of old ideas. Your readers should feel, at the end of your essay, the way they would feel after they have enjoyed a fine dinner: they know they have had enough, they are satisfied, and soon they would like to come back for more.

ASSIGNMENT 8-5

Find an essay that ends with a paragraph of fewer than fifty words. Bring your paragraph to class to compare it with those your classmates have found.

SUMMARY

- You can win the race with a strong finish. Your concluding paragraph must be clear and pointed.
- Reiterate your thesis, but do not simply copy your introduction.
- You can briefly summarize the body of your essay in the conclusion.
- You can address further implications in the conclusion.
- Quotes and anecdotes can be used effectively in conclusions—make sure they are relevant to the essay, but not forced.

QUESTIONS FOR STUDY AND DISCUSSION

1. Why should a concluding paragraph re-establish the thesis of the essay?
2. When would it be a good strategy to summarize the body of your essay in your conclusion?
3. Is it acceptable to introduce new ideas and information into your conclusion?
4. Why are quotations and anecdotes effective in certain concluding paragraphs?

SUPPLEMENTARY EXERCISES

1. Write effective concluding paragraphs that would fit with the introductory paragraphs below. You may alter the content of the introductory paragraphs if, by so doing, you feel you can make your concluding paragraphs more effective.

   a. Night owls and insomniacs might grouse about friends who can't stay awake for late-night card games. They might whine about the early (to them) closing hours of restaurants and grocery stores. But they can't any longer complain that there is nothing for them to watch on television late at night. Some of the most entertaining, innovative, and informative programs are scheduled after 11:00 p.m.

   _____

   _____

   _____

   _____

   _____

   _____

   _____

b. Footwear, in many sports, is the most important part of the athlete's equipment. Footwear *is* skiing and figure skating, of course, but it is equally important in most other sports as well. It is also among the most expensive equipment an athlete will use, the equal in price to basketballs, tennis rackets, and baseball mitts. Whether she is buying running shoes for the next marathon, cross-trainers for aerobics, or court shoes for basketball or tennis, an athlete must know what to look for when buying a good, functional pair of shoes.

c. "This wine," our guide told us, "has an earthy, spicy aroma of clove and anise, with just a hint of cinnamon. It has a fruity taste, reminiscent of apples and kiwi fruit. It is medium dry. It would make an excellent reception wine." I smelled the wine and nodded appreciatively, though I couldn't smell any spices. I tasted and nodded again, hoping an enthusiastic nod would conceal my disability. It had never before occurred to me that I was in any way disabled, but that day the painful truth came to me: apparently, I have aesthetically challenged taste buds.

d. Edmonton is the capital of Alberta and the largest city in the province, with a population close to a million people. It is situated close to the geographic centre of the province, on the North Saskatchewan River. To its south are the rich farmlands of Alberta; to its north are hinterlands, forbidding but rich in natural resources. Despite its harsh climate, Edmonton is a cosmopolitan city offering outstanding cultural attractions, well-paying jobs, and excellent educational facilities.

_____

_____

_____

_____

e.   What is the primary motivational force that guides human behaviour?
      To Freud, it was, of course, sex, the desire for sexual gratification and
      the guilt that inevitably accompanies so private yet so powerful a
      force. To Freud's less famous colleague Alfred Adler, it was not sex,
      but "compensation"—the desire to overcome an inferiority complex—
      that, he felt, was at the centre of all human personality. With such fun-
      damentally different philosophical starting points, it is hardly
      surprising that Adlerian and Freudian psychoanalysts use different
      methods to treat mental illness.

_____

_____

_____

_____

_____

_____

f.   "Take a look around you," my English professor said on the first day
      of class. "Look at ten of your classmates. By Christmas, two of them
      will have dropped out of this university. By fourth year, five of them
      will be gone." What causes so many students to drop out of college?
      Financial pressures, lack of interest in the subjects they are taking, and
      shattered self-esteem caused by insensitive people like my English
      professor are the three main causes students cite for dropping out.

_____

_____

_____

_____

_____

g.   Most people, in the course of their lives, will attend maybe 300 parties.
      Many of these parties will be endurance tests, some will be tolerable,
      some will be fun, only a handful will be sensational. Most hosts seem
      to think that loads of booze and junk food, dangerously extroverted
      guests, and loud rock music are the key ingredients of a good party.
      Actually it's variety that gives a party its spice. The hosts of a really

great party will serve food that has taken some thought and effort to prepare, they will invite guests with varied personalities, and they will turn the CD player down low enough so that their guests can talk to each other.

_____

_____

_____

_____

_____

_____

h. "I use the oral method of birth control," my friend Sally always says—"I say no a lot." Statistics suggest that Sally is not alone. College students are not as sexually active today as they were in the free-love sixties and seventies. With living costs so high, many students now must work part-time while going to school and don't have much spare time for much of a social life. Many students are wary of the health risks associated with irresponsible sexual activity. And young women have learned they lose nothing and gain much by following Sally's advice: just say no.

_____

_____

_____

_____

_____

_____

i. Astrology is the study of the influence of the stars and planets on human life. Astrologers believe that by calculating the relative positions of the planets and the fixed stars at the time a person is born and, more specifically, by determining which planet is in which sign of the zodiac and which star is rising ("in the ascendant") at the time of birth, a person's future can be charted. Some people think the notion that the position of planets and stars can determine personality and fate is bizarre, the product of the greed of con artists and the fantasies of Hollywood starlets. Others take astrology very seriously and regularly consult with their astrological charts to plan their days and help them make important decisions.

_____

_____

_____

_____

_____

_____

_____

j. On May 29, 1953, Englishman Edmund Hillary and his Sherpa guide, Tenzing Norkey, negotiated the difficult final ridge of the South Summit and made it to the top—over 8700 metres high—of Mount Everest, the highest mountain in the world. In a sense, they made it to the top because others had failed to do so. John Hunt, the leader of Hillary's expedition, carefully studied previous attempts to climb Everest and realized that, to be successful, the mountaineers would have to do three things. They would have to spend enough time climbing up the mountain to allow themselves to become acclimatized to the bitter cold and the thin supply of oxygen; they would have to establish camps as close to the top as possible, so the climbers could make the final assault refreshed and not weighed down by too much equipment; and they would have to carry with them enough oxygen to allow them to breathe on top of the world.

_____

_____

_____

_____

_____

_____

Video Case 1   CBC

Murder They Wrote: Canadian Detective-Story Writers

Three Canadian writers of detective stories are interviewed in this video segment. The main theme is the Canadian character and identity as revealed through the typical Canadian crime fighter.

Laurence Gough, author of *Killers*, says that his detectives possess that combination of "toughness and propriety" that he sees as distinctly Canadian. Canadian crime fiction, he goes on to say, differs from its American counterpart in that it tries to "disturb rather than titillate."

L.R. Wright sets her novels in the small West Coast town of Sechelt. She reveals, she says, the tension and the evil beneath that "veneer of niceness" so typical of the Canadian small town. Her hero, an RCMP detective sergeant, is devoted to maintaining a "safe moral universe" and places the rule of law before the administration of justice.

Howard Engel's stories are set in Grantham, a thinly veiled replica of St. Catharines, Ontario. He describes his hero, Detective Benny Cooperman, as "a low-key sensitive type," a typical Canadian. His detective, he claims, is the exact opposite in personality and behaviour to American counterparts like Philip Marlowe and Sam Spade.

The detective story has emerged as one of the most popular of all writing genres. Canadians especially seem to enjoy reading and writing detective fiction.

Questions

1. What is the difference between the law and justice? Is breaking the law ever justifiable, in your opinion? Write your response as an entry in your journal.

2. In an essay of approximately 750 words, compare and contrast the stereotypical American and Canadian characters. Generally speaking, how are we different in personality and character from our American neighbours?

3. Write a character sketch of the detective in a detective story that you would write. Include a physical description of your detective, along with an analysis of his or her personality.

4. Why do you think detective stories are so popular, especially in Canada?

Source: "Murder They Wrote," *Prime Time News*. CBC, May 7, 1994.

Writing Coherently

Stick Together

Repetition
Transitional Words and Phrases
Cohesion Between Paragraphs
Excessive Cohesion

Coherence: characteristic of a paragraph in which there is a smooth and logical connection between and among sentences.

To communicate clearly to its readers, an essay, or for that matter any piece of written discourse, must have **coherence**. Coherence comes from the word "cohere," which means to stick together. Both the sentences within a paragraph and the paragraphs within an essay must cohere. A paragraph is cohesive if there is a logical and rhetorical connection between each sentence in a paragraph and the sentence that precedes and follows it. An essay is coherent if there is a smooth and logical connection between and among the paragraphs that make up the essay. Let's look first at cohesion between and among the sentences within a paragraph, then at cohesion between and among the paragraphs within the entire essay.

COHESION BETWEEN SENTENCES

In Lesson Seven, you learned that body paragraphs have topic sentences and that, in order for a paragraph to be a unified whole, all other sentences in that paragraph must relate to the topic sentence. This relationship is established through the similarity in subject matter between the topic sentence and other sentences. In other words, a paragraph has *unity* if all of the sentences in the paragraph augment or elucidate the topic sentence. But to maximize clarity, sentences should be related to each other in a way that is not simply by virtue of a common topic. There should be, as well, a rhetorical connection—in other words, cohesion—between the sentences in a paragraph. This connection is most often established through the repetition of key words or of pronouns that refer to key words, the use of transitional expressions, and the use of similar sentence patterns. We will look at examples of each method of establishing cohesion between sentences.

Repetition

For an example of a paragraph that uses the repetition of key words to establish cohesion between and among sentences, look again at the first paragraph of this lesson. The first sentence ends with the word "coherence," and the next sentence begins with the word "coherence." The next four sentences all contain variations on the word "coherence." The sentences in this paragraph stick together because the key word of the paragraph is repeated. The repetition of a key word is a common way of establishing cohesion within a paragraph.

Synonyms: two or more words with essentially the same meaning.

Synonyms for key words and pronouns that refer to key words will also establish cohesion. Raj's paragraph from her essay about life in a tourist town provides a good example:

> <u>Tourists</u> are instantly recognizable by <u>their</u> physical appearance. <u>They</u> are usually dressed in baggy shorts and souvenir T-shirts and <u>they</u> usually come armed with camcorders under their arms or hoisted onto their shoulders. <u>Visitors</u> also have a way of walking that distinguishes <u>them</u> from locals. <u>They</u> meander quite aimlessly, stopping at every intersection to gaze up at the street signs or to point <u>their</u> camcorders at buildings, the architectural significance of which usually eludes their hosts. <u>Tourists</u> also tend to have happily vacant facial expressions, in contrast to the grim determination set in the expression of the locals.

In this paragraph, the pronouns "they" and "their" refer to the key word "tourists," as does the synonym "visitors." The pronouns and the synonym establish coherence without repeating the key word to the point of monotony.

ASSIGNMENT 9-1

Write, on a topic of your choice, an example of a paragraph that establishes cohesion through the repetition of key words, synonyms for key words, and pronouns that refer to key words.

Transitional Words and Phrases

Transitional expression: word or phrase that establishes a connection between sentences or paragraphs.

For an example of a paragraph that uses **transitional expressions** to establish coherence between and among sentences, look again at the second paragraph in this lesson:

> In Lesson Seven, you learned that body paragraphs have topic sentences and that, in order for a paragraph to be a unified whole, all other sentences in that paragraph must relate to the topic sentence. This relationship is established through the similarity in subject matter between the topic sentence and other sentences. In other words, a paragraph has *unity* if all of the sentences in the paragraph augment or elucidate the topic sentence. But to maximize clarity, sentences should be related to each other in a way that is not simply by virtue of a common topic. There should be, as well, a rhetorical connection between the sentences in a

paragraph. This connection is most often established through the repetition of key words or of pronouns that refer to key words, the use of transitional expressions, and the use of similar sentence patterns.

HELPFUL HINTS

When you are revising your final draft, highlight all of your cohesive ties to be certain you have used them effectively.

There are three transitional expressions used in this paragraph. The third sentence begins with the phrase "In other words," which tells readers that an important point made in the previous sentence will be reiterated and embellished in the sentence beginning with the transitional phrase. The next sentence begins with the transitional word "But," which tells the reader that a point related, but counter to, the point made in the preceding sentence will now be made. The next sentence contains the transitional expression "as well," which signals the reader that the writer will make an additional point related to the previous sentence. This paragraph also, by the way, uses the repetition of the key word "relate" and variations on it to establish coherence.

Here is another example:

> Other excellent osteoporosis-prevention activities include low-impact aerobics, dancercise, and running. For maximum gain, all activities should be performed for 30 to 45 minutes, three times weekly. However, you should be aware that not all exercise activities are created equal, particularly when it comes to building bone. For instance, while cycling and in-line skating build muscle, they don't benefit bones as much as do cross-country skiing or hiking. And some sports, such as curling, bowling and horseback riding, involve stressful actions that may put some women with thinner bones at increased risk of fracture.
>
> Beth Thompson

Four out of the five sentences in this paragraph begin with a transitional expression. The first sentence begins with the word "Other," which signals transition between its paragraph and the one that precedes it. The third sentence begins with the word "However," which tells the reader the preceding sentence will be qualified or contradicted. The fourth sentence begins with the phrase "For instance," indicating that example will be used to illustrate the preceding sentence. The last sentence begins with the word "And," indicating additional information is forthcoming.

There are many other commonly used transitional words and phrases, including

consequently	but
nevertheless	therefore
by contrast	on the other hand
meanwhile	later
soon	after a while
another	the next
at first	moreover
before	after
finally	meanwhile
similarly	now
yet	until

ASSIGNMENT 9-2 Find, in a magazine article or in one of your textbooks, a paragraph that establishes coherence mainly by using transitional expressions.

Sentence Patterns

Sentence pattern: order of arrangement of the components of a sentence.

A third way in which cohesion can be established between and among sentences within a paragraph is through the repetition of a **sentence pattern**. Read carefully Stefan's paragraph from an essay about his description of a Utopian society:

> Unfortunately, all forms of government are imperfect. Left-wing governments are strong on social justice, but weak on economic prosperity. Right-wing governments are strong on economic prosperity, but weak on social justice. Middle-of-the-road governments offer mediocrity: some economic prosperity and some social justice. What is needed is not so much a compromise as an agreement to alter government depending upon conditions. In good times, socialism will prevail so wealth is equitably distributed. In bad times, capitalism will prevail so good times can be restored and socialism can return. The motto of government in my Utopian society: economic prosperity for social justice.

Notice how similar in structure the second, third, and fourth sentences of the paragraph are, as are the sixth and seventh sentences. The sentences cohere because of this similarity.

ASSIGNMENT 9-3 Write, on a topic of your choice, an example of a paragraph that establishes cohesion mainly through the use of a repetitive sentence pattern.

COHESION BETWEEN PARAGRAPHS

HELPFUL HINTS

A paragraph can be unified but still lack coherence. Check for both unity and coherence.

Just as the sentences within a paragraph must cohere, so too must the paragraphs within the entire essay. The first sentence of one paragraph must be connected to the last sentence of the preceding paragraph. For example:

> Ask them why they are so desperate to immigrate to Canada or America and they will often say they want a better life for their children.
> A better life, for most immigrants, means a better chance to get a decent job.

Notice how, at the end of the first paragraph above and the beginning of the next paragraph, coherence is established through the repetition of the key phrase "better life."

Let's look at one more example:

> Unfortunately, history books rarely mention the aid Natives gave to these explorers, though without that aid, hazardous river exploration would not have been attempted.

> Another contribution that the aboriginal people...
> Finally, aboriginal arts and crafts...

In this example, coherence is established between the first paragraph and the next through the use of the transitional word, "Another." At the beginning of the last body paragraph, the transitional word, "Finally," establishes coherence between the last body paragraph and the preceding ones.

ASSIGNMENT 9-4

Carefully read three successive paragraphs from one of your textbooks. Explain, in one paragraph, how the author establishes cohesion among the three paragraphs.

EXCESSIVE COHESION

Cohesive ties between sentences in a paragraph and especially between paragraphs in an essay or a report should be evident but not overbearing. Students sometimes learn their lesson too well and might end one paragraph and begin the next one like this:

> In this paragraph, I have discussed the differences between the MLA and APA methods for citing academic journals, and in the next paragraph, I'm going to discuss the differences the two methods use for citing books.
>   The MLA and the APA methods differ in the way that they cite books...

The cohesion here is excessive. As a rule, paragraphs should not begin *and* end with a sentence that summarizes their content. It is a case of overkill. Readers are being kicked rather than nudged along. An essay should be cohesive, without distracting the readers by calling attention to its own process.

SUMMARY

- Create a clear and logical rhetorical connection between sentences and between paragraphs.
- Establish coherence through the repetition of key words, synonyms for key words, and pronouns that refer to key words.
- Establish coherence also through the use of transitional expressions.
- Finally, establish coherence through the use of a repetitive sentence pattern.
- Avoid excessive cohesion.

QUESTIONS FOR STUDY AND DISCUSSION

1. Why is coherence important in a paragraph and in an essay?
2. What is a transitional word or phrase? What is the function of a transitional word or phrase?
3. How can synonyms be used to help establish cohesion?
4. How can pronouns be used to help establish cohesion?
5. How can repetitive sentence patterns be used to help establish cohesion?
6. Under what circumstances is coherence "too much of a good thing"?

SUPPLEMENTARY EXERCISE

The following essay uses few cohesive ties. Improve the cohesion of this essay by inserting cohesive ties wherever you think necessary. Include transitions and other needed cohesive ties between the sentences within the paragraphs and between the paragraphs in the essay as a whole. You may alter the content of the essay or the order of sentences within paragraphs, if necessary, to improve cohesion.

Canada's Role at the United Nations Conference on Women

Salimah B.
English 100
March, 19XX

For years, Canada has enjoyed an international reputation as a compassionate country that values peace, humanitarianism, and universal human rights. A Canadian prime minister has won the Nobel Peace Prize, and peace keeping continues to be a cornerstone of Canadian foreign policy. Canada is known for its generous economic aid to Third World countries. At the fourth annual United Nations World Conference on Women, in Beijing, Canada has lived up to its reputation.

Not all of Canada's forty-two delegates are pleased with the platform the Canadian delegation has endorsed. MP Sharon Hayes of the Reform Party left the conference early as a protest against what she sees as the radically feminist agenda the Canadian delegation has supported. There has been too much emphasis on lesbian rights and pro-abortion propaganda and not enough emphasis on health and education, which are the main concerns of women from underdeveloped countries. The Canadian delegation has impressed much of the international community, which clearly respects Canadian views and which has adopted several Canadian resolutions.

The Canadian delegation sponsored a resolution that would make rape a war crime. Systematic rape would be punishable as a crime against humanity. It would be defined as genocide if directed at a specific ethnic group. Soldiers fighting in recent conflicts in the former Yugoslavia and in Rwanda have been accused of raping civilian women. The Canadian resolution will help put pressure on the international community to put pressure on the warring factions to end violence against women and to prosecute and severely punish soldiers who are found guilty of raping civilian women.

The Canadian delegation sponsored a resolution to promote and support the development of guidelines for accepting refugees seeking asylum in developed countries on the basis of gender-related persecution. Women who have suffered genital mutilation would have special status as refugees. In some strictly Islamic countries, female circumcision is standard practice. Women from countries that value male children over female children would benefit. Infanticide of baby girls in countries that highly value male children is not uncommon. Women from countries that, through inaction, tolerate or even tacitly encourage spousal abuse would receive sympathetic hearings from immigration authorities who represent countries with liberal democratic traditions.

Canadian delegate Ed Broadbent, former leader of the New Democratic Party, now president of the International Center for Human Rights and Democratic Development, has lodged formal complaints against the host country, China, for turning its police force and plain-clothes security personnel against conference delegates. A Hong Kong television crew, filming a protest in support of gay rights, was roughed up by Chinese policemen. "This is United Nations territory where freedom of expression and freedom of access are supposed to be guaranteed," Broadbent said. He is determined to force the UN to develop specific, unequivocal guidelines that will force countries that host the conference in the future to protect and not harass delegates.

Canada's reputation as the great compromiser among nations is evident in the language of the Platform of Action, the crucial document that is the culmination of the two-week conference. Many of the 189 countries represented at the conference have strict civil and religious laws against homosexuality, prostitution, and abortion, and in support of complete parental authority. Many western countries, Canada included, wanted resolutions in the Platform of Action in support of lesbian rights, of a woman's right to choose an abortion, and of a young woman's right to safe contraception without parental knowledge and consent. Conflict and controversy seemed inevitable. Canada helped draft the platform using wording that came to be known as "constructive ambiguity." Language could be used in the document in such a way to please everyone and offend no one. The platform does not say anything about "legalizing abortions." It urges countries to rescind laws that punish women for having abortions. Delegates agreed not to use the phrase "sexual rights" in the final document, substituting the phrase "human rights." The word "prostitution" was eliminated from the document; it was replaced by the phrase "sexual exploitation."

Many controversial and potentially divisive issues were discussed at the Beijing Conference. People with different customs, different religions, different values, had to come together and agree on common concerns and goals. The conference could easily have failed. Its success was due in part to the contribution of the Canadian delegation. Canadian delegates focused their energies on issues—violence against women, for example—of concern to all participants, regardless of race or religion. Canadian delegates helped find the diplomatic language needed to reach agreement on the principles contained in the Platform for Action. Canadian delegates to the UN Conference on Women enhanced Canada's reputatation as a caring nation with a gift for diplomacy and will to improve the status of women everywhere.

Writing Concisely

Wordiness
Redundancy
Passive Voice

Reading writing that is wordy and repetitious is like looking out a dirty window: it is hard to see what you are looking at. Writing is clearer when unnecessary words and phrases are rinsed away; a writer is praised for having a "clean" style. To achieve a clean and concise writing style, try as a rule to avoid wordiness, redundancy, and passive voice.

WORDINESS

Concise writing: writing that contains no unnecessary words.

In an effort to make ourselves as clear as possible, we tend in our rough drafts to overwrite, believing that more words will make our meaning clearer. When we revise, we often realize the reverse is true: **concise writing** is clear writing—less is more.

Look again at the second sentence in the first paragraph of this lesson:

Writing is clearer when unnecessary words and phrases are rinsed away; a writer is praised for having a "clean" style.

Now look at three versions of the same sentence in earlier drafts of this lesson:

1. When a writer is described as having a "clean" style, it means the writer's prose is clear because it is not obscured by unnecessary words and phrases.

2. Needless words and phrases, redundancies, circumlocutions, need to be rinsed away; a writer is praised for having a "clean" style.

3.   Writing is clearer when you rinse away unnecessary words and phrases; a writer is praised for having a "clean" style.

Sentence 1 is wordy. The two "it" clauses—"it means" and "it is not obscured"— seem awkward and unnecessary.

In sentence 2, the addition of the words "redundancies and circumlocutions" is unnecessary; indeed their inclusion, ironically enough, makes the sentence sound redundant.

Active voice: verb form in which the subject as opposed to an object performs the action.

Sentence 3 is getting very close, but the use of **active voice**—"you rinse"— does not seem to fit with the subject, "a writer." And although passive voice (explained later in this lesson) tends in general to be less effective than active, in this sentence passive voice is more efficient: "Writing is clearer when unnecessary words and phrases *are rinsed* away."

Let's look at one more example. The American writer Ernest Hemingway was famous for his concise writing style. He liked to compare his writing to an iceberg, one-tenth above the surface, the rest hidden below. Here is a passage from his book *Death in the Afternoon*, about bullfighting, one of his many interests:

In the old days the bulls were usually bigger than they are now; they were fiercer, more uncertain, heavier and older. They had not been bred down to a smaller size to please the bullfighters and they were fought at the age of four and a half to five years instead of three and a half to four and a half years. Matadors often had from six to twelve years of apprenticeship as banderilleros and as novilleros before becoming formal matadors. They were mature men, knew bulls thoroughly, and faced bulls which were brought to the highest point of physical force, strength, knowledge of how to use their horns and general difficulty and danger. The whole end of the bullfight was the final sword thrust, and actual encounter between the man and the animal, what the Spanish call the moment of truth, and every move in the fight was to prepare the bull for that killing. With such bulls it was not necessary to give emotion for the man to pass the animal as deliberately close to him with the cape as was possible. The cape was used to run the bulls, to protect the picadors, and the passes that were made with it, by our modern standards, were exciting because of the size, strength, weight and fierceness of the animal and the danger the matador ran in making them rather than by the form or the slowness of their execution. It was exciting that the man should pass such a bull at all, that a man should be in the ring with and dominate such an animal furnished the emotion rather than that he should deliberately, as now, try to pass the points of the horn as mathematically close to his body as possible without moving his feet. It is the decadence of the modern bull that has made modern bullfighting possible. It is a decadent art in every way and like most decadent things it reaches its fullest flower at its rottenest point, which is the present.

HELPFUL HINTS

It is difficult for writers to cut words and sentences they have worked hard to craft; ask a friend to check your work for wordiness and redundancy.

This is a long paragraph, written in long sentences, and as such might seem a strange choice to illustrate conciseness. But—and this is an important distinction—concise does not mean short. It means simply that unnecessary words and phrases have been eliminated. The length of Hemingway's paragraph is due in part to its developmental method, which, as you will remember from Lesson Seven, is compare/contrast. Hemingway compares and contrasts the courage and romance of the old-fashioned bullfight with the decadence of the modern version. His sentences are straightforward and forceful, and they are not cluttered with unnecessary descriptive words or phrases.

ASSIGNMENT 10-1 Find, in one of your textbooks, a three- or four-paragraph passage that you consider to be "cleanly and concisely" written. In one paragraph, explain how you think the author achieved this concision.

REDUNDANCY

Redundancy: useless repetition.

Another of concision's enemies is **redundancy**, which occurs when a writer says the same thing twice using different words. Consider this sentence:

> Readers appreciate concise writing because it is easier for them to process, and because it is more efficient and takes less time to read.

Could not the sentence end at the word "process"? Having said "easier for them to process," the writer repeats himself by adding "more efficient and takes less time to read."

Here is one more example:

> Your paragraphs will be unified if each sentence in your paragraphs develops, refines, augments, or adds to your topic sentence, thereby creating a paragraph that contains a single idea or concept.

How would you revise this sentence to make it more concise? As it is, it contains thirty-two words. Revise it to eliminate redundancy and you would probably get:

> Your paragraphs will be unified if each sentence develops or refines your topic sentence.

The sentence is half as long now, but its meaning has not changed.

Repetition can be a virtue, if it is done for a deliberate effect. Consider this paragraph:

> One sentence in a body paragraph, usually called the *topic sentence*, will contain the main idea of the paragraph, and the other sentences will develop that main idea. The other sentences might provide specific details relevant to your topic sentence. They might provide an example or two or three in support of a generalization contained in your topic sentence. They might tell a story that sheds light on the topic. They might define a key term around which your topic sentence is built.

Verb phrases containing the word "might" appear four times in five sentences. They are used to give the paragraph coherence (Lesson Nine), to make the paragraph clearer. If it clarifies rather than obscures, repetition can be effective.

But as a rule, repetition is boring, inefficient, and even slightly insulting, conveying as it does the impression that your reader is not bright enough to take your point the first time you present it. Concise writing is more interesting and generally more reader friendly.

ASSIGNMENT 10-2

Revise the following sentences to make them more concise:

1. Synchronized swimming is a dance-like performance done to music by an athlete or group of athletes who move gracefully in water and, when there is more than one of them, in a synchronized manner, to the rhythm, the cadences, and the beat of recorded sound.

2. Telecommunications on board ships is much more sophisticated today than it was years ago when ships signalled each other with lamps or flags to communicate messages to each other.

3. Plays that are classified as theatre of the absurd are characterized by qualities such as unconventional plots, bemused and inarticulate characters who seem to be lost in a confusing world that they cannot make sense of, and bare and sparsely set stage settings with minimal props and furniture.

4. Death and mortality rates from diseases such as smallpox and tuberculosis declined when hygienic conditions improved, vaccines were discovered, and those at risk began to recognize the importance of high standards of cleanliness.

5. Kayakers, canoeists, and other operators of other kinds of small boats love to paddle the calm waters around the Broken Islands, off Ucluelet on the West Coast of Vancouver Island, a favourite destination for pleasure boaters.

PASSIVE VOICE

Passive voice: verb form in which object as opposed to subject performs action.

Passive voice occurs in a sentence when a word that would normally be the object of the sentence becomes the subject. Consider, for example, this simple sentence:

The girl threw the ball.

"Girl" is the subject of the sentence, "threw" is the verb, "ball" is the object. If we made "ball" the subject, the sentence would read:

The ball was thrown by the girl.

HELPFUL HINTS

Passive voice will not make your writing sound more impressive.

Which sentence is more concise? The active voice version contains five words; the passive voice version contains seven. Active voice is usually more concise than passive voice. Moreover, the active voice version reads more smoothly.

Occasionally, however, if the subject of the sentence is indeterminate, passive voice may be preferable. Compare the active voice:

They forbid smoking in this area.

with the passive:

Smoking is forbidden in this area.

Both sentences have five words. The subject "they" in the first sentence is understood and indeterminate. The passive voice version, in this case, is better.

ASSIGNMENT 10-3

Construct a sentence first in active, then in passive voice. Which sentence is more concise? Explain why.

SUMMARY

- Revise your writing to eliminate wordiness.
- For emphasis, use repetition; otherwise, avoid redundancy.
- Use active voice, which is clearer and more concise than passive voice.
- Use passive voice if the subject of the sentence is indeterminate.

QUESTIONS FOR STUDY AND DISCUSSION

1. Why do inexperienced writers tend to use more words than necessary?
2. Is the phrase "effective use of repetition" a contradiction in terms? Explain your answer.
3. Explain the difference between active voice and passive voice.
4. What are the strengths and benefits of concise writing?

SUPPLEMENTARY EXERCISES

Rewrite each of the following sentences to make it more concise. Feel free to change the structure of the sentence and rearrange information, but do not change the meaning of the sentence.

1. Today, most people in our modern world know about the Internet, but it might not be known by them how to use the Internet efficiently and productively.

_____

_____

_____

2. In a short period of time, the class completed the in-class essays and handed in the assignments done in class before the period ended.

_____

_____

_____

_____

_____

3. Whether Quebec will remain as part of Canada or whether Quebec will not remain a part of Canada but become a separate country with close ties to Canada will be decided by the people of Quebec in a democratic referendum, when they will vote on sovereignty versus remaining a Canadian province.

_____

_____

_____

_____

_____

4. The defence proved that the gloves didn't fit by having the defendant try on the gloves in front of the jury, but the prosecution proved that, even though the gloves didn't fit, the defendant wore the gloves in photographs that the prosecution exhibited showing the defendant wearing the gloves.

_____

_____

_____

_____

_____

5. The most common cause of the breakup of a relationship in the which the man and woman have been together is financial problems.

_____

_____

_____

_____

_____

6. You can make your sentences clear and concise by eliminating wordiness, redundancies, unnecessary repetitions, circumlocutions, and passive voice when there is a definite subject for the verb in a passive-voice wordy sentence.

_____

_____

_____

_____

_____

7. The range of opinion about the proposal to build a giant warehouse store in the city centre ranged from militant disapproval to enthusiastic endorsement.

_____

_____

_____

_____

_____

8. Mountaineers attempting to scale challenging mountains like Mount Everest face overwhelming dangers and perils.

_____

_____

_____

_____

_____

9. Students who major in literature will eventually have to learn a lot about the Bible and classical mythology because mythological and biblical references are common in literature, especially in poetry.

_____

_____

_____

_____

_____

10. Conservatives feel the media has a liberal bias and liberals feel the media has a conservative bias, which suggests that views expressed by the media are really quite balanced since both sides have complaints about bias.

_____

_____

_____

_____

_____

11. The president made the suggestion that if two people from each department went to half-time work, layoffs and firings could be postponed by the company and maybe they could postpone layoffs indefinitely.

_____

_____

_____

_____

_____

12. There are scores of magazines to choose from on the magazine shelves in stores today that cater to almost any special interest any person might have.

_____

_____

_____

_____

_____

13. With some college courses, you can skip some classes and still pass the course or even get a half-decent grade, but with other courses if you miss too many classes you won't be able to pass because you will likely fail the mid-term exam and the final exam.

_____

_____

_____

_____

_____

14. Due to the fact that the school of philosophy known as existentialism began in France and then came to North America, changes were made by philosophers in the ideas of existentialism and now the term is difficult to define.

_____

_____

_____

_____

_____

15. A need for caution exists for students who want to take a full load of courses and work part-time.

_____

_____

_____

_____

_____

16. Baby boomers or people born after the end of the Second World War are beginning to think about retirement and registered retirement savings plans are proving to be very popular with baby boomers who are investing in them.

_____

_____

_____

_____

_____

17. Some students use their student loans to buy a new car, which is not necessarily a wrong thing to do, since a car is needed by some students to get to classes.

_____

_____

_____

_____

_____

18. Even oil spills much smaller than the spill that came from the oil tanker the Exxon _Valdez_ are a threat to the bird and marine life in areas where the spills occurred.

_____

_____

_____

_____

_____

19. A waiter needs a good memory, a lot of patience, a good sense of humour, an outgoing personality, and a willingness to serve anyone without thinking it is demeaning to do so.

_____

_____

_____

_____

_____

20. Gardening is a hobby that gives the gardener exercise and the feeling of satisfaction that he or she is helping things to grow and is making the world more beautiful.

_____

_____

_____

_____

_____

21. The candidate for the Liberal Party feels that MP pensions should be generous because MPs work hard and have to quit their regular jobs but the candidate, who is the current MP in the riding, for the Reform Party believes pensions for Members of Parliament should not be any more generous than pensions for those who work in the private sector.

_____

_____

_____

_____

_____

22. By subscribing to a magazine the consumer can save a lot of money, as much as 50 percent of the cost of a magazine at a store, but the disadvantage is that a magazine often arrives at a home a week or ten days after the magazine has appeared on newsstands.

_____

_____

_____

_____

_____

23. Ms. Wilson is an industrious and competent employee who works well with others and valuable, practical advice and suggestions are made by her at weekly staff meetings.

_____

_____

_____

_____

_____

24. Some people believe that ethnic jokes appear to be less offensive when directed at certain ethnic groups than they are when they are directed against other ethnic groups.

_____

_____

_____

_____

_____

25. A hotel room in a downtown hotel in any large North American city costs over a hundred dollars a night and then there is often tax and parking added on to that, which brings the actual cost of a hotel room at a downtown hotel per night to close to 150 dollars per night.

_____

_____

_____

_____

_____

Choosing Words Carefully

Word Power

Denotation and Connotation
Specific Versus Vague Words
Jargon

Ostentatious Language
Euphemisms

Think of words as gifts, and select words your readers would like.

The English language contains over 500 000 words, far more words than any other language. For writers, this is something of a mixed blessing. On the one hand, written English can be very exact and precise, because there is likely to be a word with just the shade of meaning the writer wants. On the other hand, because there are so many words from which to choose, a writer can easily make the wrong choice. To maximize your chances of making the right choice, follow the five guidelines for choosing words carefully presented in this lesson.

Words are the basic building blocks of writing. Small wonder writers are sometimes referred to as "wordsmiths." One of Canada's greatest wordsmiths, W.O. Mitchell, is profiled in the video installment at the end of this lesson.

DENOTATION AND CONNOTATION

Denotation: literal meaning—what the dictionary says a word means.

Connotation: emotional meaning—what a word suggests or implies.

Words have two types of meaning. The **denotation** of a word is its literal dictionary definition; the **connotation** of a word is what the word suggests or implies.

Consider, for example, the words "skinny" and "slender." Either one of these words might be used to describe a man who is 180 centimetres tall and weighs 67 kilograms. The *denotation* of these words is the same. But the man in question might be complimented by the word "slender" and insulted by the word "skinny." The *connotations* of the two words are diverse enough that you could make either a friend or an enemy by your selection.

Consider these examples:

1. My brother is tall, slender, and fit

2. My brother is tall, skinny, and fit.

In the second sentence, there seems to be an error made in word choice. The word "skinny" carries the wrong connotations in a sentence apparently written in praise of the writer's brother. Indeed, the sentence seems contradictory.

This does not mean, of course, that synonyms (words that have the same meaning) should not be used, only that synonyms need to have the same connotation as the word they are replacing. Substitute "slim" for "slender" and you still have a word that works.

ASSIGNMENT 11-1

Consider this sentence:

By ten o'clock, he was too drunk to drive home.

Think of a few synonyms for the word "drunk." Which synonyms would have the correct connotation for a police report? Which synonyms would be appropriate in a letter to your friend? In telling the story to your parents?

SPECIFIC VERSUS VAGUE WORDS

Writing can be made more vivid by changing a generic noun to one that is specific. Consider these four sentences.

1. The first time I saw her, she was sitting under a tree reading a book.

2. The first time I saw Miranda, she was sitting under a magnolia reading *The Bridges of Madison County*.

3. The first time I saw Dr. Sternbaum, she was sitting under a dogwood reading *Advanced Statistics for the Social Sciences*.

4. The first time I saw Mimi, she was sitting under a weeping willow reading *Cinderella*.

Simply by changing generic nouns into specific ones, the writer has given an identity to the pronoun "she." If "she" reads a "book" under "a tree," then the reader has a hard time picturing her. "She" comes more into focus by having a name, sitting under a specific type of tree, and reading an exact book title. The reader can begin to imagine what "she" looks like, how old she is, and even what type of person she is.

ASSIGNMENT 11-2

Change the word "car" in the following sentence. Use a more specific, concrete word or phrase.

On a rainy day, I was waiting for the bus, when a car drove by and splashed muddy water all over me.

In a paragraph, discuss how the meaning of the sentence changes when the vague word is replaced by a concrete word.

JARGON

In addition to conveying the appropriate meaning, words must be appropriate to the context within which they are used.

A teacher might read, in a professional journal, an article about "schema theory in reading comprehension" or about "phonics-based basal readers." Using the same terminology, she might then discuss these issues with her colleagues in the staff room. But if that teacher sent a letter to her students' parents in which she described her school's reading program, she would describe to them how she hopes to "draw on the children's previous experiences to help them learn to read" and how the children will "read stories that are designed to teach the proper spelling and pronunciation of new words." She would change her professional **jargon** into everyday language.

Every profession has its own special language that it uses to talk and write about issues that pertain to that profession. This language is called *jargon*. Lawyers, computer programmers, educators, and civil servants are all notorious jargon users. Any homogeneous group, in fact, has its own jargon. Surfers, skateboarders, and bikers can carry on conversations with other members of their group that would puzzle those who don't belong.

Jargon is acceptable, though not really necessary, when you are certain your readers will be familiar with any specialized vocabulary you might be using. But avoid jargon when writing for a general audience. A sure way to perplex and lose your readers is to use words that they won't understand and may even resent—it will make them feel they do not belong to the club.

Jargon: specialized language shared by members of a profession or a group.

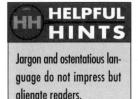

HELPFUL HINTS

Jargon and ostentatious language do not impress but alienate readers.

ASSIGNMENT 11-3

Think of a topic that can be described using specialized vocabulary with which you are familiar: computers, a specific sport, fashion design, the auto industry, any academic discipline or any field that has its own jargon. Write a paragraph on that topic in which you use several examples of specialized vocabulary. Then rewrite the paragraph replacing the jargon with language a general reader could understand.

OSTENTATIOUS LANGUAGE

Rhetorical context: refers to the language appropriate to the topic, audience, and purpose of a piece of writing.

Good writers have good vocabularies that enable them to choose just the right word for just the right **rhetorical context**. But good writers also balance their superior vocabularies with the needs and abilities of their readers. In his famous dictionary, Samuel Johnson—usually sensitive to the abilities of his readers—

defined the word "network" as "any thing reticulated or decussated, at equal distances, with interstices between the intersections." The definition might be accurate but it is not accessible to most readers, who will have to look up two or three additional words to understand the original definition.

Ostentatious synonyms: words that mean the same as a word you are replacing but that are too difficult or obscure for most readers.

Always remember that words are meant to communicate, not impress. Choose the word that best conveys your meaning to readers, not the words that make you sound brilliant. Use your thesaurus sparingly to find appropriate, but not **ostentatious**, **synonyms**.

ASSIGNMENT 11-4

Revise the following sentences so that a general reader could understand them.

1. The icing on the cake was canaliculated, making the children even more anxious to have dessert.

2. It will not be fair if he fails the test simply because of his cacography.

3. The police found an ensanguined sock and glove at the home of the defendant.

4. Management will refuse to bargain if the company employees insist that their demands are immitigable.

5. The tribute ended with a brief but moving panegyric, given by the guest-of-honour's husband.

EUPHEMISMS

Euphemisms: words or phrases that try to deflect complete truth and accuracy.

To learn about **euphemisms**—what they are, when to use them, and when to avoid them—read Oscar's essay that follows.

Lies and Whispers: The Use and Abuse of Euphemisms

Oscar S.
English 100
April, 19XX

The first time I ever saw a euphemism, though I did not know at the time that it had a name, was on my grade-five report card. The school librarian had written: "Oscar enjoys reading. Next term we will work harder on Oscar's library deportment which, this term, was at odds with his high spirits and irrepressible sense of humour." Since I had been kicked out of the library that term more times than I had been in the library, Mrs. Fairfax's comments confused me. Eventually, though, I realized she was really saying my behaviour in the library was unacceptable, only she was saying it indirectly, apparently to spare my feelings or perhaps to spare me from the wrath of my parents.

Mrs. Fairfax was using a euphemism. The word "euphemism" comes from the Greek and means literally "words of good omen" (Troyka, Buckley, and Gates 420). A euphemism is an indirect way of writing or speaking, the purpose of which is either to deceive or to soften the impact of the message being communicated.

Mrs. Fairfax's euphemism was an example of the latter. Other euphemisms that try to diminish the impact or the harsh reality of the message tend to be associated with things that threaten us the most or that make us somewhat uncomfortable. "Oh, he's dead!" might be considered indelicate in certain social situations, so we usually·say "he passed away" or "he is departed." A Member of Parliament will be kicked out of the House of Commons for the day if she calls one of her colleagues a liar. And so she says "the honourable member is 'remote from fact'" or "the honourable member is 'prone to embellishment,'" or, my personal favourite, "the honourable member has so much respect for the truth that he uses it sparingly." Euphemisms are learned very early in life. The other day, I was having coffee at my friend's house and learned a couple of new euphemisms from her two-year-old, who gave me a progress report on his toilet training.

Euphemisms are harmless, even useful, if they spare feelings or maintain social decorum. Other euphemisms, however, are dangerous because they use language indirectly in order to deceive or to conceal the truth. The military hates to use the word "kill." It's bad "PR." And so military leaders claim their troops "neutralized" the enemy or, if civilians have been killed, they claim they "were forced to pacify suspicious non-combatants." In a nuclear power plant, the word "accident" is never used; an accident is "a reportable occurrence." A big business does not lay off employees; it "reassesses its need for human resources." Governments don't like to tax us; they prefer to "initiate revenue enhancement programs."

Bad euphemisms, like the ones in the previous paragraph, weaken writing because they are wordy and deceptive. Good euphemisms, like Mrs. Fairfax's, don't necessarily improve writing, but they are acceptable in that they spare feelings or maintain decorum. Bad euphemisms are lies and should be avoided. Good euphemisms aren't truths, exactly, but they are, at least, humane.

Work Cited

Troyka, Lynn Q., Joanne Buckley, and David Gates. *Simon and Schuster Handbook for Writers*, 1st Canadian ed. Scarborough, Ontario: Prentice Hall, 1996.

ASSIGNMENT 11-5 See if you can find an example of a euphemism in a recent edition of your local newspaper. Bring the example to class for comparison with examples your classmates have found. Rewrite the passage replacing the euphemism with direct language.

SUMMARY

- Make sure that the connotation of a word is as appropriate as its denotation is accurate.
- Replace vague, abstract words and phrases with concrete, specific words.
- Avoid jargon unless you are certain your readers will understand and accept it.
- Don't try to impress your readers with ostentatious words when simpler ones are more effective.
- Use euphemisms to spare feelings but not to mislead.

QUESTIONS FOR STUDY AND DISCUSSION

1. Explain the difference between the denotation and the connotation of a word. Discuss a few examples.
2. Illustrate, through two versions of the same sentence, how concrete words are more accurate and effective than vague words.
3. When is it acceptable to use jargon?
4. When is it acceptable to use a euphemism?
5. Is there anything wrong with using words that will send your reader to the dictionary?

SUPPLEMENTARY EXERCISES

In the following sentences, change vague words to more specific ones, change words with inappropriate connotations, simplify ostentatious words, and revise any inappropriate use of jargon and euphemism. If you can't decode the jargon, write a sentence in which you explain why the language is inaccessible to you.

1. Detective Poirot was just about to abandon the search when a new idea assaulted him.

_____

_____

2. Even in smaller cities, women do not feel safe walking alone, and so they conceptualize "take-back-the-night" marches to call cognizance to their concerns.

_____

_____

3. An executive secretary has many tasks to do.

_____

_____

4. Some people are more concerned about pollution than other people are.

_____

_____

5. At the end of tragedies the heroes either pass away or are forced into exile.

_____

_____

6. Many Canadian citizens of Japanese ancestry were relocated during the Second World War.

_____

_____

7. Apportion accolades when children achieve positive behavioural objectives and endeavour to ignore aberrant behaviour.

_____

_____

8. Golf has many benefits.

_____

_____

9. To correct a dangling elliptical adverb clause, you must include in the clause a clear subject and verb, or begin the independent clause with a noun or pronoun that clearly establishes the relationship between the subordinate and main clauses.

_____

_____

10. The electronics industry is downsizing and employees with fewer than two years seniority are being deselected.

_____

_____

11. The commander of the UN military forces admitted there might have been some unfortunate collateral damage during the bombing of Serbian-held territory.

   _____

   _____

12. The Prime Minister had to shuffle her cabinet after the Minister of Natural Resources was fired for financial misconduct regarding his expense account.

   _____

   _____

13. He was an antiquated gentleman and her friends felt she might have been marrying him for his money.

   _____

   _____

14. My history professor is dull.

   _____

   _____

15. An error in the random-sampling procedure contaminated the data, rendering the results of the study invalid.

   _____

   _____

16. He was ashamed of his marital dissolution and it was two years before he told his mother about it.

   _____

   _____

17. Next season, referees will hand out more interference penalties in an attempt to prevent teams from relying too much on the neutral-zone trap.

   _____

   _____

18. One of the bank robbers panicked and assassinated a security guard.

   _____

   _____

19. To improve investor liquidity, the portfolio managers decided to sell short some of their NASDAQ holdings.

   _____

   _____

20. The border collie is the most sagacious breed of dog.

   _____

   _____

21. After an exquisite evening repast, we enjoyed a moon-lit carriage ride
   through Stanley Park.

   _____

   _____

22. He wore a six-to-one double-breasted Prince-of-Wales checked suit with
   notched lapels and slightly flared surgeon cuffs.

   _____

   _____

23. A by-product of petroleum refining, ethylene is used as a starting material
   in the industrial manufacture of intermediates.

   _____

   _____

24. Zen Buddhists strive to get in touch with their inner selves through direct
   experience and never through the adherence to the dictates of an external
   authority.

   _____

   _____

25. In an election year, the incumbent government's desire to curb inflation,
   attenuate unemployment, and realize a rise in the gross domestic product
   will determine its macroeconomic policy.

   _____

   _____

Video Case 2

An Interview with W.O. Mitchell

W.O. Mitchell is the author of the classic Canadian novel *Who Has Seen the Wind*,
which he wrote in the 1940s. In this interview with Adrienne Clarkson, Mitchell
talks about his life and how his experiences have determined the themes of his
novels.

   Writing, Mitchell notes, is inevitably influenced by the geography, the culture, and the "times" in which the author is working. But great writing tran-
scends time and place, carrying a message to every culture and every generation.

Family relationships have defined Mitchell's life and work. He writes about the stress and tensions of family life and about how the love within a family triumphs over conflict. The need for genuine friendships and the quest for immortality are other important themes in both his life and his work.

Mitchell discusses the tone of writing, the personality a piece of writing conveys to its readers. He warns writers about being so serious they move toward melodrama, or so comic they move towards slapstick. A moderate tone is appropriate for most forms of writing.

Finally, Mitchell talks about creativity, suggesting that the key to being a creative person is the ability to recapture the imagination of a child. Children are free, not bound by the learned conventions and behaviours of adults, which enables them to see and describe the world from an innocent but insightful perspective.

Questions

1. In an essay of approximately 500 words, define what Mitchell means when he talks about how much "we need each other." Describe in your paper the characteristics of a "true friend."

2. Bring to class a piece of writing that was written in the past by someone from a different culture, but that is still relevant today. Be prepared to read from the piece and/or to paraphrase it and to explain why you think it is well written and why you find it relevant to today's world.

3. Recall and describe in writing a significant experience you had when you were a child. Explain how this experience might have shaped and influenced the person you are today.

4. In a journal entry, describe a member of your family and briefly discuss how that person has influenced you.

Source: "Interview with W.O. Mitchell," *Adrienne Clarkson Presents*. CBC, 1991.

Writing Grammatically Correct Sentences

The Grammar School

Pronoun as Object of a Verb
Pronoun as Object of a Preposition
Pronoun in a Comparison
Subjective Case After a Linking Verb
"Who" and "Whom"
Pronoun-Antecedent Agreement

Subject-Verb Agreement
Indefinite Pronouns
Collective Nouns
Misplaced Modifiers
Dangling Modifiers

Grammar: the correct and appropriate arrangement of words to form sentences.

The word **grammar** comes from the Greek "grammatike," which means the art (*tekhne*) of letters (*gram*). Broadly defined, grammar encompasses the combination of letters to form words, the pronunciation of words, and the arrangement of words to form phrases, clauses, and sentences. In the context of written composition, the third meaning has become standard. Grammar is the study of the structure of language, the linguistically correct arrangement of words to form sentences.

People learn how to arrange words to form sentences very early in life, and what they learn is reinforced constantly as they grow older. From birth, they are surrounded by spoken and written language, most of which has come as standard, grammatically correct English. For this reason, student grammar is generally good, despite the fact that many people seem to think language standards are declining. In fact, students arrive at college knowing more about language than they know about any other subject. By and large, they write grammatically correct sentences automatically, without consciously thinking about what may or may not be grammatically correct.

You would probably write, for example, "My daughters *play* hockey," not "My daughters *plays* hockey," because the second version sounds all wrong. You write, "My daughter *plays* hockey," not "My daughter *play* hockey," for the same reason—the second version *sounds* wrong.

Now, if you thought too much about it, you might become quite confused. Look again at these four sentences:

1. My daughters play hockey.
2. My daughters plays hockey.
3. My daughter play hockey.
4. My daughter plays hockey.

In sentence 1, there is an "s" at the end of "daughters" but no "s" at the end of "play." In sentence 2, there is an "s" at the end of "daughters" and an "s" at the end of "plays." Shouldn't sentence 2 be correct—if there is an "s" at the end of the subject, should there not also be an "s" at the end of the verb?

Why wouldn't you write, "My daughter<u>s</u> play<u>s</u> hockey"? Ask 100 English speakers and 99 will say "because it doesn't sound right." Maybe one person will say something about adding an "s" to a noun to make it plural but adding "s" to a verb to make it singular. Most people with English as a native language make grammar choices based on sound. They write grammatically correct sentences most of the time. English as a Second Language students face a bigger challenge and have to learn the rules of English grammar in more depth than their classmates.

There are times, of course, when you do have to pause and think about the correct grammar of a sentence. Occasionally your ear might betray you. For example, which pronoun, "I" or "me," is correct in this sentence?

Fred will pick up Cathy and (I, me) on his way to the rink.

Which verb, "know" or "knows," is correct in this sentence?

Neither of my friends (know, knows) the answer to that question.

For reasons that are explained later in this lesson, "me" is the correct pronoun to use in the first sentence. "Knows" is the correct verb in the second sentence.

In this lesson, you learn how to recognize and avoid eleven grammatical errors that college students sometimes make.

HELPFUL HINTS

Improper use of pronouns is one of the most common grammatical errors. Learn the cases of pronouns and their functions.

PRONOUN AS OBJECT OF A VERB

Pronoun: Short word ("he," "him," "his") that stands in place of a noun.

Consider this sentence:

You can expect me to arrive before noon.

This sentence sounds grammatically correct, and it is grammatically correct. Consider this sentence:

You can expect my wife to arrive before noon.

This sentence sounds grammatically correct, and it is grammatically correct. Now consider this sentence:

You can expect my wife and me to arrive before noon.

This sentence is grammatically correct, but it might sound incorrect. You might want to write "I" instead of "me." We are used to hearing nouns or pronouns separated by "and" ("my wife *and* me" or "my wife *and* I") used as subjects:

My wife and I are expected around noon.

This sentence is, of course, correct because "I" is acting as a subject of the verb. But "You can expect my wife and I..." is incorrect. The "I" should be changed to "me." When the pronoun is used as the object of a verb, its form, or its **case**, changes. The subjective case, "I," changes to the objective case, "me."

Case: the form (subjective, objective, or possessive) of a pronoun.

Try to identify which of the following sentences are incorrect:

1. Him is expected around noon.
2. He is expected around noon.
3. You can expect he around noon.
4. You can expect him around noon.
5. Him and his wife are expected around noon.
6. He and his wife are expected around noon.
7. You can expect he and his wife around noon.
8. You can expect him and his wife around noon.

The first and third sentences sound ridiculous and are, obviously, grammatically incorrect. Sentence 5 might sound better, but "him" can not be used as a subject in sentence 5 any more than it could be used as a subject in sentence 1. Similarly, sentence 7 might not sound too bad, but "he" cannot be used as the object of the verb, "expect," in this sentence any more than it could be used as an object in sentence 3.

ASSIGNMENT 12-1

Identify the pronouns that could be used correctly in these sentences:

1. Dr. Smyth certainly gave John and (I, me, he, him, her, she, you, they, them) a difficult assignment.

2. The community has accepted my family and (I, me, he, him, her, she, you, they, them).

3. The university admitted Charlotte but not (I, me, he, him, her, she, you, they, them).

PRONOUN AS OBJECT OF A PREPOSITION

Preposition: often short word ("in," "on," "of," "to") that introduces a phrase that describes a noun or verb.

A **preposition** is a word like "in," "of," "by," "over," "under," "at," "for," "on," that links a noun or pronoun to the rest of a sentence. A prepositional phrase is a group of words that begin with a preposition and end with a noun or pronoun. In the following sentences, prepositional phrases are underlined. The first word underlined is the preposition.

1. Broadly defined, grammar encompasses the combination <u>of letters</u> to form words, the pronunciation <u>of words</u>, and the arrangement <u>of words</u> to form phrases, clauses, and sentences.

2. <u>In the context of written composition</u>, the third meaning has become standard.

3. This sentence contains an error <u>in grammar</u>.

4. <u>After a preposition</u>, use the objective case.

5. John got the book he wanted <u>for his birthday</u>.

Objective case: class of pronouns that act as objects of verbs or prepositions.

Subjective case: class of pronouns that act as subjects of verbs.

If a prepositional phrase ends with a pronoun, that pronoun must be in **objective case** (me, us, him, her, them).

In the above sentences, the prepositional phrases end with nouns. If they ended with pronouns, you would have to use objective case as opposed to **subjective case** (I, we, he, she, they) pronouns. See if you can determine which of these sentences are correct and which are incorrect.

1. Robert is coming for me at noon.

2. Robert is coming for Jason and I at noon.

3. Robert is coming for Jason and me at noon.

4. The boy with whom she danced was too short.

Sentence 1 is correct. "For" is a preposition, so objective case—me—is necessary. Sentence 2 is incorrect because "I" is a subjective-case pronoun and objective case is needed after the preposition "for." Sentence 3 is correct for the same reason that sentence 1 is correct. The noun "Jason" does not change the case of the pronoun. Sentence 4 is correct. The objective-case pronoun, "whom," is needed after the preposition, "with."

ASSIGNMENT 12-2

Identify the pronouns that could be used correctly in the following sentences:

1. At the Olympic Games in Lillehammer, my sister bought some wonderful pins for my brother and (I, me, he, him, her, she, you, them, they).

2. She says she will go the games in Atlanta with her boyfriend and (you, she, her, I, me, them, they).

3. It makes no difference to my friend or (you, she, her, I, me, them, they).

PRONOUN IN A COMPARISON

When you are comparing two people and the second person is identified by a pronoun, determine which pronoun to use by completing that part of the sentence that is understood. Consider this sentence:

Brian is a better actor than (she, her).

The verb in this sentence is "is." Placed after the subject of the sentence, "Brian," the verb does not have to be repeated at the end of the sentence—the second "is" is understood. If you do fill it in, however, the choice of pronoun becomes obvious:

Brian is a better actor than *she is.*

In some comparisons, either pronoun is acceptable, but the choice of pronoun determines the meaning of the sentence. Consider this sentence:

Brian likes John more than (I, me).

You would choose "I" if you wanted to say that Brian likes John more than you like John. The meaning depends on the sentence ending with the *understood* verb, "do."

Brian likes John more than *I do.*

You would choose "me" if you meant that Brian likes John more than he likes you. The meaning depends on the *understood* subject-verb combination, "he likes," preceding the pronoun.

Brian likes John more than *he likes* me.

Make sure the pronoun you use conveys the meaning you wish to convey.

ASSIGNMENT 12-3

Identify the pronouns that could be used correctly in the following sentences:

1. Eric is quite a bit taller than (you, I, me, she, him, he, her, they, them).

2. She always liked her own family more than (you, I, me, she, him, he, her, they, them).

3. Most students didn't do as well on the test as (you, I, me, she, him, he, her, they, them).

SUBJECTIVE CASE AFTER A LINKING VERB

Linking verb: verb followed by a noun, pronoun, or adjective that establishes a relationship between its subject and the noun, pronoun, or adjective that follows.

We have learned already that objective-case pronouns are used as objects of verbs:

We liked *him, her, them* as soon as we saw *him, her, them.*

There is an exception to this rule. After a certain kind of verb, called a **linking verb**, the *subjective* case of the pronoun is correct.

The most common linking verb is the verb "to be," which includes "is," "am," "are," "was," and "were." Used as the main verb in a sentence, the verb "to be" is followed by a subjective-case pronoun:

The only person interested in this book *is she.*

I thought it *was he* who was interested in this book.

ASSIGNMENT 12-4 Identify the correct pronouns in the following sentences:

1. The big winner was (you, she, he, I, me, him, her).

2. The detective is convinced that the murderer is (you, she, he, I, me, him, her).

3. The only one committed to the relationship is (I, me, him, he, she, her).

"WHO" AND "WHOM"

"Who" and "whom" are pronouns just as "he" and "him" are pronouns. "Who" is the subjective case; "whom" the objective case.

"Who" is used as the subject of a verb:

The professor *who taught* Canadian history has retired.

"Whom" is used as an object of a verb:

The professor *whom* I *had* last year for Canadian history has retired.

In the above sentence, "I" is the subject of the clause "whom I had last year," and "had" is the verb. "Whom" is the object of the verb "had."

"Whom" is also used as an object of a preposition just as other objective-case pronouns are:

The professor *from whom* you always received high grades has retired.

ASSIGNMENT 12-5 In one paragraph explain why "whom" is correct in sentences 1 and 2:

1. The candidate whom I watched did not give a very good speech.

2. The candidate to whom I gave a donation won by a landslide.

But *incorrect* in sentence 3:

3. I wondered whom would be the first candidate to speak.

PRONOUN–ANTECEDENT AGREEMENT

Antecedent: the noun that a pronoun refers back to.

An **antecedent** is a word to which a pronoun refers. In this sentence, the word "pronoun" is the antecedent of the word (the pronoun) "it."

A pronoun is in the objective case if it appears at the end of a prepositional phrase.

Consider this sentence:

> As soon as the young girl walked away from her mother and boarded the plane, she began to cry.

What is the antecedent for the pronoun, "she"? Is it "girl" or is it "mother"? It could be either. The sentence lacks clarity because the pronoun's antecedent is ambiguous. It has to be revised so that the noun (the antecedent) to which the pronoun "she" is referring is clear.

> The mother began to cry as soon as her daughter walked away from her and boarded the plane.

> The young girl began to cry as soon as she walked away from her mother and boarded the plane.

ASSIGNMENT 12-6

Compose three sentences that contain ambiguous pronouns. Give the sentences to one of your classmates to correct. Take your classmate's examples and correct them.

SUBJECT-VERB AGREEMENT

A verb must "agree" with its subject. If a subject is plural, the verb must also be plural.

> My daughters play hockey

If a subject is singular, the verb must also be singular.

> My daughter plays hockey.

A problem sometimes arises when words intervene between the subject and the verb. If, for example, a prepositional phrase comes between a subject and a verb, a writer might be tempted to make the verb agree with the object of the preposition even though it would be incorrect. For example, this sentence might not sound wrong:

> Each of my body paragraphs *contain* a different topic sentence.

But the subject of this sentence is "each," not "paragraphs." ("Paragraphs" is the object of the preposition "of.") It is the subject and the verb that must agree. Therefore, the sentence should read:

> Each of my body paragraphs *contains* a different topic sentence.

Both of the following sentences are grammatically correct:

> My body paragraphs *contain* different topic sentences.

> Each of my body paragraphs *contains* a different topic sentence.

ASSIGNMENT 12-7 Identify the correct verb in the following sentences:

1. Your essay (is, are) interesting. The ideas in your essay (is, are) interesting.

2. Paragraph development (is, are) discussed in Chapter Two. Strategies for paragraph development (is, are) discussed in Chapter Two.

3. Your readers (need, needs) to be stimulated. The interest of your readers (need, needs) to be stimulated.

4. My friends all (has, have) cars. One of my friends (own, owns) a Porsche.

5. An alliance (is, are) dangerous. An alliance with certain countries (is, are) dangerous.

INDEFINITE PRONOUNS

Indefinite pronouns: words such as "each," "every," "all" that identify unknown persons or things.

An **indefinite pronoun** refers to unknown (indefinite) persons or things. "Each," "every," "either," "neither," "none," "anyone," "everybody," "all," and "some" are among the more common indefinite pronouns. Usually, indefinite pronouns are singular and, therefore, are used with singular verbs:

1. Everybody *was* present.

2. Each *is* correct.

3. Each sentence *is* correct.

4. Each of these sentences *is* correct.

5. Every one of these sentences *is* correct.

6. Neither of these sentences *is* correct.

HELPFUL HINTS

Use computerized grammar checks cautiously—they can be unreliable.

You might be tempted to use "are" in the third, fourth, and fifth sentences above. But note that "sentences" is the object of the preposition, "of," not the subject of the verb. The subjects are "each," "every," and "neither" respectively. These are singular pronouns and so they take the singular form—"is"—of the verb.

There is an exception to this rule: Some indefinite pronouns will take the plural form of the verb if the plural form is appropriate to the context of the sentence:

All of the money *is* missing.

All of the students *are* missing.

In addition to "all," the indefinite pronouns "many," "most," and "some" also might take a plural verb depending on their context.

ASSIGNMENT 12-8

Identify the correct verb in the following sentences:

1. Neither of these teachers (was, were) willing to help me.

2. Every one of my teachers (has, have) been willing to help me.

3. Most of your education (is, are) going to occur outside a classroom.

4. Most of your teachers (is, are) going to try to give you a good education.

5. None of the police officers (understand, understands) why the Young Offenders Act can't be modified.

COLLECTIVE NOUNS

Collective nouns: words such as "team," "orchestra," "class," that refer to a common group of people.

A **collective noun** describes a group: "class," "crew," "team," and "band" are among the more common collective nouns. When a collective noun is acting as a unit, it takes a singular verb:

The orchestra is playing a Mozart symphony.

The collective noun, "orchestra," is acting as a unit in this sentence so the verb, "is playing," is singular.

When the individuals within a collective noun are acting in individual ways, the noun's verb is plural:

The orchestra were tuning up their instruments.

The activity (tuning instruments) is done on an individual basis, so the verb becomes plural—"were tuning up."

Many writers prefer to avoid a collective noun when the individuals within the collective are acting independently because the plural verb required in this case sounds awkward. However, you can always rewrite the sentence so that it is not jarring to the reader. For example, you might write instead:

The musicians were tuning up their instruments.

ASSIGNMENT 12-9

Compose four sentences using collective nouns as subjects. Write two sentences so that the collective nouns are acting as a unit; write two sentences so that the collective nouns are not acting as a unit.

MISPLACED MODIFIERS

Consider carefully these three sentences:

1. I was able to find two books and several articles in the library that will be useful to me.

2. I was able to find two books and several articles that will be useful to me in the library.

3. I was able to find, in the library, two books and several articles that will be useful to me.

Which sentence is the clearest? The clause "that will be useful to me" refers, of course, to the "two books and several articles." In the first sentence, it looks as if it is the library, instead of the books and articles *in* the library, that will be useful. In the second sentence, it sounds as if the books and articles will be useful *only* in the library.

The first two sentences, then, both contain **misplaced modifiers**. The clause "that will be useful to me" modifies "books and articles." The first sentence is written in such a way that the clause is modifying "library." The second sentence is written in such a way as to suggest that the books and articles are useful only in the library, not, apparently, if they are signed out and taken home.

Here is another example:

Hurricane Felix is threatening the coast of Nova Scotia with winds gusting up to 100 kilometres per hour.

Misplaced modifier: word, phrase, or clause that appears to modify something it does not.

Does the wind belong to the hurricane or to Nova Scotia? It belongs to the hurricane. The clarity of the sentence is improved if the modifier is placed closer to the word it modifies. It could be placed before it:

With winds gusting up to 100 kilometres per hour, Hurricane Felix is threatening the coast of Nova Scotia.

Or it could be placed after the word it modifies:

Hurricane Felix, with winds gusting up to 100 kilometres per hour, is threatening the coast of Nova Scotia.

HELPFUL HINTS

To help spot misplaced and dangling modifiers, read your sentences out loud.

ASSIGNMENT 12-10

Misplaced modifiers can create amusing sentences:

She found an antique desk for her husband, made of solid mahogany.

Compose three sentences made amusing because of misplaced modifiers. Be prepared to share your sentences with your classmates.

DANGLING MODIFIERS

Student writers sometimes compose sentences that do not contain the word that is being modified by part of the sentence. This error is called a **dangling modifier**. Here is an example:

When writing an essay, the four rules for good writing should be kept in mind.

Dangling modifier: phrase or clause that does not modify any noun in a sentence.

Who is writing the essay? Who is supposed to keep the four rules in mind? The sentence does not tell us. The phrase "When writing an essay" is left dangling at the beginning of the sentence without a word for it to modify. Corrected, the sentence would look like this:

> When writing an essay, students should keep in mind the four rules for good writing.

Now there is a noun, "students," for the phrase to modify.

Sometimes the word to be modified is in the sentence, but it is too far away from its modifier:

> When revised, the student should have an essay that does not contain errors in grammar.

The word "essay," which should be modified by "when revised," appears to be disconnected from the major thought because it is too far away from its modifier. It sounds as if it is the student, not the essay, that is being revised. Correct the sentence as follows:

> When revised, the student's essay (or "essays the student writes") should not contain errors in grammar.

ASSIGNMENT 12-11

Revise the following sentences to eliminate dangling modifiers:

1. Born and raised in Rumania, English was difficult for me to learn.

2. Flying over the Strait of Georgia, Salt Spring Island shimmered in the early morning sun.

3. Self-knowledge is often achieved by attending college.

4. With a budget that mushroomed to two hundred million dollars, many people were curious about *Waterworld*, despite what the critics had to say.

5. Not always the greatest role model, baseball fans are still devastated by the death of Mickey Mantle.

SUMMARY

- Remember that pronouns are divided into subjective, objective, and possessive cases.
- Use the objective case of the pronoun if it is the object of a verb.
- A preposition is a short word that begins an adjective or adverb phrase.
- Use the objective case of the pronoun if it is the object of a preposition.
- To determine the right pronoun to use in a comparison, complete the sentence the comparison is in.

- After a linking verb, use the subjective case of the pronoun.
- Use "who" as the subject of a verb, "whom" as the object of a verb or a preposition.
- An antecedent is a word to which a pronoun refers. Make pronouns agree with their antecedents.
- Make a verb agree with its subject, not with the object of a preposition.
- An indefinite pronoun refers to persons or things not precisely identified. Indefinite pronouns are usually singular.
- A collective noun describes a group. Collective nouns are singular when they are acting as a unit.
- A misplaced modifier is a clause or a phrase that appears to be modifying a word it should not be modifying.
- A dangling modifier is a phrase that has no word to modify or that is too far away from the word it is supposed to modify.

QUESTIONS FOR STUDY AND DISCUSSION

1. Why is good grammar important to good writing?
2. How do you determine whether or not a sentence you have written is grammatically correct?
3. Of the eleven errors in grammar covered in this lesson, which three cause you the most problem? Why?
4. What was the first rule of good grammar you remember learning in elementary school?
5. Name one grammatical error that you think should be acceptable in writing. Explain your choice.
6. What is the difference between a misplaced and a dangling modifier?

SUPPLEMENTARY EXERCISES

Revise the following sentences, eliminating any errors in grammar. Some sentences will require major revision. Other sentences will need only certain words changed.

1. When painted, you will get a better price.

   _____

2. After waiting for over an hour, the concert finally began.

   _____

3. An interesting antique, I was sorry one leg was not original.

   _____

4. The decision was not an easy one for Raj and I to make.

_____

5. Lincoln, not Mckinley, was the President who John Wilkes Booth assassinated.

_____

6. Chretien is one Prime Minister who history will treat kindly.

_____

7. I had to go along with the majority of the group who enjoy camping more than me.

_____

8. Neither the senator nor the Member of Parliament on the committee are going to vote in favour of the bill.

_____

9. A sentence fragment is a group of words that are missing a subject or a verb.

_____

10. Every one of the players promise to vote against strike action.

_____

11. The happiness of the children depend on which parent is going to get custody.

_____

12. To survive a winter in Winnipeg, warm clothing and patience is essential.

_____

13. Each of the students plan to bring along enough money to buy jewellery.

_____

14. Fitch and Sons are a good place to buy fishing equipment.

_____

15. Neither of them are willing to take the blame.

_____

16. His so-called proof about the existence of UFOs have not convinced me.

_____

17. A loaf of bread and jug of wine is essential to a romantic picnic.

_____

18. The candidate gave the same speech opposing Quebec separation in every town in the country.

_____

19. I gave my old copy of the text to my friend with all of the exercises completed.

_____

20. I thought I might be fired after I refused to pour coffee for the truckers into their own mugs.

_____

21. The professor collected all of the assignments about the civil war on Friday.

_____

22. You can't take a suitcase onto a plane that won't fit into the overhead compartment.

_____

23. The bicycle we found at the dump that is missing its handle bars can easily be repaired.

_____

24. While trying to sneak into the house past curfew, a vase crashed to the floor.

_____

25. An old man accompanied my wife who I had never seen before.

_____

26. Steve blamed Jennifer and I for failing the exam, claiming we had not helped him study enough.

_____

27. Nearly every Sunday afternoon, him and I play golf together.

_____

28. The counsellor helped convince Raj and I to apply for admission to the Faculty of Engineering.

_____

29. So many battered women feel there is no one who cares, no one who they can turn to for help.

_____

30. Alberta produces more oil than us, but we lead the country in agricultural production.

_____

Avoiding Sexist Language

Handle with Care
Gender-Specific Nouns
Masculine Pronouns

English is a responsive language, willing to change as social values and beliefs change. The English language has, for example, changed in the last two decades, in recognition of the strength and the principles of the feminist movement. In business, industry, government, and education, writing that demeans women, that perpetuates female **stereotypes**, and that seems to deny women their status as real people is considered unacceptable. Avoid, in your written work, gender-specific nouns and masculine pronouns meant to act for both genders.

Stereotype: a fixed, often biased, impression of a person or group.

GENDER-SPECIFIC NOUNS

Gender-specific noun: word such as "fire*man*" or "actress" that refers specifically to either men or women.

A **gender-specific noun** is one that refers only to men or only to women. The problem with gender-specific nouns is that they exclude one or other of the sexes when discussing subjects that, in reality, include both. Consider these sentences:

1. To be a *policeman* now, you need at least two years of college.

2. Wars punctuate the history of *mankind*.

3. If you have a complaint against a professor, you should see the department *chairman*.

The italicized nouns in the sentences above illogically imply that women do not pursue careers in police work, that they are not a part of human history, and that they are not department heads. Nothing is lost and inclusivity is gained if "policeman" is changed to "police officer," if "the history of mankind" is changed to "human history," and if "chairman" is changed to "chair."

Sometimes this discrimination can work against men. The word "homemaker" now replaces "housewife" because it allows for the fact that men sometimes bear the major domestic responsibilities in a family. The point here is that one should not discriminate.

You should avoid using nouns that refer only to women, when there are valid substitutes that don't perpetuate a stereotype. A "steward," for example, sounds like a more important person than a "stewardess." A steward is not only the man on the plane who serves lunch; he is also the manager of a great estate. But the word "stewardess" refers only to women who serve and help passengers on a plane. In other words, "steward" has more positive connotations (see Lesson Eleven) than "stewardess." For this reason, airlines now use the gender-neutral "flight attendant" to describe this job. Similarly, many waitresses feel that the connotations of their job title suggest they work in less important restaurants than do "waiters." They prefer the somewhat demeaning "ess" to be dropped.

On the other hand, if the gender-specific noun is absolute, it should be used. It is not necessary to neuter nouns that logic dictates *should* be gender specific. Freud is not the "parent" but the "father" of psychoanalysis. And even though it is a cliché and would not add much to your writing, you would still say that necessity is the "mother" of invention.

Midwives, for example, do not want to be called "midpersons." There is no acceptable gender-neutral noun for some feminine nouns, and human rights are not advanced when attempts are made to manufacture them.

ASSIGNMENT 13-1   List three nouns, not mentioned above, that are gender-specific but that should usually be avoided because they can include both genders. Provide alternatives.

MASCULINE PRONOUNS

Masculine pronoun: he, him, his.

Avoid, in your written work, using only the masculine form of a pronoun when you are identifying a noun that could refer to women as well as to men:

> Any student with more than six overdue fines will have *his* library privileges revoked.

"Student" is a gender-neutral noun; it refers to both men and women. But in the above sentence, only the pronoun "his" is used to refer to student. The sentence needs to be revised.

Feminine pronoun: she, her, her(s).

One way of revising the sentence would be to also include the **feminine pronoun**:

> Any student with more than six overdue fines will have *his or her* library privileges revoked.

The problem with including both pronouns, however, is that if they become cumulative, the writing sounds redundant and loses any sense of rhythm:

> Any student with more than six overdue fines will have *his or her* library privileges revoked. *He or she* must appeal, in writing, to the Director of

Student Services explaining why *he or she* has incurred so many fines and requesting that *his or her* privileges be restored.

Another way to revise the sentence is to make the noun plural:

Students with more than six overdue fines will have *their* library privileges revoked. *They* must appeal, in writing...

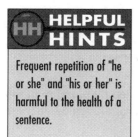

HELPFUL HINTS

Frequent repetition of "he or she" and "his or her" is harmful to the health of a sentence.

For the passage, this would be a good solution, though some of the emphasis that "Any student" connotes would be lost. Generally speaking, pluralizing a gender-neutral noun is a good, often the best, way to avoid sexist language.

At times, however, it is difficult to make a gender-neutral noun plural:

Coleridge ends the poem with a description of an inspired poet in the act of creating a poem. The poet is a powerful force, in need of protection. *His* supporters weave a circle around him three times, performing a magic ritual that will protect *his* privacy. They close their eyes in "holy dread." The inspired poet is ready; *he* has "drunk the milk of paradise."

In the Coleridge poem ("Kubla Khan"), which the above passage discusses, a particular poet is being discussed so the noun is singular; meaning would be sacrificed if the plural form, "poets," were used. It would not be wrong to add the feminine pronoun, but the flow of the passage would be adversely affected:

Coleridge ends the poem with a description of an inspired poet in the act of creating a poem. The poet is a powerful force, in need of protection. *His or her* supporters weave a circle around *him or her* three times, performing a magic ritual that will protect *his or her* privacy. They close their eyes in "holy dread." The inspired poet is ready; *he or she* has "drunk the milk of paradise."

Most English teachers would agree that, in this case, the exclusive use of the masculine pronoun is acceptable.

There are also times, of course, when the exclusive use of the feminine pronoun is perfectly acceptable. Indeed, some writers now use only "she" or "her" to refer to a gender-neutral noun, reasoning that, if for the last 500 years, only the male pronoun was used, then perhaps for the next 500 years only the female pronoun should be used:

Any student with more than six overdue fines will have *her* library privileges revoked.

Every student in my class will get the mark *she* deserves.

This is acceptable in the sentences above, and is certainly acceptable when the chances are very high that the noun does refer to a woman:

A midwife can practise in this country as long as *she* is a landed immigrant.

But common sense again dictates that for some nouns, the feminine pronoun makes little sense:

When a fighter is stunned by a punch, *he* will often look up at the clock to see how much time is left in the round.

Using the Gender-Neutral Plural Pronoun

Gender-neutral plural pronoun: pronouns such as "they" and "them" that could refer to men, to women, or to a combination of both.

Some English teachers will now accept the use of a **gender-neutral plural pronoun** ("their," "them," or "they") as a way of avoiding sexist usage, even when these pronouns are referring to a singular noun.

Even if one actor has not learned *their* lines, the entire play can be ruined. Even the player with the smallest role can ruin a production if *they* have not learned their lines properly.

By using a gender-neutral pronoun, writers avoid the problem of repetition, which the use of both the masculine and the feminine pronouns causes:

Even if one actor has not learned *his* or *her* lines, the entire play can be ruined. Even the player with the smallest role can ruin a production if *he* or *she* has not learned *his* or *her* lines properly.

Pronoun-antecedent agreement: grammatical principle that states that singular pronouns should identify singular nouns and plural pronouns should identify plural nouns.

On the other hand, many teachers still object to such usage because it violates the principle of **pronoun-antecedent agreement**, which states that only a singular pronoun can be used to refer back to a singular antecedent. "One actor" and "the player" are singular nouns, but, in the first version of the sample sentence above, they are the antecedents of the *plural* pronouns "they" and "their." Check with your teachers to find out whether they will accept the plural gender-neutral pronoun with a singular antecedent.

Indefinite pronouns: words such as "each," "anyone," "neither" that identify a person or persons who cannot be named.

With **indefinite pronouns** ("everyone," "everybody," "anyone"), the use of the neutral plural pronoun is becoming especially widespread:

Everyone complains about the taxes *they* have to pay, but no one is willing to cut those social programs that benefit *them*.

Anyone interested in applying for this job should send *their* résumé to the personnel manager.

Strictly speaking, the above sentences contain grammatical errors. The indefinite pronouns "everyone," "no one," and "anyone" are singular while "their," "them," and "they"— which refer to the indefinite pronouns—are plural. But by using the plural pronoun, a writer avoids the grating repetition of two singular pronouns:

Everyone complains about the taxes *he* or *she* has to pay, but no one is willing to cut those social programs that benefit *him* or *her*.

Anyone interested in applying for this job should send *his or her* resumé to the personnel manager.

Again, however, some teachers will not accept any violation of pronoun-antecedent agreement. Some teachers will accept a plural gender-neutral pronoun for informal, narrative essays but not for formal research papers. You should always find out from your teachers what their position on this usage is.

There are some cases where you should definitely avoid the use of the plural gender-neutral pronoun. Consider, for example, this passage:

> Coleridge ends the poem with a description of an inspired poet in the act of creating a poem. The poet is a powerful force, in need of protection. *Their* supporters weave a circle around *them* three times, performing a magic ritual that will protect *their* privacy. They close their eyes in "holy dread." The inspired poet is ready; *they* have "drunk the milk of paradise."

In the above passage, the transition from "poet" to "their" is confusing, because another noun that is plural ("supporters") also appears in the passage. A gender-neutral plural pronoun should be avoided if it creates any ambiguity.

As the above discussion indicates, there is not a "best" way of making certain that sexist language is eliminated from writing. There are, however, four good ways of avoiding sexist language; the way you choose is dependent upon context and meaning.

1. Change a singular noun into a plural noun so that a gender-neutral pronoun can be used:

   A doctor must wash his hands before he examines his patients.

   Doctors must wash *their* hands before they examine their patients.

2. Use a plural gender-neutral pronoun when referring to an indefinite pronoun, even though the indefinite pronoun is singular:

   Everyone should have *their* handwriting analyzed.

3. Use both the masculine and the feminine pronouns, as long as they are not repeated so many times that they ruin the rhythm and flow of writing:

   An influential senator can persuade *his or her* colleagues to vote against the bill.

4. Use only the singular masculine pronoun or the singular feminine pronoun if the chances are very high that the noun is gender specific:

   A synchronized swimmer needs to practise four hours a day if she wants to make it to the Olympics.

   A linebacker makes much less than a quarterback though his risk of injury is just as high.

ASSIGNMENT 13-2

Revise the following sentences to eliminate sexist language:

1. Through his work, a novelist tries to give us some insight into man's existence.

2. The ceremony was held at the tomb of the unknown soldier who sacrificed his life to preserve the freedom of his countrymen.

3. An alternate juror will be assigned to the case. She will have to take a leave of absence from work, and she will have to agree to be sequestered, possibly for as long as three months.

4. A serious marathon runner will train at least five, usually six, days a week. Usually, on those days he trains, he will run twice for at least fifteen kilometres, once in the morning and once in the evening. An obsessive marathoner will train seven days a week, and will run fifteen kilometres three times a day. Such intense training can pay dividends. The runner who trains three times a day, seven days a week, can achieve his personal best within two months. A runner who trains five days a week, twice a day, will take four months to reach his top fitness level. Without a rest day, however, a runner increases twofold his risk of an injury serious enough to cause him to miss the race he is training for.

SUMMARY

- For masculine nouns, find substitutes that can include women in the group being discussed.
- Avoid nouns that demean or stereotype.
- Do not use masculine pronouns in reference to nouns that are gender neutral.

QUESTIONS FOR STUDY AND DISCUSSION

1. Do you think the phrase "fathers of Confederation" should be changed to "parents of Confederation" in history textbooks? Support your answer.

2. Do you think the spelling of "woman" should be changed to "womyn"? Support your answer.

3. Are there any nouns ending in "ess" or "ettes" that are still acceptable in written work?

4. What, in your opinion, is the best way of avoiding masculine pronouns that refer to gender-neutral nouns?

5. Under what circumstances might the use of sexist language be acceptable?

SUPPLEMENTARY EXERCISES

Revise the following sentences to eliminate sexist, demeaning, or stereotypical language, or language that takes inclusivity to unnecessary extremes.

1. My aunt is an old maid, but she still enjoys an active social life.

   _____

   _____

2. The aptly named "Foxy Lady" is a favourite after-work hangout for businessmen.

   _____

   _____

3. Any linebacker playing in a professional league is going to get his or her share of bumps and bruises.

   _____

   _____

4. A school principal should be a good family man.

   _____

   _____

5. When the Cold War ended, there was some cause for optimism about the future of mankind.

   _____

   _____

6. Many young women believe a job as a stewardess would be glamorous.

   _____

   _____

7. Everyone has his own reasons for voting the way they do.

   _____

   _____

8. An ophthalmologist needs a supportive, understanding wife.

   _____

   _____

9. No women have ever applied to be chairman of the department.

   _____

   _____

10. She advised me to take the job and I never underestimate female intuition.

    _____

    _____

11. Their "study" concluded that the University of Saskatchewan has the most beautiful coeds on any campus across the country.

    _____

    _____

12. Sylvan Lake is manmade, the result of the damming of the Nishat River.

_____

_____

13. Every kindergarten teacher the school has hired has complained about her workload and left within two years.

_____

_____

14. Anyone found guilty of murder forfeits his civil rights.

_____

_____

15. The team owner would only say he is committed to finding the best man for the job.

_____

_____

16. The runner who crosses the finish line first will have his picture taken with the mayor.

_____

_____

17. They needed a dozen volunteers to man the information booth.

_____

_____

18. Every delegate at the UN Conference on Women wanted a chance to express her views.

_____

_____

19. The competition is open to any sculptor or sculptress who thinks they can have a piece submitted on time.

_____

_____

20. During secretaries' week, we have promised to take all the girls who work in the office out for lunch.

_____

_____

21. The senator arrived but we were sorry he didn't bring the missis.

_____

_____

22. The thief will be caught because he cut himself breaking the glass and left his blood all over the windowsill.

_____

_____

23. Anyone who teaches for twenty years in the same town will run into his students wherever he goes.

_____

_____

24. In spite of the vote, the average man on the street continues to support capital punishment.

_____

_____

25. One of the jobs of the first baseperson is to field ground balls from left-handed batters.

_____

_____

HELPFUL HINTS

On exams and in-class assignments, pay especially close attention to the spelling of frequently used words. Teachers will usually be somewhat forgiving if infrequently used words are misspelled.

Spelling

Cast a Spell on Your Writing

Reading for Spelling	Learning Some Rules
Using a Dictionary	Using Your Spell Check

Spelling errors are a serious obstacle to clear and forceful writing. Students lose marks from essays that contain errors in spelling and often ask why. The answer is that the symbols (letters and words) used to convey ideas in the written form are often as important as the ideas themselves. If the reader does not "get" what the symbols mean, then your message is blurred.

Prose that is correctly spelled is easier to read and clearer than prose that is not. For example, consider this version of the first sentence of this lesson:

Spelling *errers* are a serious *obstical* to clear and forceful writing

Written this way, the sentence is more difficult to read because you are not used to seeing "errors" and "obstacle" spelled incorrectly. The misspellings make you pause and stumble a bit as you read. Context clues and clues provided by your knowledge of letter-sound relationships make it possible to decode the sentence, but you have to work harder at it than you would if there were no spelling errors. Fluency in reading sometimes depends upon small gains in clarity in writing.

The second problem is that spelling errors prejudice your reader against your work. Your writing might be interesting and informative, but if it contains spelling errors, those errors will weaken your message. Errors diminish your reader's faith in you as someone with something valid to say. The employer who reads a letter of application containing spelling errors is less likely to interview that applicant than the applicant who sends in a letter of application perfectly spelled.

How do you make certain the words you write are correctly spelled? When you were in elementary school you were taught to "sound out" words you couldn't spell. Sometimes this is a good enough strategy; usually, it is not. Consider, for example, this sentence:

Children ar tot to "sownd owt" wurds they cant spel.

As this sentence illustrates, the letter-sound relationship in the English language is far from perfect. As a strategy to improve spelling, sounding out is overrated.

Consider this list of words:

steak	head
steal	area

Each word contains the paired vowel "ea," yet each word is pronounced differently. Similarly, the words "sugar," "shack," "ocean," "suspicion," and "mansion" all contain the same sound, the "sh" sound. But only one word, "shack," is a **phonetically spelled word**.

You can't, then, rely only on "sounding out" to avoid errors in spelling. You need some other strategies, that are discussed in this lesson.

Phonetically spelled word: word spelled by "sounding out" the letters.

READING FOR SPELLING

HELPFUL HINTS

Record in your journal those words you are not sure how to spell. Try to work those words into your journal entries over the course of a week.

How do you know that the following phonetically spelled sentence is full of spelling errors?

Children ar tot to "sownd owt" wurds they cant spel.

You know because you never see "taught" spelled as "tot" or "words" spelled "wurds." You see words in print spelled correctly often enough that gradually you learn how to spell.

Avid readers are, for the most part, good spellers. One way in which you can improve your spelling is by reading a lot, taking note as you read of the correct spelling of words you know you have had trouble spelling in the past.

ASSIGNMENT 14-1

For the next two days, keep a list of words you read that you have trouble spelling. Bring your list to class and be prepared to share it with your classmates.

USING A DICTIONARY

Unabridged dictionary: one that contains all words in a particular language.

Abridged dictionary: one that does not include obsolete, archaic, or rarely used words.

You can also improve your spelling and avoid spelling errors by buying and using a good dictionary. A dictionary will provide you with the meaning of a word, the pronunciation of a word, possibly its etymology and, of course, its correct spelling. **Unabridged dictionaries** are excellent but, because of their length, not practical for college students. The **abridged dictionaries** available in your college or university bookstore contain almost all the words students use and are good, practical dictionaries.

Mnemonic device: method used to remember something.

When you look up a word, try to master its spelling. Write it down and make up some sentences that contain it. You can also try making up **mnemonic devices** (tricks to help you memorize something) so you will remember how the word is spelled:

Exis*ten*ce is *ten* years.

M and M's acco*mm*odate me.

The initial effort it takes to master the correct spelling can prevent the frustration you will feel if you must look the word up half a dozen times before you can spell it correctly.

ASSIGNMENT 14-2

Find, in a good dictionary, the derivation of the words that you listed in Assignment 14-1. Compose sentences in which you use each of the words from your list.

LEARNING SOME RULES

English spelling, as some of the examples used earlier in the lesson illustrate, appears to be quite arbitrary. There are not many rules to guide you toward perfect spelling and those rules that do exist always come with exceptions.

You learned in elementary school to place "i before e except after c":

ach*ie*ve   dec*ei*ve
exper*ie*nce   perc*ei*ve

This rule is generally useful, but is frequently violated: *ei*ther, l*ei*sure, for*ei*gn, *ei*ghth, h*ei*ght.

Similarly, this rule can be helpful: Drop a silent "e" before a suffix beginning with a vowel:

inquire + ing = inquiring
(The "e" in "inquire" is not pronounced and the suffix "ing" begins with a vowel, so the silent "e" is dropped.)

Retain the "e" before a suffix beginning with a consonant:

force + ful = forceful
(The suffix "ful" begins with a consonant, so the unpronounced "e" in "force" is retained.)

But this rule is also violated by such words as notic*e*able, courag*e*ous, and sho*e*ing.

ASSIGNMENT 14-3 Three spelling rules, and exceptions to these rules, are discussed in this lesson. Find another rule of English spelling and note the exceptions to this rule.

USING YOUR SPELL CHECK

Spell check: Feature on most word-processing programs that allows writer to check the spelling of words used.

Most word processing programs have a **spell-check** feature. When you are revising your essay, you simply activate the spell check and the program will tell you what words have been misspelled or mistyped. The computer spell check is a useful aid to clear writing.

It is not, however, infallible. If you use "there" instead of "their" or "affect" instead of "effect," your spell check will not catch the error. Recently, this anonymous poem started to appear in word-processing labs:

> I have a spelling chequer
> It came with my PC
> It marks quite plane for my revue
> Miss steaks I cannot sea.
> I've run this poem threw it,
> I'm sure your pleased too no,
> It's letter perfect in its weigh,
> My chequer tolled me sew.

Homonyms: words like "bear" and "bare" that sound the same but have different meanings.

Be aware of any English **homonyms** (words that sound the same but are spelled differently) that might cause you to make a spelling error. Your spell check will accept "plain" or "plane," "review" or "revue," "steaks" or "stakes," "sea" or "see," "threw" or "through," "no" or "know," "way" or "weigh."

SUMMARY

- Do not rely on sounding words out to discover their correct spelling.
- As you read, note words that you might have trouble spelling.
- It is often easier to spell certain words when you know their derivation. Find the derivation of words in a good dictionary.
- Learn the basic spelling rules and the main exceptions to these rules.
- Choose word-processing programs that contain good spell checks and learn how to use them.

QUESTIONS FOR STUDY AND DISCUSSION

1. Words spelled incorrectly can almost always be decoded. (Wurds speled incorrectly can almost always be decoded). Why is it relatively easy to un-

derstand misspelled words? Since it is quite easy to understand misspelled words, why is spelling important?

2. Why are there so many exceptions to spelling rules?

3. Do you think good spelling is a sign of overall intelligence? Explain your answer.

4. What is the title of your dictionary? When was the last time you used it?

5. Do you use word-processing software that contains a spell check? How useful do you find spell-check programs?

SUPPLEMENTARY EXERCISES

Study the following sentences carefully and correct any spelling errors you find. A sentence might contain more than one misspelled word. A few sentences do not contain any spelling errors.

1. Her absense had a detrimental affect on my outlook on life.

   _____

   _____

2. When we analyse poetry in my English class, I'm always surprised by students' comments.

   _____

   _____

3. He apologized for the inconveniance, but I was still unhappy about the delay.

   _____

   _____

4. According to the college calender, there are still ninty days of classes left.

   _____

   _____

5. Eighteen parking spaces have been alotted to staff, which is more than necesary.

   _____

   _____

6. Voting, I argued, is not a privlege but a right.

   _____

   _____

7. The professers on this campus have so many idiosycrisies, it's a wonder we pay attention to them.

_____

_____

8. We will cover the rules of grammer in this course.

_____

_____

9. In Hong Kong, you can buy good jewellery for half the price you would pay here.

_____

_____

10. Morgage rates will have to decline another point before we can afford to by a house.

_____

_____

11. Parents always seem to embarrass their teenage children.

_____

_____

12. After my ballet class, my muscels are sore.

_____

_____

13. In February, they celebrate their nineth wedding aniversery.

_____

_____

14. In Flin Flon, there is a serious shortage of physiscians.

_____

_____

15. It was a difficult manouevre, but its success would ensure victory.

_____

_____

16. Hamlet promises his father he will seek vengence.

_____

_____

17. Elderly people are suseptible to colds and the flu.

_____

_____

18. The RCMP supercedes the local police in dealing with interprovincial crime.

    _____

    _____

19. She wrote me an outstanding letter of recomendation, but I still did not get an intervue.

    _____

    _____

20. My niece is eligible for unemployment insurance, but she is reluctant to apply for it.

    _____

    _____

21. Sillitoe's *The Lonliness of the Long-Distance Runner* is not on our reading list.

    _____

    _____

22. He has a tendancy to exagerate, so he does not have allot of close friends.

    _____

    _____

23. Iago decieves Othello right from the start of the play.

    _____

    _____

24. Every conceivable treatment was tried, but nothing seemed to work.

    _____

    _____

25. She is a buisness major, so they are suited to each other.

    _____

    _____

26. They very cooly entered the bank and produced their weapons.

    _____

    _____

27. The sweater was made of course cloth, and it was too itchy to wear.

    _____

    _____

28. Warring factions in the former Yugoslavia seem to be trying to annilate one another.

    _____

    _____

29. I was on the horns of a dilemma because she is such a good friend, but I did not want to live in that dormitory.

    _____

    _____

30. Consistancy is one mark of a good athelete.

    _____

    _____

Lesson Fifteen

Punctuating

Punctuation Rules

Rule 1: No Comma Between Two Complete Sentences
Rule 2: Semicolon Between Conjunctive Adverbs
Rule 3: No Commas for Restrictive Elements
Rule 4: No Commas Between Cumulative Adjectives
Rule 5: Semicolons for Phrases or Clauses in a Series
Rule 6: A Colon for an Explanation or Series
Rule 7: A Dash for a Break in Thought
Rule 8: Quotation Marks for Quotations or Emphasis
Rule 9: Apostrophes for Possession

Proper placement of punctuation marks is easier if you read your essay out loud as you punctuate.

Proper punctuation, like proper grammar and spelling, is essential to sentence clarity. Indeed, punctuation marks were designed to improve clarity in written composition. Read aloud this sentence in which punctuation marks have been eliminated:

> By the time we reach college our vocabularies have expanded and we know which words are exceptions to the rules of elementary school spelling counterfeit foreign heir are among the many exceptions to the i before e rule ninth and truly are among the exceptions to the retain the silent e rule mileage is an exception to the drop the silent e rule

Here is the same sentence, correctly punctuated:

> By the time we reach college, our vocabularies have expanded, and we know which words are exceptions to the rules of elementary school spelling: "counterfeit," "foreign," and "heir" are among the many exceptions to the "i before e" rule; "ninth" and "truly" are among the exceptions to the "retain the silent e" rule; "mileage" is an exception to the "drop the silent e" rule.

This version is clear not because any words have been changed or their order rearranged but simply because punctuation marks have been added.

There are few absolute rules that govern the use of punctuation marks.

There are thirteen punctuation marks and close to thirty rules that govern their use. You know already that you have to put a period, a question mark, or an exclamation point at the end of a sentence and that you have to use a comma to separate words or phrases in a series, as is done earlier in this very sentence:

...a period, a question mark, or an exclamation point...

In addition, you know you must use a comma after an introductory element such as the phrase "in addition," which begins the sentence you are now reading. And you know, as well, that commas are used at each end of a parenthetical expression; for example, the phrases "as well" and "for example," used earlier in the sentence you are now reading.

This lesson does not cover those rules of punctuation—the use of the period, for example—that college students already know well. It focuses, instead, on those rules of punctuation that students might not know quite as well. There are nine of them.

RULE 1: NO COMMA BETWEEN TWO COMPLETE SENTENCES

Comma-splice or run-on sentence: sentence error resulting from two sentences separated only by a comma.

A comma is not a strong enough pause to separate two complete sentences. The following sentence contains an error, usually referred to as a **comma-splice** or **run-on sentence**:

The topic sentence should contain the main ideas of the paragraph, the other sentences should develop the main idea.

This "sentence" is punctuated incorrectly because it places only a comma between two sentences. There are four ways of correcting a run-on sentence.

Coordinate conjunction: short word ("and," "but," "or") that joins two sentences together when preceded by a comma.

1. Add a **coordinate conjunction** (and, but, or) before the comma:

   The topic sentence should contain the main ideas of the paragraph, *and* the other sentences should develop the main idea.

2. Separate the two sentences with a period.

   The topic sentence should contain the main ideas of the paragraph. The other sentences should develop the main idea.

3. Separate the two sentences with a semicolon.

   The topic sentence should contain the main ideas of the paragraph; the other sentences should develop the main idea.

Subordinate conjunction: a conjunction such as "when," "if," "while," "because," etc., that makes a clause subordinate to or dependent on the main clause of the sentence.

4. Add a **subordinate conjunction** (when, if, while, because, etc.) to one of the sentences. This will reduce one of the sentences to a dependent or subordinate clause. A comma is not a strong enough pause to separate two sentences, but it can be used between a sentence and a dependent clause.

The topic sentence should contain the main ideas of the paragraphs, while the other sentences should develop the main idea.

or

While the topic sentence should contain the main ideas of the paragraph, the other sentences should develop the main idea.

There is one other way of correcting a run-on sentence, but it applies only to those run-on sentences whose verbs can be matched with the subject of *both* sentences. Consider this run-on sentence:

A concluding paragraph should summarize the content of an essay, it should also reiterate the essay's central idea.

The two verbs, "summarize" and "reiterate," can go with or agree with the subject of the first sentence, "paragraph." For this reason, the run-on sentence above can be corrected simply by removing the second subject, "it." Now the sentence would read as follows:

A concluding paragraph should summarize the content of an essay and reiterate the essay's central idea.

Note that with the elimination of the second subject, "it," the comma is also eliminated.

ASSIGNMENT 15-1

Correct the following run-on sentences according to the instructions given.

1. Use a coordinate conjunction.

a. We planned to serve key lime pie, my brother is allergic to citrus fruit.

b. Tyson will be fighting an inexperienced opponent, experts are predicting an early knockout.

2. Eliminate the second subject.

a. Your essay should be double-spaced, it should have one-and-a-half-inch margins on both sides of the page.

b. He knew he had a strong case, he decided not to press charges.

3. Change one of the sentences to a dependent (or subordinate) clause.

a. We couldn't serve key lime pie, my brother is allergic to citrus fruit.

b. My uncle played basketball in college, he taught me how to dribble behind my back.

4. Use a semicolon.

a. Your essay should be double-spaced, it should also have one-and-a-half-inch margins on both sides of the page.

b. She decided to retire early, she could not handle the stress any longer.

RULE 2: SEMICOLON BEFORE CONJUNCTIVE ADVERBS

Conjunctive adverb: connecting word such as "however" or "therefore" that, when preceded by a semicolon, joins two sentences together.

Like a coordinate conjunction, a **conjunctive adverb** links together two sentences. More precisely, a conjunctive adverb is an adverb that links and defines the relationship between two sentences. Common conjunctive adverbs include these words: "however," "therefore," "nevertheless," "consequently," "otherwise," and "indeed."

There is, however, a crucial difference between a coordinate conjunction and a conjunctive adverb: a coordinate conjunction linking two sentences together must be preceded by a comma; a conjunctive adverb linking two sentences together must be preceded by a semicolon or a period. Study closely the way the following sentences are punctuated:

1. Both a coordinate conjunction and a conjunctive adverb link sentences together, a conjunctive adverb is preceded by a semicolon. (incorrect)

2. I would love to take up skiing, but the equipment is too expensive. (correct)

3. Many students need student loans to attend school full-time, however not all students qualify. (incorrect)

4. Jake's application for a student loan was turned down; therefore he has to find a part-time job. (correct)

5. The schools in the minister's riding now have access to the Internet. Inner-city schools, however, are still waiting to get basic computer equipment. (correct)

Sentence 1 is a run-on; the comma after the word "together" is not strong enough to link the two sentences together.

Sentence 2 is correct; the comma after the word "skiing" plus the coordinate conjunction, "but," are sufficient to link the two sentences together.

Sentence 3 contains an error in punctuation frequently made by college students, who reason that if a comma plus "but" can link together two sentences, a comma plus "however" should be able to do the same. "But" and "however" are synonymous words; they are not, however, the same parts of speech. A conjunctive adverb can not be preceded by a comma in order to link two sentences together. It has to be preceded by a semicolon. (A period, followed by "However" with a capital "H," would also be correct). As written above, sentence 3 is a run-on sentence.

Sentence 4, with the semicolon before the conjunctive adverb, "therefore" is correct.

What about sentence 5, in which "however" is also preceded by a comma? Is this sentence also a run-on? No, it isn't. Sentence 5 is correct as written because, in this sentence, "however" is not linking two sentences together. It is used within a sentence, not at the start of a sentence. For this reason, it is preceded (and followed) not by a semicolon (or a period) but by a comma.

HELPFUL HINTS

Do not overuse the semicolon, especially in place of commas.

ASSIGNMENT 15-2 In your own words, explain in one paragraph why the following sentence contains an error in punctuation. Include in your paragraph two versions of the same sentence correctly punctuated.

> Ellis did not hand in two of his assignments, therefore, he did not get a passing grade in his sociology course.

RULE 3: NO COMMAS FOR RESTRICTIVE ELEMENTS

Compare these two sentences:

> Sheehy's *Guide to Reference Books*, which should be at the reference desk of your library, will list sources that will be useful to you.

> All of the books that I need to research my essay have been signed out of the library.

Non-restrictive clause: word group *not* essential to the meaning of a sentence and so separated from the sentence by commas.

In the first sentence, the clause "which should be at the reference desk of your library" is not essential to the meaning of the sentence. Eliminate this clause and the sentence still makes sense. The clause does not restrict the meaning of the sentence and is, for this reason, called a **non-restrictive clause**. For this reason, as well, this clause should be separated from the rest of the sentence with commas.

In the second sentence, the clause "that I need to research my essay" is essential to the meaning. Eliminate this clause, and the sentence no longer makes sense:

> All of the books have been signed out of the library.

Restrictive clause: word group essential to the meaning of a sentence and so *not* separated from the sentence by commas.

This clause restricts the meaning of the sentence and is, for this reason, called a **restrictive clause**. For this reason, as well, this clause must not be separated from the rest of the sentence by commas.

Replacing Commas with Parentheses or Dashes

Parentheses or dashes can be used, in place of commas, to either side of non-restrictive elements. Each of the following sentences is correctly punctuated:

> I didn't major in English, even though it was my favourite subject in high school, because I wanted to make a lot of money after I finished college.

> I didn't major in English (even though it was my favourite subject in high school) because I wanted to make a lot of money after I finished college.

> I didn't major in English—even though it was my favourite subject in high school—because I wanted to make a lot of money after I finished college.

The difference among the three sentences above is in the emphasis each one places on the non-restrictive clause, "even though it was my favourite subject in high school." Parentheses (sentence 2) de-emphasize the information contained in the non-restrictive clause, that is, the information contained between the parentheses. Dashes—sentence 3—highlight the information between them. The commas in the first sentence neither downplay nor highlight the information between them: the clause "even though it was my favourite subject in high school" is considered no less important, no more important, than the other information in the sentence. For this reason commas are usually, but by no means exclusively, used to separate non-restrictive elements from the rest of a sentence.

Optional Commas

In some sentences, the use of a comma is optional. In a series, especially a series of single words, the comma before "and" can be eliminated. Similarly, if a phrase at the beginning of a sentence is brief and if you want the pace of your sentence to move quickly, you may eliminate the comma after the introductory element. In the following four sentences, the optional commas are circled:

> When we write, we sometimes discover new values, attitudes⊙and ideas.
> El Sorento serves Greek, Italian, French⊙and Mexican food.
> At sunrise⊙the condemned man is escorted to a small padded cell at the end of the hall.
> In some sentences⊙the use of a comma is optional,

Note, however, that if the dependent clause is at the beginning of the sentence, a comma must follow the dependent clause:

> While we are writing, we sometimes discover new ideas.

ASSIGNMENT 15-3

Add necessary punctuation marks to the following sentences:

1. In 1992 Windsor Castle the Queen's house on the banks of the Thames was damaged by a serious fire.

2. Tia Maria Drambuie Benedictine and Curacao are among the most popular liqueurs and are sold throughout the world.

3. The silver that is mined in Mexico is considered superior to the silver mined in Colorado.

4. The tern is a slender gull-like bird and with its long pointed wings and a deeply notched tail it flies with grace and strength.

5. The upper limit of the biosphere the part of earth where life can exist is about 9000 metres above sea level the lower limit is approximately 3000 metres beneath the surface of the ocean.

RULE 4: NO COMMAS BETWEEN CUMULATIVE ADJECTIVES

Study carefully the following two sentences:

> She has never before included black leather skirts in a spring collection.

> Models in bright, colourful skirts paraded down the runway.

Coordinate adjectives: two words together modifying a noun and separated from each other by commas.

Cumulative adjectives: two words together, the first of which modifies the second, which modifies a noun; they are not separated from each other by commas.

Both sentences contain two adjectives modifying the noun "skirts." In the first sentence the two adjectives are cumulative, so commas do not come between them. "Black" would modify "leather" if the word "skirts" were eliminated from the sentence. In the second sentence, both adjectives directly modify "skirts," which could not be deleted from the sentence. Commas come between **coordinate adjectives**, but not **cumulative adjectives**.

An often-used test to determine if adjectives are coordinate or cumulative is to see if the word "and" can be placed between the adjectives. If it can, the adjectives are coordinate and so need commas: "a bright and colourful skirt." If "and" does not sound quite right placed between the adjectives—"a black and leather skirt"—the adjectives are cumulative and are not separated from each other by a comma.

ASSIGNMENT 15-4

Make up a sentence that contains coordinate adjectives and a sentence that contains cumulative adjectives. Punctuate each sentence correctly. Compare your sentence with the sentences your classmates have written.

RULE 5: SEMICOLONS FOR PHRASES OR CLAUSES IN A SERIES

Words in a series are separated by commas:

> All you need to know about words, phrases, clauses, and sentences is found in that book.

Phrases in a series are also separated by commas:

> Little Red Riding Hood ran through the forest, over the bridge, across the meadow, and between the bushes to get to her grandmother's house.

Phrases or clauses that are in a series and that also contain commas are separated by semicolons:

> You want your essay to be well-organized; you want your sentences within your paragraphs and your paragraphs within the essay to be logically connected, in other words to cohere; you want your diction to be accurate and

appropriate; you want your prose to be concise; and you want to avoid errors in grammar, spelling, and punctuation.

ASSIGNMENT 15-5

Make up and correctly punctuate a sentence that contains phrases or clauses in a series. At least one of the phrases or clauses must contain a comma. Be prepared to share your sentence with your classmates.

RULE 6: A COLON FOR AN EXPLANATION OR SERIES

A colon is used before an explanation promised earlier in the sentence. In the following sentence, the "experience" alluded to before the colon is explained after the colon:

> You might have had this experience in the past: you are watching a play and you feel you know one of the characters.

A colon is also used before a series. Here is an example:

> As you watch the play, you feel many emotions: joy, sorrow, despair, and elation.

But a colon is *not* used before a series if the sentence is structured in such a way that there is not the sense of a "break" between the series and the way the series is introduced. Compare this sentence with the nearly identical sentence above, but note that this sentence does not need a colon:

> As you watch the play you feel such emotions as joy, sorrow, despair, and elation.

ASSIGNMENT 15-6

Write two versions of the same sentence: one in which a colon would be required and one in which a colon would not be required. Bring your sentences to class to share with your classmates.

RULE 7: A DASH FOR A BREAK IN THOUGHT

A dash is used to indicate a change in thought or a break in thought. Here is an example:

> You can pay for a database search and access obscure journals through interlibrary loan—but this might prove to be a waste of time and money.

A dash and a colon are sometimes interchangeable. In the following two sentences, either a dash or a colon could be used:

> Organization, cohesion, diction, and concision: all of these elements are necessary for writing to be clear.

> Reading writing that is wordy and repetitious is like looking out of a dirty window: it's hard to see what you're looking at.

ASSIGNMENT 15-7 Write a sentence that uses a dash correctly, and a sentence that could be punctuated using either a colon or a dash.

RULE 8: QUOTATION MARKS FOR QUOTATIONS OR EMPHASIS

When writing essays about literature, students often place quotation marks around book titles. This is incorrect. Book titles are underlined or placed in italics. Minor titles—those of poems, short stories, songs—are placed in quotation marks.

> Mullen's blank-verse narrative poem, "My Rain Barrel," from her 1994 collection, *Satan's Rainbow*, illustrates the same striking use of metaphor.

Quotation marks are also used to indicate that someone's exact words, written or spoken, are being quoted:

> "I write slowly," Mullen told one interviewer. "Even my short poems like 'Apple Trees' can take weeks to complete."

> In her Preface to *Satan's Rainbow*, Mullen responds to criticism that her work is impenetrable, arguing that complexity "should not obstruct readers but allow them some freedom in interpretation" (xix).

In the second sentence above, quotation marks appear at the beginning and end of quoted written words. Long quotations are set off from the text and would *not* contain quotation marks, unless the source being quoted also contained them.

In the first sentence above, spoken words are quoted. Note that the poem's title, which would normally be in regular quotation marks, is here in single quotation marks to distinguish it from the direct quotation. Quotations within quotations are also in single quotation marks. For example:

> "I revise constantly," Mullen told one interviewer. "I believe in Olson's advice: 'The time to begin writing is when you think you have finished your final draft.'"

Quotation marks, finally, are used to indicate something different or special about the word or phrase. Also, words as words are indicated with quotation marks. Irony and sarcasm, for example, are often indicated with quotation marks:

I would never accuse her of plagiarism but perhaps she was "unduly influenced" by the content and style of the reviewer in *The New Yorker*.

How many "ands" are in this sentence?

ASSIGNMENT 15-8

1. Use quotation marks correctly in the following sentence:

   Analyzing Keats's sonnet Bright Star, Foster writes: the repetition of the adverb, still, is typical of Keats's style.

2. In one paragraph, explain why you used quotation marks as you did in the sentence above.

RULE 9: APOSTROPHES FOR POSSESSION

Apostrophes are used in nouns to indicate ownership. Study carefully the following sentences:

1. The professor claimed he had misplaced his student's essay.

2. The professor claimed he had misplaced his students' essays.

3. For that assignment, the men's essays were not as well written as the women's.

In the first sentence, the apostrophe comes before the "s" because the noun "student" is singular. In the second sentence, the apostrophe comes after the "s" because the noun "students" is plural. The rule, then, is put an apostrophe before the "s" to indicate singular possession, after the "s" to indicate plural possession.

What about the third sentence? Men and women are plural: why does the apostrophe come before the "s"? It comes before the "s" because "men" and "women" are nouns that form their plural not by adding an "s" but by changing a vowel: Man becomes men; woman, women. The apostrophe always comes before the "s" in nouns that form their plural by changing a vowel: children's toys, not childrens' toys.

"It's" and "Its"

Apostrophes are not used in pronouns that are already in the possessive case: his, hers, theirs, yours, its. The misuse of the apostrophe in "its" is a very common error. Most college English teachers could retire if they had a dollar for every time they have circled, in a student's essay, the possessive pronoun "its" written with an apostrophe. Notice the use of and the absence of the apostrophes in these sentences:

It's missing one of *its* pages.

It's unlikely that both of *its* headlights would burn out at the same time.

As these sentences indicate, the only time you use an apostrophe in the word "it's" is if the word is a contraction for "it is." If "its" indicates possession, there is never an apostrophe before the "s." Nor is there ever, under any circumstances, an apostrophe after the "s" in the word "its."

ASSIGNMENT 15-9

Insert the necessary punctuation marks in the following sentences.

1. A portion of the play the third scene of the final act to be precise was excluded to meet the two-hour time limit.

2. The anteaters tongue is covered with sticky saliva which allows it to trap ants termites and other insects on which it feeds.

3. Daves new interest is cybernetics the science that among other things compares brain functions to the functions of machines especially computers.

4. France lost Alsace and Lorraine to Germany in 1871 after a war in which the Germans who were better prepared than the French won nearly every battle.

5. The greyhound wolfhound and deerhound hunt by sight the bloodhound foxhound and beagle hunt by scent.

6. Diabetics lack insulin which controls the supply of sugar from the blood to the muscles however with proper insulin injections diabetics can live a normal life.

7. Film adaptations of novels are usually disappointing but the film version of Kinsellas Field of Dreams is better than the book.

8. Since the beginning of the century the Nobel Prize has been awarded to men and women for outstanding contributions to the following fields physics chemistry medicine literature peace and economics.

9. As T.S. Eliot says in Little Gidding one of the poems in his Four Quartets What we call the beginning is often the end And to make an end is to make a beginning.

10. Originally the word tycoon from the Japanese taikun referred to the commander-in-chief of the Japanese army but now its used often in a derogatory sense to describe a powerful influential businessperson.

HELPFUL HINTS

Punctuation marks should always clarify, never obscure writing.

SUMMARY

- Proper punctuation is essential for sentence clarity.
- A run-on sentence is an error because it consists of two sentences separated only by a comma.
- Conjunctive adverbs such as however, therefore, and nevertheless are preceded by a semicolon when they link sentences together.
- Commas are put on either side of non-restrictive words, phrases, and clauses.
- In some sentences the use of a comma is optional.
- Commas are placed between coordinate, but not between cumulative, adjectives.
- A series of phrases or clauses that contain commas are separated from each other by semicolons.
- A colon precedes an explanation or a series.
- A dash indicates a break in thought.
- Quotation marks are used to indicate minor titles, direct speech or a direct quotation, special emphasis, and words used as words.
- An apostrophe indicates ownership.

QUESTIONS FOR STUDY AND DISCUSSION

1. Why must writers know the rules of punctuation?
2. How can you recognize and correct a run-on sentence?
3. Explain this rule in your own words: Semicolons can only be used between parts of a sentence of equal grammatical rank.
4. What is the difference between a restrictive and a non-restrictive clause?
5. When would you put parentheses instead of commas around a non-restrictive clause?
6. When would you put dashes instead of commas around a non-restrictive clause?
7. The comma is the most arbitrary punctuation mark. Discuss.
8. Explain the difference between coordinate and cumulative adjectives.
9. Explain the difference in function between a dash and a colon.
10. When would you use single quotation marks?
11. Explain the difference between "its" and "it's."
12. When would an apostrophe precede the "s" in a plural noun?

SUPPLEMENTARY EXERCISES

Rewrite the sentences with the proper punctuation marks. Change incorrect punctuation marks and delete any unnecessary punctuation marks. Some sentences are correctly punctuated and do not need to be changed. Do *not* change any sentence into two separate sentences by using a period.

1. I quit smoking fifteen years ago now I can't be near anyone who smokes.

2. In Brandon there are many interesting shops; and the shopkeepers welcome you even if you just want to browse.

3. The plane will make a ninety-minute stop in Moncton where you are free to disembark for thirty minutes, a twenty-minute stop in Toronto where you must not disembark, and another ninety-minute stop in Calgary where again you may disembark for twenty minutes.

4. According to the *Daily Express* this season the Regina Theatre Company will produce the following plays; *The Importance of Being Earnest* by Oscar Wilde *Trifles* by Susan Glaspell and *The Ecstasy of Rita Joe* by George Ryga.

5. Plato thought the world we see was a mere reflection a 'spume' to use Yeats's word—of the real world.

6. Tornadoes can reach speeds up to 60 km/h the circling winds within the vortex of the tornado can reach speeds of 600 km/h.

     _____

     _____

     _____

7. Steroids enhance athletic performance but to quote Professor W.A. Benson the short-term gain in strength is not worth the long-term health risks to which a steroid user exposes himself.

     _____

     _____

     _____

     _____

     _____

8. We think recycling is a progressive, new idea, but many reusable goods were recycled fifty years ago, during the war.

     _____

     _____

     _____

9. A Quisling named after Vidkun Quisling whom the Germans brought to power after they conquered Norway in 1940 is a term used to denote a fifth-columnist a traitor or a collaborator.

     _____

     _____

     _____

     _____

     _____

10. Flowers used in the making of perfume include: the rose jasmine acacia and violet: aromatic herbs that can also be used include: rosemary thyme and lavender fruit peel especially from the citrus fruit can also be used.

     _____

     _____

     _____

     _____

     _____

11. My mothers' pearls came from the waters off the coast of Mexico, considered to be one of the finest places for pearl fishing.

     _____

     _____

     _____

12. Despite the protests despite the dangers Canada will need nuclear power plants to meet the energy needs of a growing population.

_____

_____

_____

13. One of the poems Ode on a Grecian Urn in the anthology Literature in English ends with the lines Beauty is Truth Truth Beauty That is all / Ye know on earth and all ye need to know.

_____

_____

_____

_____

_____

14. The reviewer in the Times gave *Priscilla Queen of the Desert* four stars but I found it to be a dull, inane movie.

_____

_____

_____

15. On November 21 1945 at Nuremberg an international military tribunal consisting of four judges representing four different countries America France Britain and the Soviet Union put twenty-four Nazi leaders on trial.

_____

_____

_____

_____

_____

16. The teachers staff room at my childrens school has a brand new microwave oven.

_____

_____

_____

17. The llama is a cousin to the camel but llamas are smaller; they do not have humps, and they have a thicker coat.

_____

_____

_____

18. Any mother who had to make the choice Sophie had to make would sooner sacrifice her own life most fathers would feel the same way.

_____

_____

_____

19. In the middle of the summer a mountain, covered with skiers, is an unusual sight to see.

_____

_____

_____

20. Over 90 000 moths and butterflies characterized by large colourful wings and scaly bodies belong to the Lepidoptera order of insects.

_____

_____

_____

21. "Libretto" the Italian word for booklet is the text of an opera.

_____

_____

_____

22. On January 10 1920 the League of Nations, formed to promote international peace and security held its first meeting in Geneva, Switzerland.

_____

_____

_____

23. Alternative forms of medicine and therapy acupuncture meditation and herbal to name just a few are becoming more popular.

_____

_____

_____

24. Coleridge and Wordsworth lived in the Lake District in the northwest of England where they wrote many of the poems included in their book Lyrical Ballads including Tintern Abbey and Kubla Khan.

_____

_____

_____

_____

_____

25. The largest planet, eleven times the diameter of Earth, Jupiter is composed, like the sun, mainly of helium and hydrogen.

_____

_____

_____

Avoiding Errors in Sentence Structure

Avoid

Sentence Fragments
Run-on Sentences
Awkward Definitions
Awkward Syntax
Lack of Unity

You learned, in Lesson Twelve, how to avoid errors in grammar when you are writing sentences. This lesson focuses on errors in the *structure* of a sentence as a whole unit. There are five errors in sentence structure that you must try to avoid.

Good sentence structure, like good writing generally, is appropriate to the age and education of its readers. The sentence structure of an academic essay is usually quite sophisticated. The sentence structure of a children's book must be simple and natural. One of Canada's most successful writers of children's stories, Susanne Martel, is profiled in the video installment at the end of this lesson.

SENTENCE FRAGMENTS

Sentence fragment: group of words punctuated like a sentence but not forming a complete sentence.

A **sentence fragment** is a group of words that begins with a capital letter and ends with a period but that does not form a complete sentence. Here is an example:

> A typical introduction will have one or two paragraphs. Depending on the nature and length of the assignment.

The phrase "Depending on the nature and length of the assignment" begins with a capital letter and ends with a period but cannot possibly be a sentence. Where is the subject? What is doing the "depending"? Change the phrase to:

> The decision depends on the nature and length of the assignment.

Now you have a complete sentence because you have included a subject, "decision."

You could also, of course, correct the fragment by changing the period to a comma and the capital "D" on "Depending" to a lower-case "d":

A typical introduction will have one or two paragraphs, depending on the nature and length of the assignment.

Similarly, if a group of words is punctuated as a sentence but is missing a verb, the group of words will be a fragment:

The second body paragraph of this essay is developed through definition. The term defined being "oxymoron."

The phrase "The term defined being 'oxymoron'" cannot be a sentence because it does not contain a verb. The word "defined" can be a verb, but in this sentence it is acting as an adjective modifying the noun "term." The word "being" is only part of a verb: We say "you *are* being silly, not "you being silly."

How do we correct a sentence fragment that is missing a verb? Either include a complete verb or attach the fragment to the complete sentence:

The second body paragraph of this essay is developed through definition. The term defined is "oxymoron."

The second body paragraph of this essay is developed through definition, the term defined being "oxymoron."

It is possible to make a sentence fragment error even when the group of words the writer is trying to pass off as a sentence does contain a subject and a verb. For example:

You should not have to define specific terms or provide general background information. Unless you are asked to do so.

The clause "Unless you are asked to do so" does contain a subject and a verb and, for this reason, we call it a clause instead of a phrase. But it is a subordinate or dependent clause, dependent on the complete sentence that precedes it. It should not be separated from that sentence.

You should not have to define specific terms or provide general background information, unless you are asked to do so.

Note that replacing the comma in the above sentence with a semicolon would not be correct. The use of the semicolon to separate a dependent and an independent clause is a common error that college students make.

Here is another example:

A sentence fragment is a group of words that begins with a capital letter and ends with a period. But that does not form a complete sentence.

"But that does not form a complete sentence" is a subordinate or dependent clause—it depends for its existence on the sentence to which it is attached. It cannot exist as a sentence on its own. The sentence should read:

HELPFUL HINTS

While sentence fragments are sometimes acceptable, it is wise to avoid them altogether in college writing.

A sentence fragment is a group of words that begins with a capital letter and ends with a period but that does not form a complete sentence.

A sentence fragment can be used deliberately and correctly if it is used for a particular effect. The first two paragraphs of *Bleak House* by Charles Dickens are full of fragments, but they are used brilliantly to set the scene and the tone of the novel. Here are the first three sentences of the book.

London. Michaelmas Term lately over, and the Lord Chancellor sitting in Lincoln's Inn Hall. Implacable November weather.

Were we to "correct" the fragments, the opening would lose much of its impact:

This story is set in London. Michaelmas Term is lately over, and the Lord Chancellor is sitting in Lincoln's Inn Hall. The city is in the grip of implacable November weather.

The bleak and cheerless ambience so important to the novel's impact is lost when the fragments are "corrected."

It will be obvious to your English teacher if a sentence fragment in your essay is used deliberately, for effect, or if you have made an error in sentence structure.

ASSIGNMENT 16-1

Revise the following sentences to correct sentence fragments.

1. The separatist movement will lose some of its momentum. If the Quebec Nordiques win the Stanley Cup.

2. Red Deer is located in the rich farmland midway between Calgary and Edmonton. A location that enhanced its development as an agricultural service and distribution centre.

3. Many comedians who got their start on SCTV went on to star in American films. Including Rick Moranis, Martin Short, and John Candy.

4. William Beer, a dentist by profession, helped popularize lacrosse. Spearheading a drive in 1867 to have lacrosse accepted as Canada's national game.

5. After the Second World War, the demand for public education increased dramatically. This mainly as a result of the baby boom.

RUN-ON SENTENCES

Another common error in sentence structure is the run-on sentence, which consists of two complete sentences joined together by a comma. Because the run-on sentence is an error in punctuation, it has already been discussed in Lesson

Fifteen. Because it is also an error in sentence structure, one more example is presented here, followed by four ways of correcting the error.

Another common error in sentence structure is the run-on sentence, a run-on sentence consists of two complete sentences joined together by a comma.

1. Use a period.

   Another common error in sentence structure is the run-on sentence. A run-on sentence consists of two complete sentences joined together by a comma.

2. Use a semicolon.

   Another common error in sentence structure is the run-on sentence; a run-on sentence consists of two complete sentences joined together by a comma.

3. Make one sentence a subordinate clause.

   Another common error in sentence structure is the run-on sentence, which consists of two complete sentences joined together by a comma.

4. Reduce one sentence to a phrase.

   Another common error in sentence structure is the run-on sentence, consisting of two complete sentences joined together by a comma.

ASSIGNMENT 16-2

Revise the following sentences to eliminate run-on sentences:

1. Cats have excellent vision, they can see as well at night as they can during the day.

2. Leonard Cohen was an influential song writer, especially during the 1960s, his songs were recorded by artists in several different countries.

3. A contract is an agreement between two people to allow for the exchange of goods and services, one person provides a product or a service, the other person pays for it.

AWKWARD DEFINITIONS

When you write academic essays, you will often have to define a term related to the discipline you are studying. Avoid using the phrases "is where" or "is when" when you are writing a definition sentence. Linking verbs such as "is" are normally followed by nouns or adjectives, not adverbs. Combining adverbs with linking verbs can make the sentence sound awkward. Here are two examples:

A thesis statement is when there is a central or controlling idea in the essay's introduction.

Psychotherapy is where a variety of methods are used to treat mental illness.

The problem in the first sentence is the phrase "is when you have," and in the second sentence, the phrase "is where." These phrases are clumsy and get in the way of the other words in the sentence. Avoid these awkward phrases. Correctly worded, the sentences should read:

A thesis statement is a central or controlling idea in the essay's introduction.

Psychotherapy is the practice of treating mental illness using a variety of methods.

ASSIGNMENT 16-3

Improve the following definitions:

1. A black hole is when a star has so strong a gravitational force that nothing, including light, can escape from it.

2. A stable nuclide is where the nuclear forces in a nucleus are so strong that no particles escape from the nucleus.

AWKWARD SYNTAX

Syntax: the way in which words are ordered in a sentence.

Phantom verb: verb without a subject, creating a confusing sentence.

HELPFUL HINTS

A sentence that contains an error can seem correct when surrounded by correct sentences. If you suspect an error in sentence structure, write that sentence out and examine it apart from the other sentences in its paragraph.

Some sentences have an error in structure that results from awkward **syntax**. Syntax refers to the way in which words are ordered in a sentence. Awkward syntax occurs if unnecessary words are included in a sentence, if necessary words are omitted, or if the words are ordered incorrectly.

Read these two sentences carefully:

Since writing an essay is so time consuming, explains why the class was annoyed that the essays are due early next week.

It is possible to make a lot of money buying and selling a single stock, but reduce the risk of loss by having a varied and balanced portfolio.

In the first sentence, the verb "explains" does not have a subject—who or what is doing the explaining? Edit out the unnecessary verb "explains" and the relative pronoun "why," which is only there because the **phantom verb** (a verb without a subject) is there, and the sentence regains its balance:

Since writing an essay is so time consuming, the class was surprised that the due date is early next week.

In the second sentence, the verb "reduce" does not have a subject. Give it one and the sentence is clear:

It is possible to make a lot of money buying and selling a single stock, but an investor will reduce the risk of loss by having a varied and balanced portfolio.

ASSIGNMENT 16-4

Clarify the relationship between the subjects and the verbs in the following sentences:

1. Hundreds of tourists from all over the world enjoying the innovative architecture, the excellent art gallery, and the variety of shops accounts for the crowds in the streets of Vancouver.

2. Astronomers can study the outer layers of the sun and its corona when the light from the sun is obscured by the moon during an eclipse and are eager to travel across the world to do so.

3. An example of unfair labour practice is an employer, when he refuses to pay minimum wage.

Awkward syntax also results if a sentence does not contain enough words to communicate clearly on first reading. Here are two examples:

This essay could be structured on a comparison/contrast but there aren't enough differences.

Dixieland jazz originated in New Orleans in the early 1900s, and became popular later on from famous people like F. Scott Fitzgerald, whose glamorous friends and characters danced to it.

It is possible, with some effort, to puzzle out what these writers are trying to say, but their sentences are weak because they do not contain enough information or enough clear links between ideas. These writers need to make life a little easier for their readers by filling in some blanks:

The structure for this essay could be compare/ contrast, but there aren't enough differences between the two items being compared and contrasted.

Dixieland jazz originated in New Orleans in the early 1900s and was popular throughout America by the 1920s, partly because F. Scott Fitzgerald, his glamorous circle of friends, and the characters in his stories all listened and danced to Dixieland music.

ASSIGNMENT 16-5

Revise the following sentences to improve their clarity:

1. Newgate Prison was destroyed in the Great Fire of 1666 and was not rebuilt until 1778, then destroyed by fire again during the Gordon Riots of 1780.

2. People suffering from hypothermia become lethargic and eventually unconscious, needing blankets and warm, non-alcoholic liquids.

3. Creon thought Polynices was a traitor, refusing a state funeral, but Polynices's sister Antigone defied Creon, burying her brother with full military honours.

LACK OF UNITY

Lack of unity: describes a sentence that has two parts that do not seem related to each other.

The fifth error in sentence structure is **lack of unity**. Lack of unity occurs when a sentence has two parts that do not seem to fit together. Here are two examples:

> We don't know what we have to do to get a top grade, but the teacher has a wonderful sense of humour.

> Hydrogen is the lightest of all the elements that can be explosive when mixed with air, and has been used for making bombs.

As is often the case with errors in sentence structure, readers can figure out what the writer is trying to say, but to do so, they must read the sentence three or four times. Good sentences communicate the first time they are read. Compare the sentences above with these revisions that establish a clearer connection between the parts of the sentences:

> We like the teacher's wonderful sense of humour, but we don't like his reluctance to let us know what we have to do to get a top grade.

> Although hydrogen is the lightest of all the elements, it has been used for making bombs because it is explosive when mixed with air.

ASSIGNMENT 16-6

Revise the following sentences to improve their unity:

1. The Canadian dollar is weak compared with the American dollar, and many feature films are now being shot in Canada.

2. The forests on Texada Island have been cut down, so limestone is mined.

3. The hawk is a diurnal bird of prey, but the eagle is more common on the West Coast.

SUMMARY

- Write sentences with complete subjects and complete verbs.
- Do not attempt to make a subordinate (or dependent) clause stand alone as a sentence.
- To avoid a run-on sentence, put a period or a semicolon between two sentences, or reduce one of the sentences to a subordinate clause.
- Write clear, precise definitions.
- Be sure the relationship between the subject and verb of your sentences is clear.
- Include enough information in your sentences so that they communicate clearly and accurately.

- If there are two parts to your sentence, make sure the relationship between the parts is clear.

QUESTIONS FOR STUDY AND DISCUSSION

1. Of the five errors in sentence structure discussed in this lesson, which one gives you the most trouble? What steps will you take to avoid this error?
2. How is it possible for a group of words to have both a subject and a verb but still be a sentence fragment?
3. When is a sentence fragment acceptable?
4. How can you spot a run-on sentence when you are revising your written work?
5. Write definitions for each of these terms: "subject," "verb," "syntax."
6. What is the danger of trying to make your writing too concise?
7. What is the difference between paragraph unity (Lesson Seven) and sentence unity?

SUPPLEMENTARY EXERCISES

Revise the following sentences to eliminate errors in sentence structure. Some sentences can be corrected simply by changing a word or two; others will need more substantial revisions.

1. The Berlin Wall was built at the end of World War II. Dividing the eastern part of Berlin into a communist sector and the western part of the city into a capitalist sector.

   _____

   _____

   _____

   _____

2. The aardvark is a nocturnal mammal about 1.5 m long, it feeds on termites and ants.

   _____

   _____

   _____

   _____

3. Acid rain is where there is too much nitric and sulphuric acids in rain and snow.

   _____

   _____

_____

_____

4. Normally, rain would have a pH level of 5, however in some areas of North America pH levels as low as 3 have been recorded.

_____

_____

_____

_____

5. Rain with a pH level of 3 has 100 times more acid than normal, it gets into the soil harming the fruit and leaves on trees.

_____

_____

_____

_____

6. We try to attend church during Advent. The four Sundays that precede Christmas.

_____

_____

_____

_____

7. Halloween is not celebrated in Jamaica explaining why our neighbours were frightened by all the children in strange outfits.

_____

_____

_____

_____

8. George I was King from 1714 to 1727, his son George II was King from 1727 to 1760.

_____

_____

_____

_____

9. Queen Victoria was the granddaughter of George III. Who apparently experienced a period of insanity.

_____

_____

_____

_____

10. The West Coast Trail is paradise for hikers, but many tourists have to travel too far.

_____

_____

_____

_____

11. New episodes of *Friends* and *Melrose Place* are on this week, but I have too much homework.

_____

_____

_____

_____

12. Federally, the Conservative party was reduced to two seats, in Ontario the Conservative party won the election.

_____

_____

_____

_____

13. The wording of the referendum is controversial because is it complete independence or sovereignty-association?

_____

_____

_____

_____

14. Although in the rural ridings there is widespread support for the Liberals, does not mean they can win enough seats to form a government.

_____

_____

_____

_____

15. By looking through calendars is the best way you can decide which college or university is right for you.

_____

_____

_____

_____

16. A decrease in enrollment and an increase in tuition fees were the end of the music program.

_____

_____

_____

_____

17. Subject-verb agreement and pronoun case were the lesson in today's class.

_____

_____

_____

_____

18. Alliteration is when a series of words begin with the same sound.

_____

_____

_____

_____

19. The hare has longer ears and legs than the rabbit, hares do not burrow as rabbits do. Relying for safety on their speed and ability to hide.

_____

_____

_____

_____

20. Thermodynamics is where the relationship of heat to work is studied.

_____

_____

_____

_____

21. Thunder follows lightning because thunder is caused by the intense vibrations in the air. That are the byproducts of the rapid heating followed by the rapid cooling of the air that the lightning has caused.

_____

_____

_____

_____

22. By tightly weaving together wool and cotton, gabardine is produced. Which is used in the making of raincoats.

_____

_____

_____

_____

23. Galleons are sometimes referred to as "treasure vessels." Because precious minerals were transported in galleons from the South American colonies back to Spain.

_____

_____

_____

_____

24. Canada converted to the metric system years ago, many Canadians still prefer to use the imperial system of measurement.

_____

_____

_____

_____

25. In Montreal, two rival motorcycle gangs, the Hell's Angels and Rock Machine, are fighting for control of drug trafficking and prostitution; creating, in the process, a wave of violence that is straining the resources of the Montreal Police Department.

_____

_____

_____

_____

Video Case 3

CBC 🌐

A Christmas Story: A Profile of Susanne Martel

French-Canadian author Susanne Martel writes children's stories. She has written compulsively, eight hours a day, for fifty years, publishing twenty-five books. At present, she is at work on her memoirs.

Martel loves to write; she loves both the creative aspect of the writing process and the physical act of writing. She entertains her readers with adventure stories, featuring a hero whom she compares to Errol Flynn but whom her children compare to James Bond and Indiana Jones. She has as much fun writing her books as her readers have in reading them. She writes longhand with pencil and pad; she appears to be quite indifferent to the wonders of the modern word-processor.

Her memoirs are a departure from her usual genre, but she is clearly bringing the same energy to this project that she has brought to all her others. She has written 400 pages already, she says, and is only up to age twenty.

Questions

1. Write the most recent chapter of your own memoirs, the chapter that describes your life and loves over the past year.

2. Write a letter to Susanne Martel in which you try to convince her to abandon her method of writing her books by hand in favour of using a computer.

3. Try writing a two- to three-page children's story.

Source: "Xmas Story," *Prime Time News.* CBC, December 23, 1994.

Achieving Sentence Variety

Sentence Combining

Coordination
Subordination
Coordination and Subordination Combined
Achieving Sentence Variety

Good writers avoid a series of sentences that are short and choppy. A series of short, choppy sentences can have a hypnotic effect on readers and can take their attention away from the message the writer is trying to communicate. This type of writing is similar to monotonous speech. Good writers vary the structure of their sentences by using coordination and subordination.

COORDINATION

Coordination: method of combining sentences using coordinate conjunctions "and," "but," and "or."

Coordination is a method of combining sentences by using coordinate conjunctions such as "or," "but," or "and." Read these two sentences, for example:

> African slaves adapted the music of their homeland to the seven-note European musical scale. A new style of music, the blues, was born.

By using the coordinate conjunction "and," the two sentences become one:

> African slaves adapted the music of their homeland to the seven-note European musical scale, *and* a new style of music, the blues, was born.

> Consider the following:

> In football the glory usually goes to offensive players. Defensive players, however, are equally important.

These two sentences become one sentence with the coordinate conjunction, "but":

> In football the glory usually goes to offensive players, *but* defensive players are equally important.

ASSIGNMENT 17-1 Use coordinate conjunctions to combine the following sets of sentences.

1. A "hand" is equal to four inches. It is a unit of measure for calculating the height of horses.

2. A heat pump can save money in the long run. It is costly to install.

3. The hemp plant is native to Asia. It is now cultivated widely because of its strong fibre.

SUBORDINATION

Subordination: method of combining sentences using subordinate conjunctions such as "because," "since," and "although" or relative pronouns "who," "whose," "that," and "which."

Subordinate or dependent clause: group of words that contains a subject and a verb but that cannot stand alone as a sentence.

Independent clause: a complete, properly structured sentence.

Subordination is a method of combining sentences by reducing a sentence to a phrase or a subordinate clause and by joining that phrase or subordinate clause to a complete sentence. A **subordinate clause** is a group of words that contains a subject and a verb but that can not stand alone as a sentence. A subordinate clause is also known as a **dependent clause**. The term **independent clause**, sometimes used in the context of discussions on subordinate or dependent clauses, is the same as a sentence.

The first sentence in the previous section could be changed to a subordinate clause if the word "when" is placed at the beginning:

When African slaves adapted the music of their homeland to the seven-note European musical scale, a new style of music, the blues, was born.

Similarly, the "football" sentences, joined together through subordination, might become:

Although the glory in football usually goes to offensive players, defensive players are equally important.

Let's look at one more example:

Doctors in the eighteenth century sometimes treated their patients with bloodletting. Bloodletting usually compounded the patient's ailment.

These two sentences might become one sentence if the second sentence is changed to a subordinate clause using the word "which:"

Doctors in the eighteenth century sometimes treated their patients with bloodletting, which usually compounded the patient's ailment.

Note, again, that the three subordinate clauses in the above sentences cannot stand alone even though they do contain subjects and verbs. If they were punctuated as sentences, they would be sentence fragments.

Phrase: group of words that does not contain a subject or a verb and that modifies a noun or verb.

A sentence can also be reduced to a phrase and combined with another sentence to achieve sentence variety. A **phrase** is a group of words that does not contain a complete subject and verb. Here is another version of the "blues" sentences, this time combined by reducing the first sentence to a phrase:

By adapting the music of their homeland to the seven-note European musical scale, African slaves created a new style of music, the blues.

Here is another version of the "bloodletting" sentence, this time combined by reducing the second sentence to a phrase:

Doctors in the eighteenth century sometimes treated their patients with bloodletting, usually compounding the patient's ailment.

Let's look at one more example:

Jersey is the largest of the Channel Islands. It is just a few miles west of France.

These two sentences might become one if the first sentence is reduced to a phrase:

The largest of the Channel Islands, Jersey is just a few miles west of France.

Or the second sentence could be reduced to a phrase:

Located just a few miles west of France, Jersey is the largest of the Channel Islands.

ASSIGNMENT 17-2

Use subordination to combine the following sets of sentences.

1. The Hippopotamus can be found throughout most of Africa. It lives in herds.

2. Shrove Tuesday is the day before the first day of Lent. It was the custom to "shrive" or go to confession on that day.

3. Organic materials can be dated by gauging their radioactivity. Archaeologists can use radiocarbon dating to estimate the age of objects that were made 50 000 years ago.

COORDINATION AND SUBORDINATION COMBINED

Sentence variety: describes writing that uses sentences of differing lengths and structures.

HELPFUL HINTS

Practise sentence combining. It is a proven method of improving sentence style.

To achieve sentence variety, good writers use any effective combination of coordination and subordination. Read carefully this paragraph written without **sentence variety**:

This lesson discussed sentence variety. You were introduced to the concepts of coordination and subordination. Coordination is a method of combining sentences. You use a coordinate conjunction: "and," "but," "or." Subordination is also a method of combining sentences. First you reduce a sentence to a phrase or a subordinate clause. Then you join that phrase or clause to a complete sentence. A *subordinate clause* is a group of words. It contains a subject and a verb. It can not stand alone as a sentence. A subordinate clause is also know as a *dependent clause*. The term *independent clause* is sometimes used. It is used in the context of discussions on subordinate or dependent clauses. It is synonymous to a sentence.

Without sentence variety, the paragraph has no rhythm or cadence. It is without style. It reads as if it were written by a drill sergeant. Here is the same paragraph, written with more varied sentence structure. Compare the two versions for clarity and readability. Notice how coordination and subordination are used to improve the style of the original version:

In this lesson on sentence variety, you were introduced to the concepts of coordination and subordination. Coordination is a method of combining sentences using a coordinate conjunction such as "or," "but," or "and." Subordination is a method of combining sentences by reducing a sentence to a phrase or a subordinate clause and by then joining that phrase or subordinate clause to a complete sentence. A *subordinate clause* is a group of words that contains a subject and a verb but that can not stand alone as a sentence. A subordinate clause is also know as a *dependent clause*. The term *independent clause*, sometimes used in the context of discussions on subordinate or dependent clauses, is synonymous with a sentence.

Let's look at one more example. Here are four short sentences. They are clear, but choppy:

The evidence strongly suggests that the defendant is guilty. But he is also rich. He has hired the best lawyers. Many experts are predicting a hung jury.

Even a moderate use of coordination would improve the style of the passage:

The evidence strongly suggests that the defendant is guilty. But he is also rich, and has hired the best lawyers. Many experts are predicting a hung jury.

Or all four sentences could be joined together, using the coordinate conjunctions "but," "and," and "so":

The evidence strongly suggests that the defendant is guilty, but he is rich and he has hired the best lawyers, so many experts are predicting a hung jury.

Or the sentence could be improved by using only the coordinate conjunctions "but" and "and":

The evidence strongly suggests that the defendant is guilty, but he is rich, he has hired the best lawyers, and many experts are predicting a hung jury.

The style of the passage could also be improved through the use of subordination. The first sentence could be changed to a subordinate clause:

Although the evidence strongly suggests that the defendant is guilty, he is rich and can hire the best lawyers, convincing many experts the trial will end in a hung jury.

Or the second and third sentences could be changed to a clause:

> The evidence strongly suggests that the defendant is guilty but, because he is rich and can hire the best lawyers, many experts are predicting a hung jury.

A combination of subordination and coordination could also be used:

> Although the evidence strongly suggests that the defendant is guilty, he is rich, he can hire the best lawyers, and many experts are predicting a hung jury.

ASSIGNMENT 17-3

Combine each group of sentences below so choppiness is eliminated and style is improved. You do not necessarily have to reduce each passage to a single sentence. Bring your improved sentences to class and compare your version with those of your classmates. Discuss with your classmates the effectiveness of the various ways of improving the style of each passage. Watch for run-on sentences and awkward sentence structure.

1. Counsellors often encourage their clients to keep a journal. They think it's a good idea for people to write about their feelings and activities. They will learn more about themselves. This can help people find ways to cope with their problems.

2. A sonnet is a short poem. It has fourteen lines. A Shakespearian sonnet has three quatrains and a rhyming couplet. A Petrarchan sonnet has an octave and a sestet.

3. We didn't think *The Honeymoon* was a very funny movie. We thought the attempts at humour were offensive. The humour was based on clichés and stereotypes. The bride was depicted as a hopeless driver. She was a spendthrift. She was irrational to the point of absurdity.

4. Tone refers to the personality or attitude a piece of writing projects. An essay about AIDS would have a serious tone. The tone of an essay describing your bout with laryngitis might be humorous and light-hearted.

5. Hamlet has an extraordinary run of bad luck. First his father dies. Then his mother marries his uncle Claudius. Hamlet has never liked Claudius. Next, Hamlet sees a ghost. The ghost turns out to be Hamlet's dead father. The ghost tells Hamlet that Claudius murdered him. Claudius poured poison in Hamlet's father's ear.

6. An introductory paragraph should present the essay's central or controlling idea. The central or controlling idea is called the thesis. An introductory paragraph should also capture the reader's interest.

7. *The Man from U.N.C.L.E.* was a popular TV show during the 1960s. It starred Robert Vaughn and David McCallum. They played spies. U.N.C.L.E. stands for the United Network Command for Law Enforcement.

8. The Philippines are a chain of islands in Southeast Asia. The islands are surrounded by the Pacific Ocean. The population of the Philippines is approximately 50 000 000 people.

9. The Eiffel Tower was built by Alexandre Eiffel. He was a French engineer. He built the Tower for the Paris Exhibition. The Exhibition was held in 1889. The Tower is 300 metres high.

10. Daniel Defoe wrote *Robinson Crusoe*. This novel was published in 1719. It is based on the adventures of Alexander Selkirk. Selkirk was a sailor and an explorer.

ACHIEVING SENTENCE VARIETY

Writing with coordination and subordination and, in the process, achieving sentence variety, is rarely a conscious act. Try to write smoothly and clearly and, in so doing, you will achieve at least a measure of sentence variety. In time a writer knows, without consciously thinking about it, that a series of short, simple sentences will not please readers and so, intuitively, will tend to write sentences of varying length and structure.

HELPFUL HINTS

Never sacrifice clarity for the sake of sentence variety.

Still it is important, when revising, to be on the lookout for passages that could be more effective if the sentence structure varied. There is a simple but highly effective method for avoiding dull sentences: Read your essay out loud. If you have written a paragraph or a part of a paragraph in need of varied sentence structure, you will recognize that passage, and you can make the necessary revisions.

One final point: Sentence variety does not mean that long sentences are more effective than short ones. Short sentences work. They can add emphasis in a paragraph, and they can break the monotony of a series of long sentences with complex structures. As a rule, however, a series of three or more short sentences should be avoided.

ASSIGNMENT 17-4

Ask three different people to combine the following four sentences in order to make one sentence.

> I had conjunctivitis. I could not write the final exam on Monday. Fortunately, my professor allowed me to write the exam at the end of the week. By then, the infection had subsided.

Choose the version you think is the most effective and, in one or two paragraphs, explain why you think the sentence you chose is better than the other two.

SUMMARY

- Avoid a series of short, choppy sentences. Combine related sentences.
- Use coordinate conjunctions to combine related sentences.
- Change a sentence to a subordinate clause and combine it with a related sentence.
- Change a sentence to a phrase and combine it with a related sentence.
- Use any combination of subordination and coordination to combine sentences.
- Practise sentence combining to achieve sentence variety.

QUESTIONS FOR STUDY AND DISCUSSION

1. What is coordination? Why can too much coordination have an adverse effect on writing?
2. What is the difference between a clause and a phrase?
3. What is the difference between a main (or independent) clause and a subordinate (or dependent) clause?
4. Explain why the ability to subordinate is considered to be a sign of a "mature" writing style.
5. How can you tell if the draft of one of your essays could be improved with sentence variety?

SUPPLEMENTARY EXERCISES

Rewrite each of the following passages to eliminate choppy structure and to improve sentence variety. Most passages can be reduced to a single sentence. Use two sentences if necessary.

1. Yaletown is the latest trendy place to be in Vancouver. It is being called the new Gastown. Yaletown used to be basically a warehouse district. Now highrise condominiums are springing up where warehouses used to be. Many upscale clothing stores are opening in Yaletown.

_____

_____

_____

_____

_____

_____

_____

2. There are some interesting gifts in the museum gift shop. There are some fabulous ornaments for Christmas trees. There are three-dimensional silver snowflakes for sale.

_____

_____

_____

_____

_____

_____

3. Wool sweaters can be machine washed. Use mild soap. You can tumble dry your sweaters. This is contrary to popular belief. Tumble-drying will lift the fibres. This will give the sweater a new appearance.

_____

_____

_____

_____

_____

_____

4. The Los Angeles Dodgers have a new pitcher. His name is Hideo Nomo. He is from Japan. He has an awesome split-fingered fastball. He is leading the league in strike-outs.

_____

_____

_____

_____

_____

_____

5. A backpack is very versatile. Students consider a backpack an essential item. You can fit all of your school books in a backpack. They are easy to carry. You can keep your hands free. You can also get your lunch into your backpack.

_____

_____

_____

_____

_____

_____

_____

_____

6. The Rock and Roll Hall of Fame and Museum is located in Cleveland. A Cleveland deejay named Alan Freed coined the term "rock and roll." The "Rock Hall," as it is called, contains many interesting artifacts. Jimi Hendrix's original lyrics to his song "Angel" are there. A piece of the plane in which Otis Redding crashed and died is also there.

_____

_____

_____

_____

_____

_____

_____

7. In 1973, the Ontario communities of Galt, Preston, and Hespeler were amalgamated. The new city is called Cambridge. It has a population of about 82 000.

_____

_____

_____

_____

_____

_____

8. Canada is renowned for its strange place names. One example is Fort Whoop-Up. Fort Whoop-Up is near Lethbridge. It was originally built to sell whiskey. This function changed with the arrival of the North West Mounted Police in 1874.

_____

_____

_____

_____

_____
_____
_____
_____

9. Daphne Odjig is one of Canada's best-known artists. Her father was a Potawatomi. Her mother was an English war bride. Her work is distinctively Native. Yet she was also influenced by cubism and surrealism. Her mural *The Indian in Transition* is in the National Arts Centre in Ottawa.

_____
_____
_____
_____
_____
_____
_____

10. Wampum is made from white and purple seashells. The seashells are found on the Atlantic coast. The shells were threaded onto string or woven into belts. In the early days of the fur trade, wampum was a form of currency.

_____
_____
_____
_____
_____
_____
_____

Writing with Style

Cultivate Style!
Metaphors
Balanced Elements

Image consultants tell us that "just the right" necktie can improve an already well-matched shirt and suit, that the right belt can perfect an already expensive designer dress, and that the right earrings can set off an already beautiful face. In other words, accessories can add style to a good look and make it look *great*.

Style: choice of words and sentence structures and use of figurative language to add pizzazz and flavour to writing.

Style in fashion is something like style in writing. **Style** refers to the small but important touches that add polish and flair to a writer's work and, in so doing, heighten the impact of the writer's message. Style is the difference between good and excellent writing.

Here is an excerpt from a letter that Samuel Johnson wrote to Lord Chesterfield on February 7, 1754. Chesterfield had offered his patronage to Johnson, who was finishing his now-famous dictionary. Unfortunately, the offer came after it had become clear that the dictionary would be a real contribution to English culture. Johnson was annoyed that Chesterfield would wait until he knew the project would be successful before he was willing to have his name associated with it. He wrote to Chesterfield, in part, as follows:

HELPFUL HINTS

Style, as defined in this lesson, is essential to creative writing, important for academic writing, and less important for technical and professional writing.

> Is not a patron, my lord, one who looks with unconcern on a man struggling for life in the water, and when he has reached ground encumbers him with help? The notice which you have been pleased to take of my labors, had it been early, had been kind; but it has been delayed till I am indifferent, and cannot enjoy it; till I am solitary, and cannot impart it; till I am known, and do not want it.

Metaphor: comparison between two objects to clarify the meaning of one or both objects and to add style to writing.

Parallel clauses: word groups with the same word patterns within a sentence.

Johnson's reply stings not only because of what it says, but also because of the *way* Johnson says it. It is Johnson's style that makes his response to Chesterfield so strong and forceful. In the first sentence the **metaphor** comparing a patron to a man who offers help to a drowning man *after* the man has saved himself is both clever and pointed. In the second sentence, repetition combined with **parallel clauses** separated from one another by semicolons provides a strong sense of rhythm and balance. Johnson's letter is effective because he has used so skillfully the two hallmarks of a deft writing style: metaphor and balance.

In expressive writing, an effective style is essential to enhance descriptions and to bring nature alive for readers. Saskatchewan writer Sharon Butala is known for her intense, lyrical descriptions of the natural world. She is the subject of our last video profile at the end of this lesson.

METAPHORS

A metaphor is a comparison between two objects, the purpose of which is to clarify the meaning or significance of one or both of the objects being compared. Metaphors, as Johnson's letter illustrates, can, through their ingenuity, make writing more interesting, pointed, and readable.

At the beginning of this lesson, a metaphor is used—writing style is compared to style in fashion. Comparing accessories to writing techniques and comparing an overall fashion statement to the overall effect of a piece of writing is done to help you understand what style is and how it can benefit your writing. Let's look at another example:

> During question period in the House of Commons, La Chance is a real pit bull. Once he sinks his teeth into a vulnerable cabinet minister, he will not let go until the minister is howling from the pain.

Notice how the metaphor gives a vivid picture of the nature of the person being described.

In the narrow sense of the term, a metaphor is a direct comparison through which a writer says that one thing *is* something else—La Chance *is* a real pit bull. In the broad sense of the term, a metaphor can encompass other comparisons, such as simile, personification, and hyperbole.

A **simile** is similar to a metaphor, the difference being that a simile uses the words "like" or "as" to compare two things:

> La Chance *is like* a pit bull in the House of Commons.

> Coffey skates as effortlessly *as* an eagle flies.

Simile: type of metaphor that uses "like" or "as" to compare two objects.

Personification is another kind of comparison, which involves ascribing to inanimate objects, human behaviour or characteristics:

> For the first thirty minutes the film is gripping and absorbing, but once the crime has been committed and the trial begins, the film begins to plod along. It takes a bizarre turn when the victim is found alive, and eventually it gets lost completely in the maze of its own convoluted plot.

Here a movie is compared to a person who begins a brisk walk, slows down, takes a wrong turn, and finally gets lost. A movie cannot literally do this, of course, but by animating or personifying the film, the writer gets the point across clearly and forcefully.

Personification: type of metaphor in which something not human is given human attributes.

Hyperbole, a deliberate exaggeration not meant to deceive but used for a dramatic effect, can also be considered a form of metaphor. This example of a hyperbole compares a writing assignment to an impossibly time-consuming task:

Hyperbole: exaggeration for rhetorical effect, not meant to be taken literally.

I couldn't complete this assignment if I were given 1000 years to work on it.

Literally, of course, the writer could finish the assignment within 1000 years. The hyperbole is used for emphasis, to get across the writer's anxiety about the difficulty of the assigned task.

Effective metaphors make a complex concept more understandable and make writing more pointed, memorable, and entertaining. They must, however, be used carefully and discriminately.

ASSIGNMENT 18-1

Find in a magazine article, in one of your textbooks, or in one of your own essays

1. Two examples each of a metaphor and a simile

2. One example of personification

3. One example of hyperbole

Bring your examples to class to share with your classmates and to discuss with them the effect these devices have on the works in which they appear.

There are two pitfalls you need to avoid when you are writing metaphorically. They are the mixed metaphor and the cliché.

Mixed Metaphors

As effective as metaphors can be, they can be disastrous if overused or used incorrectly, as is the case when two metaphors are mixed together. This is called a **mixed metaphor**. For example:

> She has a crystal clear writing style and uses it to hammer home her arguments.

Mixed metaphor: blending together of two metaphors, creating an effect confusing to the reader.

This unfortunate mix of crystals and hammers illustrates that a sentence is too short a rhetorical unit to sustain more than one metaphor. Metaphors can be very effective but must not be overused or mixed together. One way to revise the sentence would be to write

> Her crystal clear writing style makes her arguments all the more emphatic.

Here is another example:

> He would not be such a stuffed shirt if he occasionally took time to stop and smell the roses.

The image of this poor man trying to bend over and smell flowers while his shirt is stuffed does not work. One of the metaphors can stay, but one should go if this writer wants the work to be taken seriously.

He would not be such a stuffed shirt if he took time to relax and enjoy the beauty of the world around him.

ASSIGNMENT 18-2

Rewrite the following sentences, eliminating the mixed metaphors.

1. While the rest of Europe was poised on the brink of war, Great Britain still tried to turn the other cheek.

2. The other provinces acted like spoiled children and the accord went down the tubes.

3. After the fight he looked like a racoon with both eyes black as the night.

Clichés

Cliché: metaphor used so often that it has lost its original effect.

Writers should avoid overused metaphors or **clichés**. Their use gives the impression of a writer who lacks originality and imagination. How do you know if a metaphor has been used enough to classify it as a cliché? Try this test: Can you complete the expression after only part of it has been given to you? If you can, it is probably a cliché. See if you can fill in these blanks:

1. He was like a kid in a _____.

2. He was like a bull in a _____.

3. In her white T-shirt, she looked as fresh _____.

4. She was phoning from another continent but her voice was as clear _____.

5. Today's sportscars are as fast as _____.

6. In spite of the charges, the defendant stood there, as cool _____.

7. This assignment will really separate the men _____.

8. The water was as smooth as _____.

If you can fill in the blanks, you should avoid these phrases in your written work. Familiarity, to coin a _____, breeds _____.

BALANCED ELEMENTS

Parallelism: the quality of two or more sentence elements or sentences being balanced.

A second characteristic of an effective writing style is balance or, as it is sometimes called, **parallelism**. Two sentences can say exactly the same thing, but if one of the two is expressed with a sense of balance, it will be more forceful and effective. Balance can do for a writer's style what coordination can do for an athlete: improve performance.

Look first at this simple example of a badly balanced sentence:

I like to participate in all sports, but I especially love to ski, to golf, and swimming.

The word "swimming" is out of balance; it is a different part of speech from "to swim" or "to ski." This flaw is usually called **faulty parallelism**—one word or phrase is not of the same construction as other words or phrases, though its placement within the sentence requires it to be. The sentence would be parallel or balanced if it were written as follows:

Faulty parallelism: characteristic of a sentence in which one of a series of phrases or clauses is not expressed in the same way as the others.

I like to participate in all sports, but I especially love to ski, to golf, and to swim.

I like to participate in all sports, but I especially love skiing, golfing, and swimming.

Here is another example of a passage written without parallelism:

Even errors you might consider minor will likely annoy your readers. Spelling errors make the reader stumble as he reads and this will be confusing to him, as will be a missed comma. A dangling modifier means your reader will have to reread the sentence. Fluency in reading depends on whether or not written work is clear.

Here is the same passage written with well-balanced clauses and phrases:

Even errors you might consider minor will likely annoy your readers. A spelling error can make your readers stumble; a missed comma can confuse your readers; a dangling modifier can cause them to reread a sentence in order to understand it. Fluency in reading depends on clarity in writing.

Notice how the parallel structure of the three clauses in the second sentence gives that sentence a sense of balance, and as a result, makes it clearer and easier to read. Notice, too, how in the third sentence the same effect recurs because the phrase "Fluency in reading" balances the phrase "clarity in writing."

In descriptive writing, parallelism is especially effective. Look, for example, at the effect that these beautifully balanced sentences have on Joyce's description of a snowfall at the end of his story "The Dead":

Yes, the newspapers were right: snow was general all over Ireland. It was falling on every part of the dark central plain, on the treeless hills, falling softly upon the Bog of Allen and, farther westward, softly falling into the dark mutinous Shannon waves. It was falling, too, upon every part of the lonely churchyard on the hill where Michael Furey lay buried. It lay thickly drifted on the crooked crosses and headstones, on the spears of the little gate, on the barren thorns. His soul swooned slowly as he heard the snow falling faintly through the universe and faintly falling, like the descent of their last end, upon all the living and the dead.

Read the passage out loud and you can sense, from the rhythm and the balance of the phrases and sentences, the slow pan of a camera crossing the Irish plain, coming to rest at the lonely churchyard. You can sense, as well, the falling of the snow. Joyce's use of parallelism, the alliteration in the last sentence ("soul swooned slowly"), the tone of the passage, even the way the passage is punctuated, all combine to create a wonderfully rhythmic, almost mesmerizing effect.

ASSIGNMENT 18-3

Revise the following sentences to improve parallelism or balance.

1. She arrived dressed in jeans and a T-shirt and there were all the other women wearing suits.

2. Sports psychologists feel that some athletes take steroids not so much because they crave victory but it's from having low self-esteem.

3. By the end of the movie, the main character has become quite unstable, losing his identity and then ultimately, he commits suicide.

4. The company would either go bankrupt or there was a leveraged buyout possibility that could save it.

5. You will write two kinds of exams in this course: subjective exams that will require you to write essays and multiple-choice exams which are objective exams.

6. Alan is planning to attend the local two-year college, Chris is going straight to the local university, while going to work in her mother's business is the choice Jenny has made.

7. My essay will explore this question: Do humans have language because they can think, or is thinking the result of humans having language?

8. Literature can be entertaining, gives us insight into human experience, and the artistic dimension of language is displayed.

9. While he was Secretary General of the United Nations, Dag Hammarskjold worked tirelessly for peace in the Middle East and the Congo, and the Nobel Prize for peace was awarded to him in 1962.

10. Under Shaughnessy's leadership, the CPR not only expanded its rail lines but shipping and mining became successful aspects of the company as well.

 **HELPFUL HINTS**

Cultivate your own style; avoid imitating the style of others.

SUMMARY

• A good style adds grace and flair to written work.

• An effective metaphor can make a sentence pointed and memorable.

- A simile uses "like" or "as" to compare two things.
- Personification makes inanimate objects animate and so can animate your written work.
- A hyperbole is a deliberate exaggeration used for emphasis and effect.
- Avoid mixing two metaphors together in a single sentence.
- Avoid clichés, metaphor phrases that have been used too much.
- Use effective balance; avoid faulty parallelism.

QUESTIONS FOR STUDY AND DISCUSSION

1. What are the characteristics of a good writing style?
2. Are there any written assignments you would do in college or in a job where metaphors would not be appropriate?
3. What, in your experience as a reader, are some of the most overused clichés?
4. Why should you avoid using more than one metaphor in one sentence?
5. Why is faulty parallelism considered to be a sign of a weak writing style?

SUPPLEMENTARY EXERCISES

Improve the style of the following passages. Use simple English in place of clichés and mixed metaphors, or replace the clichés and mixed metaphors with your own examples of fresh figurative language. Correct the balance within any sentences containing faulty parallelism.

1. He would go out with her at the drop of a hat if she would stop treating him like dirt.

   _____

   _____

   _____

2. Experienced gardeners use mulch, which acts as a fertilizer and also so water drains effectively.

   _____

   _____

   _____

3. Initially Freud's ideas were considered to be dangerous and to be a threat to the moral fabric of society.

   _____

   _____

   _____

4. They say the controversy is a tempest in a teapot, but there's more than meets the eye in his refusal to negotiate.

    _____

    _____

    _____

5. In Russia, blue jeans are still worth their weight in gold because in Russian clothing stores jeans are few and far between.

    _____

    _____

    _____

6. By Thursday, I knew it was time to buckle down or I would never get my essay off the ground.

    _____

    _____

    _____

7. It would be nice to have both, but if it came down to a choice, most people would rather be wealthy than to have fame.

    _____

    _____

    _____

8. Fralt and Jokint hire the top graduates and this results in them attracting a lot of new clients.

    _____

    _____

    _____

9. There is no such thing as a sure-fire stock, but the blue-chip stocks that make up the Dow are safe bets, nine times out of ten.

    _____

    _____

    _____

10. We will run into a roadblock when we try to convince the feminists on staff, but we will cross that bridge when we come to it.

    _____

    _____

    _____

11. Churchill had his own ax to grind and was not about to be upstaged by Stalin whom he saw as a fox in the henhouse.

_____

_____

_____

12. An affluent consumer society will have to find efficient ways of disposing waste or is recycling a possibility?

_____

_____

_____

13. The human personality is shaped by both our heredity and the environment in which we were raised also plays a part.

_____

_____

_____

14. A true friend will offer all the help we need and not demand our help in return though he might expect it.

_____

_____

_____

15. Politicians need to learn that money doesn't grow on trees, and their constituents will resent pensions that are out of whack with the pensions of ordinary working people.

_____

_____

_____

16. When the negotiations ended, the union had exactly what it wanted and the new contract was signed by the union president.

_____

_____

_____

Video Case 4

Apprenticeship in Nature: A Profile of Sharon Butala

Sharon Butala's story demonstrates clearly and irrevocably how empowering the process of writing can be.

A young urban professional, Butala fell in love with and married a Saskatchewan rancher and moved to a prairie farm. At first, she says, she felt lonely and isolated, awkward and invisible, a stranger in a strange land. Then she began to write, and through her writing she began to understand, appreciate, and connect with her new surroundings. "I wrote myself out of my isolation," she says. Indeed, she established a spiritual bond with the prairie landscape by describing it in beautifully lyrical books such as *The Perfection of the Morning*.

Having developed so strong a sense of place through her writing, Butala is now using her work for more practical purposes. She is lobbying the government to help protect the rural way of life, which is beginning to be threatened by the same agribusiness interests that have nearly destroyed the family farm in the United States.

Butala's work as a writer illustrates both the spiritual and the practical sides of a writer's life. Writing can heal a "psychic crisis," as it did for her, and powerful writing can also influence social and economic policies. "A writer speaks for her people," Butala says. Writing is at once an internal and an external enterprise.

Questions

1. In your journal, explain in your own words the old saying "The pen is mightier than the sword."

2. In an essay of approximately 750 words, compare and contrast the life and people in the city and in the country. Which do you prefer? Explain why.

3. Nearly everyone has shared Butala's experience of feeling out of place. In your journal, describe an experience you have had that made you feel as if you were an outsider. What did you do to overcome these feelings?

Source: "Apprenticeship in Nature," *Prime Time News.* CBC, August 6, 1994.

Revising Your Writing

This book, *Lessons in Essay Writing*, describes and explains the elements of the writing process. In the previous eighteen lessons, you have learned, among other things, how to organize an essay, how to write clear and effective sentences and paragraphs, how to avoid errors in grammar and spelling, and how to write with style.

You have also learned that these elements do not proceed in a logical sequence, and that writing is more of a recursive than a linear process. In other words, writing and revising writing do not occur in a prescribed order—writers revise *as* they write.

Revision: literally "re-seeing"; rewriting a draft of an essay.

Revision is not really a "separate stage" of the writing process. By the time you have completed a draft of your essay, you have already revised some sentences and paragraphs and corrected errors in grammar and spelling. It is highly unlikely, however, that your essay is ready to be turned in after you have completed a draft, even though you will have made revisions as you worked through that draft. You must go through at least one more revision process. You must step back and look at your paper as a whole. If you have time, let a day or two pass before you reread and revise your draft. This way you put some distance between yourself and your work, and you might see flaws and ways of improving your work that you might otherwise have missed.

To give structure and focus to revising your draft, reread your essay very carefully, then work through the "Checklist for Evaluating and Revising Writing" that follows. The checklist presents a summary of the elements of good writing described in this text. Simply put a check mark beside the items in the list if you are satisfied your essay meets the criterion described; put an "X" wherever there is still room for improvement; then revise your essay accordingly. The lesson number in which you can locate the material that covers the point on the checklist has been included to help you out. You might have to repeat the process a second or third time before you are completely satisfied your essay meets all the requirements for good writing summarized in the checklist. The good news is that if your essay does satisfy the checklist criteria, you will get a top grade.

CHECKLIST FOR EVALUATING AND REVISING WRITING

❏ 1. I have written an essay that my reader(s) should find thoughtful, interesting, and informative. (Lesson 1)

❏ 2. Where necessary, I have supported the ideas and arguments in my essay with current and reliable secondary sources. (Lesson 2)

❏ 3. I have acknowledged secondary sources accurately and appropriately, using the MLA or APA method of parenthetical citation. (Lessons 3, 4)

❏ 4. My essay is well organized. My reader(s) will recognize a beginning, a middle, and an end. (Lesson 5)

❏ 5. My introductory paragraph or paragraphs engage my reader, present my thesis, and establish the tone of my essay. (Lesson 6)

❏ 6. My body paragraphs have topic sentences. The topic sentence of each paragraph is adequately developed with other sentences that add any necessary combination of details, examples, comparisons, contrasts, causes, effects, and anecdotes. (Lesson 7)

❏ 7. My concluding paragraph or paragraphs summarize the body of my essay, reiterate the thesis, and clearly indicate that what was promised in the introduction has been delivered. (Lesson 8)

❏ 8. There is a smooth and logical transition from one sentence to the next sentence and from one paragraph to the next paragraph. (Lesson 9)

❏ 9. My writing is concise. I have eliminated any instances of wordiness and redundancy. (Lesson 10)

❏ 10. The words I have used in my essay have the correct connotation as well as the correct denotation. (Lesson 11)

❏ 11. My words are specific and concrete, not vague and abstract. (Lesson 11)

❏ 12. I have not used jargon, euphemisms, or ostentatious language in my essay. (Lesson 11)

❏ 13. I have checked all of my sentences to make certain they contain no errors in grammar. (Lesson 12)

❏ 14. My essay does not contain any sexist language. (Lesson 13)

❏ 15. I have checked carefully the spelling of words I am unsure of and corrected spelling errors. (Lesson 14)

❏ 16. I am satisfied that my essay has no errors in punctuation. (Lesson 15)

❏ 17. My essay does not have any sentence fragments or run-on sentences. (Lesson 16)

❏ 18. My sentences are clear and unified. (Lesson 16)

❏ 19. My sentence structure is varied. No part of my essay contains a series of short, choppy sentences. (Lesson 17)

❏ 20. My sentences do not contain any mixed metaphors or clichés. (Lesson 18)

❏ 21. My sentences are well balanced. I have no sentences that contain faulty parallelism. (Lesson 18)

ASSIGNMENT 19-1

Read the following essay carefully. Evaluate and correct the essay, using the list of 21 criteria for good writing summarized in this lesson. Put a check mark beside those criteria the essay meets and an "X" beside those criteria the essay fails to meet. For each criterion beside which you put an "X," explain in one paragraph why the essay does not meet this criterion and how the essay needs to be improved.

Forever in Blue Jeans

Tony D.T.
English 101
March 19XX

During the second half of the twentieth century, no article of clothing has sold so consistanly well as jeans have. The Nehru jacket has come and gone, tie died T-shirts are now an occasional curiosity in retro-clothing stores, and tacky parties are the only place you're going to wear bell bottoms. But jeans are as popular today as they have ever been.

Blue jeans were first introduced into America around the turn of the entury by a Bavarian immigrant. His name was Levi Strauss. His first name still provides a generic description for jeans.

Strauss used a very sturdy cotton cloth to make trousers for miners in San Francisco. The cloth came from Genoa, Italy. The term "jeans" is a corruption of the word "Genoa" (Jeans). Originally the cloth was meant for covered wagons, but Strauss's genius was in realizing that this strong cloth would be perfect for the grinding work the miners did.

Eventually, he found an even better cloth, similar to Genoa cloth, but lighter, this cloth was <u>serge de Nimes</u> (Jeans), that is, serge from the town of Nimes in France. The word "denim" is a corruption of the town's name. The term "denim jeans," then, is actually a contradiction in terms, literally meaning "de Nimes Genoa" and really describing two different kinds of fabric from two different towns.

Throughout the first half of the twentieth century jeans were the favourite clothing for working class men, farmers, miners, and factory workers. Because of this working-class association, wearing jeans came to be a form of protest for middle-class children who wanted to shock the establishment by wearing radical clothing. In the 50s, James Dean and Marlon Brando popularized the connection between jeans and rebels, with or without causes.

During the counter culture 60s and into the 70s, jeans became the the main part of the unofficial uniform of young adults. College campuses were a sea of blue as students and their professors conformed to the dress code of the day. Students in Eastern European countries craved jeans and would offer travelling students from the West double what they paid for their blue jeans.

Jeans should have disappeared in the 80s, when the mantra of young adults changed from "love and peace" to "greed is good." Instead, they went, like the rest of the decade, as upscale as possible. Designer Calvin Klein brought out a line of supposedly high-quality jeans and marketed them brilliantly, with the help of a young and sleek woman who seductively told us nothing came between her and her Calvins. Soon other designers were also cashing in. Yuppies began to wear their designer jeans in fancy restaurants and wine bars. White jeans, black jeans, green jeans, pre-shrunk and acid washed jeans gained popularity.

The phenomenal success of denim jeans continues to this day and shows no sign of waning. Look at the legs of today's college students and you will see jeans covering most of them.

Their popularity shows every sign of continuing. Jeans are durable, they last for years, they are easy to care for, look better with each washing, and don't need to ironed. It looks as if we will be, as Neil Diamond predicted in his song, forever in blue jeans.

References

"Jeans." *The Hutchinson Encyclopedia*, 1992 ed.

SUMMARY

- Revise your writing *while* you are working on a draft and *after* you have completed a draft.
- Evaluate and revise your draft against the Checklist for Evaluating and Revising Writing in this lesson.
- Hand in a neat and clean copy of your essay, formatted according to your professor's instructions.

QUESTIONS FOR STUDY AND DISCUSSION

1. Consider your own writing process. Would you describe this process as linear or recursive?

2. How many drafts of an essay do you usually write before you hand the essay in?

3. What criteria for good writing would you add to the list of 21 in the Checklist for Evaluating and Revising Writing presented in this lesson?

4. Which of the criteria on the checklist have given you trouble in the past? How could you overcome these weaknesses in your own writing?

5. Do you think you will do much writing when you have finished college or university? What information do you have that leads you to that conclusion?

SUPPLEMENTARY EXERCISES

Read the following paragraphs carefully. Then, using the Checklist for Evaluating and Revising Writing, give each paragraph a mark out of ten. Write a few sentences after each paragraph explaining why you gave it the score you did.

1. Celebrity restaurants are the latest craze in the food industry. Some of the biggest Hollywood stars including Arnold Schwartenegger, Bruce Willis, and Sylvester Stallone own a chain of restaurants called Planet Hollywood which feature memorabilia from famous movies. There is a Hard Rock Cafe now, filled with rock and roll memorabilia, in virtually every major city in North America and Europe. Recently in New York, a group of super models, including Claudia Schiffer and Cindy Crawford opened a new restaruant along the same lines called the Fashion Cafe.

Score _____

_____
_____
_____
_____
_____
_____

2. Canada's Elvis Stojko has won the men's skating title at the last two world championships. He will defend his title in Edmonton in March. He is preparing a new short program. Based on a motor racing theme. It lasts for two-and-a-half minutes. He is preparing a new long program, four-and-a-half minutes, which is inspired by aboriginal dances Stojko has studied. During upcoming Canadian and European tours, he will refine

his new programs. He will tour with other world-class skaters including Phillipe Candelero, Surya Bonaly, and Michelle Kwan.

Score _____

_____
_____
_____
_____
_____
_____

3. In 1987 Prime Minister Brian Mulroney and the provincial premiers negotiated an agreement that came to be known as the Meech Lake Accord. The Accord granted consessions to Quebec in order to encourage them to remain a part of Canada. French would be recognized as the dominant language of Quebec. Quebec would have the right to control its own immigration. Quebec would have a say in the appointment of its senators, as would the other provinces. To become law, the Meech Lake Accord had to be passed by all ten provincial legislatures. It was not. Manitoba refused to pass it because it failed to adequately address aboriginal rights. Newfoundland did not pass it because Premier Clyde Wells felt his province was being bullied by the federal government.

Score _____

_____
_____
_____
_____
_____
_____

4. Literally, omniscient means "all knowing." The narrator of a story told from the omniscient point is not a character in the story, but someone who knows who the characters are, what they are doing, and what they are thinking and feeling. Some novels written from an omniscient point of view seem artificial because the author seems to have too much power and control. He not only describes actions, thoughts, and feelings but also seems to manipulate his characters and their actions. The reader feels as if he is watching a chess game, the outcome of which is predetermined. The narrator seems to be God. In the hands of masters like Dickens and Austen, however, the omniscient point of view seems perfectly natural and unobtrusive. Readers feel as if they are inside the story, watching the

game of life, neither welcome nor unwelcome, but inexorably present. The narrator has disappeared; he is more of a holy spirit than a god.

Score _____

_____
_____
_____
_____
_____

5. The interim agreement was a masterpiece of compromise and diplomacy. The leader of the party that won the most seats would become president, but the leader of any party which won 20 percent of the vote would become vice-president. The compromise assured Mandela's victory, but assured, as well, a significant, if not strong, voice for white South Africans. The cabinet would also be multiparty, hence multiracial. The new president would appoint up to twenty-seven cabinet ministers, any party which won 5 percent of the vote would have a representative in cabinet. To win the support of Chief Buthelezei, the committee members, while stopping short of recommending an autonomous Zulu state, did recomend some decentralization by creating nine provinces. Each of which would have its own legislature.

Score _____

_____
_____
_____
_____
_____
_____

6. Most people were surprised to learn that Orville Redenbacher did actually develop the product he promoted. First, there was his name. It must have been an invention. Then there was his appearance. Some ad-man must have created this caricature of middle America with his bow tie, hair parted down the middle, and then there was that goofy smile. Orville Redenbacher was his real name and he really did develop the gourmet popcorn he sold. He graduated from Purdue University with a degree in agronomy. It took him several decades to develop the hybrid corn plant that would produce the popping corn that would lead to his fame and fortune.

Score _____

_____

_____

_____

_____

_____

_____

7. Men, by virtue of their sex, were given the right to vote in both provincial and federal elections. Women had to fight for and "earn" the right to vote. On the Prairies, Nellie McClung launched a concerted campaign for women's suffrage, and finally, in January, 1916, the Manitoba provincial government granted women the right to vote and they could elected to the holding of provincial office. They were after all indispensable to the running of the farms which was the Prairie economy. Gradually other provinces fell into line and then in May of 1918, the federal government granted the right of women to vote. In recognition of their contribution to the war effort during the First World War of 1914 to 1918, in which Canada did participate. A year later they could be elected to the house of Commons though it is interesting to note that women still could not become appointed to be senators in Canada until 1929. It was a gradual and sometimes demeaning process. Kim Campbell became the first Woman Prime Minister in 1993.

Score _____

_____

_____

_____

_____

_____

_____

8. Monet's early work contains solid forms and shapes. Terrace at Le Havre, which he painted in 1866, is an example. As he developed as an artist, he became more interested in light until light dominated his work and form and shape faded into the background. The paintings he made between 1892 and 1894 of Rouen Cathedral are examples.

Score _____

_____

_____

_____

_____

_____

_____

9. In a large skillet, heat two tablespoons of extra virgin olive oil over medium-high heat. Sauté two large red onions, which have been thinly sliced for two minutes, gradually adding four cloves of garlic, five peeled and julienned carrots, two peeled and julienned parsnips, four scallions chopped up, one fennel bulb which has been julienned, and one cup of chopped cilantro. After you have cooked this mixture for four minutes, add five ounces of cooked angel hair pasta. Season the whole mixture with salt and pepper. Cool it before you stuff your salmon with it.

    Score _____

_____

_____

_____

_____

_____

_____

10. Zoos are sometimes described as prisons for exotic animals, but this description is far too kind. The word prison implies crime and punishment for committing that crime. The only crime zoo animals are guilty of is that they are of interest to people who enjoy watching forlorn animals pace back and forth behind iron bars. Zoo animals are given life sentences, yet they have not even been accused of committing a crime. Zoos which are currently in operation throughout the world must be phased out of existence as their animals die off, and, by international law, no new zoos should be allowed to open at any time, in any place.

    Score _____

_____

_____

_____

_____

_____

_____

Appendix A

Detailed Analysis of a Model Composition

Throughout *Lessons in Essay Writing*, there are model essays designed to illustrate certain principles of good writing. The essays in Lesson Five, for example, illustrate effective structure; the essays in Lessons Three and Four illustrate the effective use of secondary sources and the proper ways of acknowledging secondary sources.

In this Appendix, we are going to take a careful look at one of these essays, not only for minute stylistic details but for the overall qualities of good writing discussed in this book. The aim here is to help you understand how and why this essay exemplifies the qualities of good writing discussed in *Lessons in Essay Writing* and to remind you of the elements of good writing covered in this text.

The essay we are going to examine is the research paper, "English: The First One Thousand Years," from Lesson Three. You will likely have to write one major research paper in your composition course, and your grade on this paper will likely have a significant effect on your final grade. Consider this analysis carefully. It will help you understand the qualities of a successful research paper and remind you of what you need to keep in mind as you work through the process of writing your own research essay.

The text of the essay appears on the left-hand page; running commentary and analysis appear on the facing right-hand page

English: The First One Thousand Years

Roberta M.
English 100
February, 19XX

A thousand years ago, an English poet wrote a poem about the Battle of Maldon, a heroic attempt by English forces to defeat a Viking attack against the town of Maldon in Essex. Facing defeat, the old warrior Byrhtwold, the leader of the English forces, tries to rally his troops with these words:

> Hige sceal þe heardre, heorte þe cenre
> mod sceal þe mare, þe ure maegen lytlad. (311-312)

Byrhtwold was speaking English and his English soldiers would, of course, have understood him. To modern speakers of English, this is a foreign language requiring translation:

> Courage must be the firmer, heart the bolder, spirit the greater,
> the more our strength wanes. (Crossley-Holland and Mitchell 14)

Only the word "heorte" (heart) is recognizable in the original.

Old English is a Germanic language, born in the wake of the invasion of England by German tribes, most notably the Angles and the Saxons, during the fifth century. Their language was a branch of Indo-European, which dates back to about 5000 B.C. and from which modern European and some Asian languages sprang. Indo-European might, in turn, be a branch of another language, possibly a literal mother tongue, from which all other human languages might have emerged (Wright).

When the Germans (the Angles and the Saxons) landed on the English shores, they were met by an even earlier group of Indo-Europeans, the Celts, whom they forced north and west, where today live Celtic descendants: the Welsh, Scots, and Irish. The Celts were not strangers to invaders, having been victims of Roman imperialism beginning in 55 B.C. and ending early in the fifth century, when the mighty Roman Empire began to collapse. Some English place names, Manchester and Winchester, for example, are derived from the Roman word "castra," meaning "camp" (McCrum, Cran, and MacNeil 52).

The Celts fought hard against the German invaders, and, under one King, Artorius—probably the legendary King Arthur—had some success. But the Anglo-Saxons were determined to mine the rich minerals and settle the fertile soil of this beautiful island, and soon routed the Celts, adding insult to injury by calling them "wealas," which means foreigners and is the Anglo-Saxon root word for Wales and Welsh (McCrum, Cran, and MacNeil 56).

1

2

3

4

COMMENTARY

1. Roberta uses a good technique to engage the reader's interest, something an introductory paragraph must do. She begins with an interesting anecdote and a related quotation. The first paragraph also introduces her topic but does not state her thesis. In research papers, the introduction often stretches over two, even three paragraphs. Note that the parenthetical citation for the lines of poetry includes only the line numbers. The translation includes the name of the translators.

2. Here, at the end of the essay's introduction, it is obvious that Roberta is going to present to her readers a brief history of the English language. In the first sentence, she mentions the event—the fifth-century invasion of England by the Angles and Saxons—that activated the birth of English.

3. At the beginning of this paragraph, notice the transition that links it to the preceding paragraph. Note the parenthetical citation at the end of the paragraph; there are commas between the authors' names but, in the MLA method, no comma before the page number.

4. Roberta's discussion of the derivation of the words "Wales" and "Welsh" is interesting and it links this paragraph to the previous one. Note the use of the dashes in the first sentence. Commas or parentheses could have been used, but the dashes emphasize the phrase between them.

Old English literature, especially poems like <u>Beowulf</u> and <u>The Battle of Maldon</u>, quoted above, show how much the Anglo-Saxons admired courage, honour, and strength. But they were farmers as well as warriors, and modern words that relate to the land—words like "shepherd," "earth," "plow," "swine," "wood," and "field"—are Anglo-Saxon in origin. Other words of Anglo-Saxon origin—such as "glee," "laughter," and "mirth"—reveal yet another aspect of their culture (McCrum, Cran, and MacNeil 58).

5

In 597, Christian missionaries came to England, bringing with them hundreds of Latin words that gradually became anglicized. Words related to Christianity—"angel," "disciple," "priest," "litany," "shrine"—entered the language. Words already in the language—"God," "heaven," "hell"—originally pagan, acquired Christian connotations (McCrum, Cran, and MacNeil 63).

6

Late in the eighth century Scandinavian invaders—the notorious Vikings—began to arrive. By the middle of the ninth century, they had conquered half of the country, the South saved thanks largely to the leadership of King Alfred the Great. As time went by, the two cultures blended, a process that was eased by the similarity in language. Old English and Old Norse, the language spoken by the Vikings, are so similar in fact that it is not always easy to tell which words have Viking origins. Place names ending in "by" and "wick," such as Derby and Chiswick, are probably Old Norse, as are words beginning in "sk": sky, skin, skirt. Old Norse also enriched English with words that were nearly the same as existing English words but with subtle distinctions in meaning. The Old English had "craft;" the Vikings gave them "skill." An Old English farmer might "want" a new horse; after the Vikings had settled, the farmer could also "wish" for a new horse (McCrum, Cran, and MacNeil 71).

7

After the Vikings came the Normans from the north of France, who, under William the Conqueror, defeated the English King Harold at the Battle of Hastings in 1066. The Normans established French and Latin as the languages of law and government. As a result, words with French and Latin roots—"perjury," "attorney," "nobility," "royal," and "sovereign," for example—entered the language (McCrum, Cran, and MacNeil 73-74). Thirteenth-century English is still a puzzle to modern speakers, but is easier to decode than the English in which <u>Beowulf</u> and <u>The Battle of Maldon</u> were written. In <u>Kyng Alisaunder</u>, written 300 years after <u>The Battle of Maldon</u>, one of Alexander's enemies taunts the Greek King, complaining that Alexander has "brent myne tounes, myne men yslawe." The modern translation, "burned my towns, slain my men," (Burnley 127) is markedly closer to the original than is the modern translation of the passage from <u>The Battle of Maldon</u>, quoted above.

8

COMMENTARY

5. This paragraph contains interesting examples of the Anglo-Saxon contribution to the English language. The mention of The Battle of Maldon creates coherence within the essay, referring back as it does to the first paragraph.

6. Roberta's organizational structure is well established. With this paragraph, she brings her historical survey up to the sixth century. She is developing her topic chronologically, highlighting key events in the history of English. This is another in a succession of quite short paragraphs developed by the use of examples. This would not always be advisable, but a historical essay lends itself to this type of structure.

7. Notice the transitional phrase with which the paragraph begins. The essay continues to proceed in chronological order: the survey is now up to the eighth century. This is a well-developed paragraph. The first sentence is the topic sentence, and the other sentences present interesting details and examples in support of the topic sentence.

8. Roberta is now at about the half-way point in her historical survey. Note the style of this paragraph. In the first sentence, the phrase "came the Normans" reverses the usual subject-verb order. The second and third sentences are quite short and to the point. The other sentences are longer and more complex. Good sentence variety like this helps to hold the reader's interest in what the writer is saying.

Norman French influenced English but posed no threat to its survival. For 300 years the language of the court, it still did not trickle down to the common people who, too busy to worry too much about the goings on at court, calmly continued to speak their mother tongue in day-to-day life. In time, young Norman men began to marry young English women and young Norman women began to marry young English men; their children and their children's children learned English as their first language. In time, hostility developed between France and England and the new generations of Normans declared their allegiance to their new homeland and fought in its defence. English re-asserted itself in legal and government circles. By the middle of the fourteenth century, English farmers, judges, bishops, and Kings were again conversing, praying, and conducting the affairs of state in English.

All that was needed to entrench English permanently was a great poet of the people, one who would write in English and immortalize the array of colourful English men and women of all social classes and occupations. Geoffrey Chaucer was born in 1340 and wrote The Canterbury Tales, probably around 1390. The opening lines remain the most famous example of Middle English writing:

Whan that April with his showres soote
The droughte of Marche hath perced to the roote,
And bathed every veine in swich licour
Of which vertu engendred is the flowr;
Whan Zephyrus eek with his sweete breeth
Inspired hath in every holt and heeth
The tendre croppes, and the yonge sonne
Hath in the Ram his halve cours y-ronne;
And smale fowles maken melodye,
That sleepen al the night with open ye—
So priketh hem Nature in hir corages—
Than longen folk to goon on pilgrimages,
And palmeres for to seken struange strondes,
To ferne halwes, couthe in sondry londes;
And specially, from every shires ende
Of Engelond to Caunterbury they wende,
The holy blisful martyr for to seeke,
That hem hath holpen, whan that they were seke.
(1-18)

COMMENTARY

9. After a series of paragraphs developed mainly by the use of examples, this paragraph built upon anecdotes is effective. Notice the cohesive ties within the paragraph, which covers a lot of historical ground. Phrases such as "For three hundred years," "In time," and "By the middle of the fourteenth century" help the reader follow the flow of the discussion.

10. With this paragraph, the essay begins to take a somewhat different slant on its subject. Here, and for the next few paragraphs, the influence that a couple of major writers had on the evolution of English will be discussed. Readers will enjoy attempting to make sense of their language as it was written and spoken six hundred years ago.

Chaucer's English, as the opening lines to <u>The Canterbury Tales</u> illustrate, is easier to decode than Old English but is still a challenge to modern English speakers. Students who must read Chaucer's work require texts that are heavily annotated. In one recent edition, for example, every line of the above excerpt, except lines 15-16, is annotated (Kolve and Olson 3). A full translation is not required, however, as it is for Old English texts.

11

Many letters that are silent in today's spoken English were pronounced by Chaucer and his fellow English speakers. The final "e" in words like "ride" and "hope" would usually have been pronounced, as would the "k" in "knife" and the "gh" in "thought." Verbs often ended in "en," the verb "to seek," for example, being "to seken." Past participles were often prefixed by "y," as in "hadde y-ronne" (Kolve and Olson xvi).

12

Around 1477, William Caxton brought a new European invention, the printing press, to England (Bolton 17). He printed his books in the English used in London, Chaucer's English. The printing press revolutionized literacy, making books readily available to all segments of society. London English became and remains the standard because of Caxton's decision to print his books in the English used in London. As Bolton notes:

13

> We can...say that spelling was by and large stabilized by the time Shakespeare was born, and that the standard of stability was the literary dialect of London English exemplified by and descended from Chaucer. (18)

Shakespeare was born in 1564, and wrote his plays and poems in the 1590s and early 1600s, before his death in 1616. His influence on the language was enormous. Scores of words never in print before, appear, for the first time, in Shakespeare's work: "accommodation," "assassination," "dexterously," "indistinguishable," "obscene," "pedant." This is a minuscule list of words coined by or put into print for the first time by Shakespeare (McCrum, Cran, and MacNeil 98).

14

Shakespeare, moreso even than Chaucer, shows us how versatile and flexible the English language is, how well it lends itself to the expression of a thought that is at once concise, metaphorical, and profound. He remains the most quoted of all English authors. If your lost property has "vanished into thin air," notes Levin "you are quoting Shakespeare. "You are quoting Shakespeare, he continues, if

15

> you have ever refused to budge an inch or suffered from green-eyed jealousy, if you have played fast and loose, if you have

COMMENTARY

11. This paragraph is developed by the compare/contrast method. The first sentence is the topic sentence, as it often is. The challenge of reading Middle English is compared and contrasted with the challenge of reading Old English.

12. This paragraph will interest any reader who has ever been frustrated by English spelling. Try pronouncing the "gh" in the word "thought," as English speakers in Chaucer's day would have done!

13. Again, note the paragraph's first phrase, "Around 1477," reinforcing the chronological structure of the essay. This is the first paragraph to discuss the influence of technology on language, a point which will brought up again later in the essay. Note the quote from Bolton. Because it is quite long, it is not integrated into the body of the essay but is indented and separated from the rest of the text. Note that there are no quotation marks around the quote, as there would be if it were shorter and not set apart. Note also that only the page number appears at the end of the quote because the author's name has already been mentioned.

14. Notice how Roberta neatly picks up the mention of Shakespeare's name, which appeared in the Bolton quote in the previous paragraph. This is an example of an effective, natural transition between paragraphs. Notice also that, in this paragraph, the topic sentence is the second one.

15. Note the parenthetical citation. "Qtd." stands for "quoted." If you quote from a source you don't have but that you have found in another source and want to use, you include "qtd. in" in your parenthetical citation. Note how the structure of this paragraph mirrors the structure of an essay. It begins with a topic sentence, the equivalent to an essay's thesis. It contains four sentences that elucidate the topic. It ends with a sentence that summarizes the content of the paragraph and reiterates the paragraph's main idea.

been tongue-tied, a tower of strength, hoodwinked or in a pickle, if you have knitted your brows, [or] insisted on fair play. . . (qtd. in McCrum, Cran, and MacNeil 98)

Perhaps you make "a virtue of necessity"; perhaps you can't sleep "a wink" some nights; maybe you "stand on ceremony" occasionally, or get "too much of a good thing," or live in "a fool's paradise." All of these everyday expressions have their origins in Shakespeare's work.

In 1611, when Shakespeare's career as a writer was coming to a close, the King James version of the Bible was published. Beautifully written in simple and straightforward English, the King James Bible can easily be read today by anyone who can read English. The printing press allowed for wide distribution at home and abroad of the King James Bible. The English language as we know it now was already firmly entrenched. `16`

The English of the 1690s, then, is easily read by readers in the 1990s. But even after 1700, the language continued to grow and change, as it continues to do so now. The changes are minor compared to the change from the English of The Battle of Maldon to the English of Shakespeare, but significant nevertheless. `17`

Since the early seventeenth century, for example, English has continued to borrow and adapt hundreds of words from other languages. While the King James Bible was being written and published, explorers were meeting the Native people of North America. From their languages came words like "hickory," "chipmunk," "moose," "tomahawk," and "kayak" (McCrum, Cran, and MacNeil 123). As years passed, European immigrants began to arrive, bringing with them many words from many languages—words that were soon incorporated into English. Gefvert provides a small list of examples: `18`

From French we borrowed "brochure" and "chaperone;" from Portuguese, "veranda;" from Spanish, "cafeteria" and "marijuana;" from Italian, "serenade" and "umbrella;" from Swedish, "ski;" from Dutch, "cookie;" from German, "hamburger" and "kindergarden;" from Arabic, "algebra;" from Persian, "paradise." (344)

Asian languages have enriched English with words like "tea" and "silk." From African languages, words like "banana" and "jazz" have come into English (Gefvert 344). Today, of course, the process continues. English-speaking countries welcome immigrants whose many gifts include new words that soon find their way into English dictionaries.

COMMENTARY

16. For the second sentence, Roberta originally wrote, "Beautifully written in simple and straightforward English, anyone today can easily read the King James Bible." What is wrong with this earlier version? It contains a dangling modifier that confuses meaning by suggesting that "beautifully written" refers to "anyone" rather than to "the King James Bible."

17. This is a short transitional paragraph, common in research papers. Transitional paragraphs tell readers that one major section of the paper is over and a new section is about to begin. In this case, Roberta notes that by 1700 English as we know it today was established, but that changes continue to occur. The rest of the essay will discuss the development of English after 1700.

18. Notice in the first sentence the phrase "for example," which establishes continuity between this paragraph and the one that precedes it. The topic sentence (the first) is very well developed in this paragraph, using a wide range of interesting examples. Two authoritative and reliable sources are cited.

Scientific and technological inventions and discoveries also bring new words into the language. When the telephone and telegraph were invented, for example, they needed names. The word-makers of the day took the Greek root "tele," meaning "far or distant," and added to it other Greek roots like "phone," meaning "sound," and "graph," meaning "write or mark" (Francis 319). Scores of other words have entered the language this way. New English words entering the language in the wake of the computer revolution could fill a small dictionary. Our fathers' dictionaries did not include "on-line," "software," "computer hacker," or "interface." [19]

Even in the last forty years, then, English has changed. Its flexibility and adaptability are perhaps the outstanding characteristic of English—the reason why it has, at about 500 000 words, the largest vocabulary of any language, and the reason why it is the closest thing we have to an international language, spoken by a billion people scattered throughout every country in the world (McCrum, Cran, and MacNeil 10). This flexibility and adaptability is also the reason why English has changed so much over its first thousand years of use and why it continues to change and develop. When the history of the next thousand years of English is written, it will be written in a language that will have an even larger vocabulary than the one we have now and with a grammar that has changed to reflect the changes in the society that uses it. [20]

COMMENTARY

19. The influence of technology on language is a broad topic. Roberta provides key examples, and brings her history right up to the present with a discussion of how computer technology has influenced language. Again, she provides interesting examples in support of the topic sentence.

20. Notice how Roberta's concluding paragraph briefly summarizes the body of the essay and, in the third sentence, reiterates its thesis. A concluding paragraph, especially in an essay with a historical slant, often points to future concerns related to its topic. Roberta's concluding sentence notes that language will continue to change as people and society change.

Works Cited

Bolton, W.F. <u>A Short History of Literary English</u>. London: Edward Arnold, 1967.

Burnley, David. <u>The History of the English Language: A Source Book</u>. New York: Longman, 1992.

Chaucer, Geoffrey. <u>The Canterbury Tales: Nine Tales and the General Prologue</u>. Ed. V.A. Kolve and Glending Olson. New York: W.W. Norton, 1989.

Crossley-Holland, Kevin., trans. and Bruce Mitchell, ed. <u>The Battle of Maldon and Other Old English Poems</u>. New York: St. Martins, 1967.

Francis, W. Nelson. "Word Making: Some Sources of New Words" <u>Language: Introductory Readings</u>, 3rd. ed. Eds. Virginia P. Clark, Paul A. Eschholz, and Alfred F. Rosa. New York: St. Martins, 1981. 316-328.

Gefvert, Constance J. <u>The Confident Writer: A Norton Handbook</u>. New York: Norton, 1985.

Kolve, V.A. and Glening Olson, eds. <u>The Canterbury Tales: Nine Tales and the General Prologue</u>, by Geoffry Chaucer. New York: W.W. Norton, 1989.

McCrum, Robert, William Cran, and Robert MacNeil. <u>The Story of English</u>. Rev. ed. London: Faber and Faber, 1992.

Roberts, Paul. "A Brief History of English." In <u>Language: Introductory Readings</u>, 3rd. ed. Eds. Virginia P. Clark, Paul A. Eschholz, and Alfred F. Rosa. New York: St. Martins, 1981. 585-595.

Wright, Robert. "Quest for the Mother Tongue." <u>The Atlantic</u> April 1991: 39-68.

COMMENTARY

21. Roberta has chosen the MLA method to cite her sources. She has cited ten sources, about the right number for the type of research paper you will write in your composition class. Notice the format, the punctuation, the underlining, and the use of quotation marks in the entries in the Works Cited list. It is important to cite all sources accurately.

Overall Comments

Roberta's essay is interesting and informative. She has made good use of reliable and authoritative secondary sources. One or two of her paragraphs, notably the one about the printing press, could perhaps be developed in just a bit more detail. She might also have said something about the influence of social movements—the feminist movement, for example—on the development of English. Otherwise, the content of her essay is excellent.

The essay is clear and concise. Roberta has obviously proofread her work carefully, eliminating errors in grammar, spelling, and punctuation. The paragraphs within the essay and the sentences within each paragraph are linked together with transitional words and phrases and other cohesive ties.

The essay does not contain any errors in sentence structure: no sentence fragments, run-on sentences, errors in subject-verb agreement, or misplaced modifiers. The sentence variety is excellent throughout. Roberta does use at least one cliché—"adding insult to injury"— but for the most part her word choice is good.

This research essay was assigned early in the term, as in all likelihood yours will be. It is best to get started on it right away; a research essay is not one to leave until a few days before it is due. It will take time to gather the sources you need, to sift through them, and to decide which ones will be most useful. You will likely need to discuss your topic and your outline—possibly even a rough draft—with your teacher. You may get class time for peer conferencing, and you will have to have enough work done on your paper to get the benefits of your classmates' input.

Remember that, in a composition course, the research paper is often considered to be the most important assignment and is often the one worth the most marks.

Appendix B

Evaluating Writing

How did you decide on the grade you gave me? This is the question English teachers hear probably more than any other. In this Appendix, we are going to look at three versions of two essays and discuss the grades each version would likely receive from experienced English teachers.

The criteria English teachers use to mark essays are essentially the same as those (presented in Lesson Nineteen) for evaluating the final draft of your essay before you revise it one last time and hand it in. Here, these criteria are expressed from the marker's point of view.

CHECKLIST FOR EVALUATING WRITING

1. This is a thoughtful, interesting, and informative essay.

2. Current and reliable secondary sources have been used to support the ideas and arguments in this essay.

3. Secondary sources have been acknowledged accurately and appropriately, using the MLA or APA method of parenthetical citation.

4. The essay is well organized. It has a clear beginning, a middle, and an end.

5. The introductory paragraph or paragraphs engage the reader's interest, present the writer's thesis, and establish the tone of the essay.

6. Body paragraphs have topic sentences. The topic sentence of each paragraph is adequately developed with other sentences that add the necessary combination of details, examples, comparisons, contrasts, causes, effects, and anecdotes.

7. The concluding paragraph or paragraphs summarize the body of the essay, reiterate the thesis, and clearly indicate that what was promised in the introduction has been delivered.

8. There is a smooth and logical transition from one sentence to the next and from one paragraph to the next.

9. The essay is concise. The writer has eliminated wordiness and redundancy.

10. The words used in the essay have the correct connotation as well as the correct denotation.

11. Words are specific and concrete, not vague and abstract.

12. The writer has avoided jargon, euphemisms, or ostentatious language.

13. The sentences contain no errors in grammar.

14. The essay does not contain any sexist language.

15. There are no spelling errors.

16. There are no punctuation errors.

17. The essay does not have any sentence fragments or run-on sentences.

18. The sentences are clear and unified.

19. The sentence structure is varied. No part of the essay contains a series of short, choppy sentences.

20. Sentences do not contain any mixed metaphors or clichés.

21. Sentences are well balanced. There are no sentences which contain faulty parallelism.

Evaluating student writing is not a precise science. The criteria listed above are the ones most English teachers use, but the weight given to each criterion will differ from one teacher to the next. Some teachers are sticklers for grammar and punctuation and will take marks off for errors; others will be more concerned with content and organization and might not take too many marks off for errors in grammar, spelling, and punctuation.

Nevertheless, it is possible to generalize to a certain extent. It is certainly safe to say that if an English teacher can check-mark each of the twenty-one criteria listed above on an essay he or she is marking, the essay is going to get a top grade. Similarly, if the marker has to put an X beside half or more of the evaluative criteria, the essay is likely to receive a failing grade. An average essay might be weak on five or six of these criteria; a good but not excellent essay might show weakness in two or three of them.

In this Appendix, three versions of two essays are examined, discussed, and evaluated. Study carefully the three versions and the comments made by the marker. This will help you understand how and why teachers decide on the grade they will give your papers. It will also, of course, remind you of the characteristics of good writing discussed throughout *Lessons in Essay Writing*.

The text of the essay appears on the left-hand page; the evaluative comments appear on the facing right-hand page. A general comment, including a justification for the grade each version of each essay would likely receive, follows each essay.

Choosing a Bottle of Wine

Martin G.
English 100

Choosing the right wine is usually the most difficult of the decisions you are going to have to make when you are planning a dinner
party. You need to follow a few basic guidelines when choosing the
right wine.

    You first must decide if you want to serve a light, medium, or
full-bodied wine. The wine's "body" is determined by its alcohol content. Which is indicated on the label of the bottle. A light-bodied
wine has an alcohol content of between eight and ten percent; a
medium-bodied wine has an alcohol content of eleven or twelve percent; a full-bodied wine has an alcohol content of thirteen or fourteen percent.

    You need to know something about the grapes from which wines are
made, in order to make just the right choice for your guests. The
name of the grape should be on the label of the bottle. A wine made
from the cabernet sauvignon grape will be rich and deep red and serve
it with red meats, especially pot roasts, steaks, ribs, and lamb.
Wines made from the Chardonnay grape, on the other hand, produce dry
white wines that go well with main courses made from fish, shellfish,
poultry, and veal. Wines made from the pinot noir grape will be red
but the cabernet sauvignon is not as light. Pinot noir wines are the
perfect complement to barbecued red meat and chicken. The gewürztraminer grape, native to Germany, produces dry white wines with exotic perfumes that make them perfect complements to Asian food.
Japanese and Thai dishes especially. If you plan to serve a vegeterian meal, go with a wine made from the Sauvignon blanc grape. Your
wine will be light and crisp and your vegeterian guests will love
it's aroma of grass and pea pods.

    Finally, you need to know where the wine came from, its country
of origin. And, even more important, the specific region within that
country. The Chablis region of France, for example, produces dry,
medium-bodied white wines, a Chablis is perfect with white seafoods
such as sole and halibut. The south of Italy produces some very dry
but light white wines. Which go well with virtually any salad which
you plan to serve before your entree. The Beaujolais region of France
produces exquisite light bodied red wines.

    Wine can be the world's most intimdating beverage. But you can
choose, from the hundreds of choices available, just the right wine
for just the right occassion, if you know something about the wine's
body, what the grape was, and the region in which it was produced.

1

2

3

4

5

COMMENTARY

1. Martin's opening paragraph is weak. It contains a thesis, the last sentence of the paragraph. However, it does not really engage the reader's interest.

2. Again, this paragraph lacks detail. Martin should describe some foods that go well with each of the three body types of wine. Readers would want to know this. The third sentence is a sentence fragment.

3. The transition from the preceding paragraph to this one is vague. The first sentence should read: You *also* need... The verbs in the third sentence are not parallel. The verb "serve" does not balance "will be" earlier in the sentence. Change "serve" to "will go well with..." The fifth sentence is awkwardly structured and unclear. The eighth sentence is a fragment. The word "vegeterian" is misspelled. The pronoun "it's" in the last sentence should be "its." A comma should follow "crisp." The paragraph is well developed.

4. This paragraph is not adequately developed. Martin should provide at least one more example of a region and the wine it produces. The second sentence is a fragment; the third is a run-on; the fourth is another fragment. The expression "light bodied" in the last line should be hyphenated.

5. Martin's concluding paragraph is weak. The word "intimdating" in the first sentence is misspelled, as is the word "occassion" in the second. The paragraph does summarize the body of the essay and reiterate the essay's main idea, but, like the opening paragraph, it is somewhat flat and dull.

Overall Comments

Martin has chosen a topic that would be interesting to most readers. He appears to know a lot about the topic, though more information could be provided on some of the points discussed.

The essay is well organized. Martin covers three points in three body paragraphs and provides separate introductory and concluding paragraphs. The introduction and conclusion are weak. Some of the body paragraphs are not developed in enough detail. Cohesion within the paragraphs is generally good; the link between paragraphs 2 and 3 needs to be clarified.

Martin has a few problems with sentence structure. He needs especially to review the sentence fragment. He must also revise his paper to catch spelling errors.

In its present form, then, Martin's essay has some major problems. A marker could not put a check mark beside at least eight of the items on the criteria list. If this were the first essay Martin wrote in his composition class, he might get a C. If it were written later in the semester, he would likely get a D from an easier marker, an F from a harder marker.

Look now at an improved, revised version of Martin's essay.

Choosing a Bottle of Wine

Martin G.
English 100

Planning a dinner party involves several difficult but crucial decisions. You must decide who you are going to invite and be confident that the guests will get along well. You must plan a menu which all of the guests will enjoy and appreciate. Finally, you must choose just the right wine to compliment the food you plan to serve. Choosing the right wine is usually the most difficult of the decisions you are going to have to make. You will choose your guests from a comparatively small pool of friends and prepare food you know how to cook and present effectively. But there are hundreds of different wines from a dozen different countries. How are you to know which wines will be the perfect complement to the food you serve? You need to follow a few basic guidelines when choosing the right wine.

    You first must decide if you want to serve a light, medium, or full-bodied wine. The wine's "body" is determined by its alcohol content, which is indicated on the label of the bottle. A light-bodied wine has an alcohol content of between eight and ten percent; a medium-bodied wine has an alcohol content of eleven or twelve percent; a full-bodied wine has an alcohol content of thirteen or fourteen percent. A light-bodied wine is best with light dishes, salads and desserts, for example. A full-bodied wine is the one to serve if your main course is rich and hearty; beef Wellington, baked salmon with stuffing, pasta with a rich cream or meat sauce, chicken breast stuffed with meat and/or cheese. A medium-bodied wine is best for dishes that are moderately rich; pasta primavera, most shellfish and white seafoods, chicken garnished with vegetables or citrus fruit.

    You also need to know something about the grapes from which wines are made, in order to make just the right choice for your guests. The name of the grape should be on the label of the bottle. A wine made from the cabernet sauvignon grape will be rich and deep red and serve it with red meats, especially pot roasts, steaks, ribs, and lamb. Wines made from the Chardonnay grape, on the other hand, produce dry white wines that go well with main courses made from fish, shellfish, poultry, and veal. Wines made from the pinot noir grape will be red, but lighter than those made from the cabernet sauvignon. Pinot noir wines are the perfect complement to barbecued red meat and chicken. The gewürztraminer grape, native to Germany, produces dry white wines with exotic perfumes that make them perfect complements to Asian food, Japanese and Thai dishes

1

2

3

COMMENTARY

1. This is a much better introductory paragraph. Martin uses an effective method, sometimes known as the "funnel opening." He begins with a broad statement related to his topic: the many decisions to make when planning a dinner party. He describes a few examples, then gradually funnels or narrows down his topic to one decision: choosing the right wine. This paragraph will engage the interest of most readers. The practical value of the essay—to provide useful information to its readers—is emphasized. The "who" in sentence two should be in objective case: "whom." The word "compliment" in sentence three should be "complement."

2. This is a well-written and well-developed body paragraph. Examples of the foods which go well with the wines are now provided. The semicolons in the fifth and sixth sentences should be changed to colons.

3. The faulty parallelism in sentence three has still not been corrected. The other errors have been corrected. This is now a well-written and well-developed body paragraph.

especially. If you plan to serve a vegetarian meal, go with a wine made from the Sauvignon blanc grape. Your wine will be light and crisp, and your vegetarian guests will love its aroma of grass and pea pods.

Finally, you need to know the wine's country of origin and, even more important, the specific region within that country. The Chablis region of France, for example, produces dry, medium-bodied white wines. A Chablis is perfect with white seafoods such as sole and halibut. The south of Italy produces some very dry but light white wines, which go well with virtually any salad you plan to serve before your entree. The Beaujolais region of France produces exquisite light-bodied red wines. Serve a Beaujolais with a grilled medium-rare filet mignon, garnished with peppers and brocolli, and your dinner guests will be dazzled by your savoir faire. The Bordeaux region of France, one of the most famous of all wine-producing districts, is renowned for its full-bodied red wines, ideal for red meats covered in rich sauces.

Wine can be the world's most intimdating beverage. But you can choose, from the hundreds of choices available, just the right wine for just the right occassion, if you know something about the wine's body, its grape, and the region in which it was produced.

COMMENTARY

4. This is a better paragraph than the earlier version. Another example has been added; one more is still needed to give the paragraph a strong sense of completion. The word "brocolli" in the sixth sentence is misspelled. In the fifth sentence, Martin has added a mention about the dinner guests, neatly establishing a link between this paragraph and the first.

5. This is an improved final paragraph. It is still a little flat and dull for so interesting a topic. There are still spelling errors in the first and second sentences. One more revision might produce a more effective conclusion.

Overall Comments

Martin has now brought his essay up to a B level. He still needs a more effective conclusion, and he still needs to correct a couple of errors in sentence structure and punctuation. The final version of Martin's essay follows.

Choosing a Bottle of Wine

Martin G.
English 101

Planning a dinner party involves several difficult but crucial decisions. You must decide whom you are going to invite and be confident that the guests will get along well. You must plan a menu that all of the guests will enjoy and appreciate. Finally, you must choose just the right wine to complement the food you plan to serve. Choosing the right wine is usually the most difficult of the decisions you are going to have to make. You will choose your guests from a comparatively small pool of friends and prepare food you know how to cook and present effectively. But there are hundreds of different wines from a dozen different countries. How are you to know which wines will be the perfect complement to the food you serve? You need to follow a few basic guidelines when choosing the right wine.

1

You first must decide if you want to serve a light, medium, or full-bodied wine. The wine's "body" is determined by its alcohol content, which is indicated on the label of the bottle. A light-bodied wine has an alcohol content of between eight and ten percent; a medium-bodied wine has an alcohol content of eleven or twelve percent; a full-bodied wine has an alcohol content of thirteen or fourteen percent. A light-bodied wine is best with light dishes—salads and desserts, for example. A full-bodied wine is the one to serve if your main course is rich and hearty: beef Wellington, baked salmon with stuffing, pasta with a rich cream or meat sauce, chicken breast stuffed with meat and/or cheese. A medium-bodied wine is best for moderately rich dishes: pasta primavera, most shellfish and white seafoods, chicken garnished with vegetables or citrus fruit.

2

You also need to know something about the grapes from which wines are made, in order to make just the right choice for your guests. The name of the grape should be on the label of the bottle. A wine made from the cabernet sauvignon grape will be rich and deep red and will go best with red meats, especially pot roasts, steaks, ribs, and lamb. Wines made from the Chardonnay grape, on the other hand, produce dry white wines that go well with main courses made from fish, shellfish, poultry, and veal. Wines made from the pinot noir grape will be red, but lighter than those made from the cabernet sauvignon. Pinot noir wines are the perfect complement to barbecued red meat and chicken. The gewürztraminer grape, native to Germany, produces dry white wines with exotic perfumes that make them perfect complements to Asian food, Japanese and Thai dishes especially. If

3

COMMENTARY

1. This is a clear, well-written introductory paragraph that engages the reader's interest and presents the essay's thesis.

2. This is an effective body paragraph with a clear topic sentence (the first) and good support for the topic sentence. The topic sentence is developed by the use of definitions and example. The semicolon errors have been corrected.

3. The faulty parallelism has been corrected. This paragraph has a clear topic sentence (the first) and good support for the topic sentence. Martin discusses five types of grapes and the foods that go with the wines made from each type.

you plan to serve a vegetarian meal, go with a wine made from the Sauvignon blanc grape. Your wine will be light and crisp, and your vegetarian guests will love its aroma of grass and pea pods.

Finally, you need to know where the wine's country of origin and, even more important, the specific region within that country. The Chablis region of France, for example, produces dry, medium-bodied white wines. A Chablis is perfect with white seafoods such as sole and halibut. The south of Italy produces some very dry but light white wines, which go well with virtually any salad you plan to serve before your entree. The Beaujolais region of France produces exquisite light-bodied red wines. Serve a Beaujolais with a grilled medium-rare filet mignon, garnished with peppers and broccoli, and your dinner guests will be dazzled by your savoir faire. The Bordeaux region of France, one of the most famous of all wine-producing districts, is renowned for its full-bodied red wines, ideal for red meats covered in rich sauces. If it is seafood with a rich sauce you plan to serve, look for a white wine that comes from the Rhone Valley.

Wine can be the world's most intimidating beverage. But you can choose, from the hundreds of choices available, just the right wine for just the right occasion, if you know something about the wine's body, its grape, and the region in which it was produced. With this knowledge, you can respond to your guests' compliments with the haughty demeanour of the wine connoisseur: "Oh, thank you. It's a light-bodied Chablis made from the Chardonnay. Don't you love its taste of tropical fruits with just that hint of spiciness!"

4. Martin has included one more example at the end of this paragraph, making for a fuller development of the topic sentence (the first). He has now discussed five wine regions and foods that go well with wine from each region. The word "broccoli" is now correctly spelled.

5. Martin has added some dialogue to his concluding paragraph. This makes it much more effective. He brings the guests back again, effectively linking his last paragraph to his first. This conclusion complements the essay's casual, informative tone.

Overall Comments

Most teachers would give this essay a top grade, an A or an A-. It conforms to all of the twenty-one items on the criteria list. It is interesting and informative. It has a strong, clear thesis. The body paragraphs have topic sentences and enough additional sentences to develop the topic sentences effectively. The writing is clear. The style is pleasing and sophisticated.

Three versions of another essay follow, with evaluative comments for each paragraph and a general overall comment at the end of each version. Again, read each version carefully and consider the marker's comments.

The Art of the Close Clean Shave

Don J.
English 100

You need the right equipment first of all to get a close clean shave. To get a close clean shave, a man will need a bar of soap. One of the brands which is one-third cold cream. Cold cream soaps do not dry the skin out as ordinary soap tends to do. Dove and Camay have moisurizing in cream in them but they are quite feminine. Look for an unscented moisturizing soap. He will need a face cloth or, even better, a buff puff. He will need a good-quality shave cream, preferably a gel. He will need a clean double-blade safety razor. Finally, he will need a moisurizer. An unscented one!

The shaver should not wash his face, he should scrub it. A face cloth works well as a face scrubber. A buff puff works better. A buff puff looks like a small hockey puck. It is made of rough nylon that really cleans the face. It removes all the dead skin cells, and exposes fresh skin. This is the easiest smoothest skin to shave.

The shaver should wash his face with the cold cream soap, leave the lather from the soap on his face, then scrub his lathered face about a hundred times with the buff puff, paying special attention to the shaving area. Then he should rinse his face off by placing it directly under the shower head so it collides with hot water.

Then you apply your shave cream or gel. More is not better; shaving creme should be applied sparingly. You should leave the creme on your face for a minute to really give your whiskers time to get soft.

The shaver must draw his razor in short gentle strokes across his face, rinsing excess lather from the razor with hot water after every two or three strokes, getting rid of the lather as he goes. The shaver must move his razor acorss his face in the same direction his whiskers lie. He must shave with the grain, so to speak. Many men, in an effort to get as close a shave as possible, shave against the grain. When they do this their beard and their razor are fighting against each other. When a man shaves against the grain of his beard, he risks cuts, bumps, and ingrown hairs.

After his beard has been smoothly shaved away, the shaver must rinse off all excess lather, particulaly that which collects around the ears. The shaver needs to dry off his face with a clean towel, and apply a light unscented moisturizer. The moisturizer will replenish and revitalize the skin. Alcohol-based aftershave lotions should be avoided which dry out the skin. Similarly, scented moisturizers usually contain alcohol, which cancels out the moisturizing benefits.

This is what you need to know to get a clean and a close shave.

COMMENTARY

1. Don jumps right into the body of his essay; he lacks any introduction. Even as a body paragraph, this one is weak. It lacks unity, drifting away from its topic sentence (the first), especially in the fifth and sixth sentences. The words "moisurizing/-er" are misspelled. The fifth sentence is full of careless errors. The third and last ones are fragments. Don has not proofread his paper carefully.

2. Sentence variety is needed in this paragraph. It begins with short, choppy sentences. No comma should come after "cells" in sentence six; it is not a compound sentence. The adjectives "easiest smoothest" in sentence seven are coordinate and should be separated with a comma. The paragraph is underdeveloped. Don needs to say enough about each stage of this process to enable his readers to perform it.

3. This and the preceding paragraph are on the same topic and should be joined. Two short paragraphs in a row often suggest a problem with structure.

4. Don has suddenly shifted his point of view from "the shaver" to "you." This is another underdeveloped paragraph. More than two sentences are needed to develop the topic sentence (the first). "Creme" is misspelled.

5. The topic sentence of this paragraph is well developed, but no transition links the paragraph to the preceding one. The first sentence is wordy and redundant. A spelling error occurs in the second sentence.

6. This paragraph begins with a good transitional phrase. Another careless typo, "particulaly," appears in the first sentence. A better sense of transition is needed between the first two sentences. Commas should be placed between the coordinate adjectives "light unscented." The fourth sentence contains a misplaced modifier: the clause "which dry out the skin" should go after "lotions," or the sentence should be revised altogether.

7. This is a perfunctory concluding paragraph. The point of view has been changed again. In such a light-hearted topic, a more imaginative conclusion, perhaps one that contains an anecdote, would be more effective.

Overall Comments

Don needs to proofread his work with much greater care before he hands it in. He needs better introductory and concluding paragraphs. Several of his paragraphs are not developed in enough detail. This topic lends itself to paragraphs developed by the use of anecdote, but Don has missed this opportunity.

Don's grammar, spelling, and punctuation are often shaky. His style is flat, the result, mainly, of poor sentence variety. In its present form, this essay would probably not get a passing grade.

Let's look now at the first revised version of Don's essay.

The Art of the Close Clean Shave

Don J.
English 100

It is really quite simple to get a close, clean shave. All you need is the right materials and the right technique. — 1

We begin with the equipment, the right tools for the job. To get a close clean shave, a man will need a bar of soap, one of the brands which is one-third cold cream; cold cream soaps do not dry the skin out as ordinary soap tends to do. He will need a face cloth or, even better, a buff puff. He will need a good-quality shave creme, preferably a gel. He will need a clean double-blade safety razor. Finally, he will need a moisurizer, preferably an unscented one. — 2

The best shaves occur not at the sink but in the shower. The face gets cleaner in the shower than at the sink, and a clean face is essential for a good shave. The steam from the shower will help moisten the man's beard, and help the whiskers stand up. The better the whiskers stand up; the closer the shave will be. — 3

The shaver should not wash his face, he should scrub it. A face cloth works well as a face scrubber; a buff puff works better. A buff puff looks like a small hockey puck and is made of rough nylon that cleans the face, removes all the dead skin cells, and exposes fresh skin, the easiest, smoothest skin to shave. The shaver should wash his face with the cold cream soap, leave the lather from the soap on his face, then scrub his lathered face about a hundred times with the buff puff, paying special attention to the shaving area. Then he should rinse his face off by placing it directly under the shower head so it collides with hot water. Hot water separates the whiskers and generates the steam that will keep the whiskers moist and vertical. — 4

The shaver then applies his shave cream or gel. More is not better; shaving cream should be applied sparingly. The shaver should leave the cream on his face for a minute to really give his whiskers time to prepare for their fate. Here, another advantage of shaving in the shower becomes obvious: the shaver can wash the rest of his body while he lets the lather soak into his face. — 5

COMMENTARY

1. Don has added an introductory paragraph and a thesis. It's better than no introduction at all, but it does not really engage the reader's interest or set a tone for the essay. There is a subject-verb agreement error in the second sentence: The verb "is" should be changed to "are."

2. This is a much better body paragraph. The unity problem of the first version has been corrected. The style could still be improved. "Creme" is misspelled, as is "moisurizer."

3. Don has added this paragraph, which improves the overall essay by adding an essential step to the process he is describing. There are some punctuation problems: The third sentence is not a compound sentence, so the comma after "beard" should be scrapped. The semicolon in the last sentence should be changed to a comma.

4. This is a much-improved body paragraph. Don has joined together the two paragraphs about the same topic. The topic sentence (the first) is now well developed using a combination of definition and detail. Don has improved his writing style with some sentence variety.

5. Don has re-established the correct point of view: the "you" of the earlier version is back to "the shaver." The paragraph is more fully developed. An additional sentence—the last one—has been added. The spelling errors have been corrected.

Finally, skin meets steel. The shaver must draw his razor in short gentle strokes across his face. Rinsing excess lather from the razor with hot water after every two or three strokes. The shaver must move his razor across his face in the same direction his whiskers lie. He must shave with the grain, so to speak. Many men, in an effort to get as close a shave as possible, shave against the grain. When they do this their beard and their razor are fighting against each other, just as a plane and a piece of wood would be if the carpenter planed against the grain of the wood. When a man shaves against the grain of his beard, he risks cuts, bumps, and ingrown hairs.

6

After his beard has been smoothly shaved away, the shaver must rinse off all excess lather, particulaly that which collects around the ears. Finally, the shaver needs to dry off his face with a clean towel and apply a light unscented moisturizer. The moisturizer will replenish and revitalize the skin. Alcohol-based after-shave lotions should be avoided because they dry out the skin.

7

Getting a close, clean shave is not rocket science. With the right equipment, the right preparation, and the right technique, any man can master this simple but satisfying art.

8

COMMENTARY

6. Using the cohesive word "finally," Don has now established a transition between this paragraph and the preceding one. He has eliminated the wordiness in the second sentence, but unfortunately he has made the third sentence a fragment. The careless spelling error has been corrected. Don has made the style of this paragraph more interesting by using the simile in sentence seven.

7. This paragraph could be developed in a bit more detail. There are still no commas between the coordinate adjectives in sentence two. The misspelling of "particulaly" has still not been corrected.

8. This is a better concluding paragraph. The thesis statement is effectively reiterated and, in the process, the body of the essay is summarized. It will still strike some readers as too short and abrupt.

Overall Comments

Don has certainly improved his essay. It is fairly informative and interesting, though an essay on a topic like this could also be quite entertaining which, in its present form, it is not. His introductory and concluding paragraphs could still be more effective, but at least he has made more of an effort to provide readers with a beginning and an end. His body paragraphs are better developed.

Don's grammar and sentence structure, while still shaky in a few places, are more solid. He has improved his style with better sentence variety and some figurative language. Don has probably brought his paper up to a C+ or a B- level.

Let's look now at the final version.

The Art of the Close Clean Shave

Don J.
English 100

My roommate shaves by washing his face with ordinary bar soap, leaving the lather from the soap on his face and shaving the lather off. Every morning, he emerges from the bathroom with tiny pieces of toilet paper stuck pathetically to tiny bleeding nicks on his face. One morning I counted seven of these makeshift bandages. Like many young men, my roommate has not yet mastered the fine art of shaving. This essay is for him and for his many brothers who can't quite get the hang of this most essential of male grooming rituals. It is really quite simple to get a close, clean—and safe—shave.

1

We begin with the equipment, the right tools for the job. To get a close clean shave, a man will need a bar of soap, one of the brands which is one-third cold cream; cold cream soaps do not dry the skin out as ordinary soap tends to do. He will need a face cloth or, even better, a buff puff. He will need a good-quality shave cream, preferably a gel. He will need a clean double-blade safety razor. Finally, he will need a moisturizer, preferably an unscented one.

2

The best shaves occur not at the sink but in the shower. The face gets cleaner in the shower than at the sink, and a clean face is essential for a good shave. The steam from the shower will help moisten the man's beard and help the whiskers stand up. The better the whiskers stand up, the closer the shave will be.

3

The shaver should not wash his face, he should scrub it. A face cloth works well as a face scrubber; a buff puff works better. A buff puff looks like a small hockey puck and is made of rough nylon that cleans the face, removes all the dead skin cells, and exposes fresh skin, the easiest, smoothest skin to shave. The shaver should wash his face with the cold-cream soap, leave the lather from the soap on his face, then scrub his lathered face about a hundred times with the buff puff, paying special attention to the shaving area. Then he should rinse his face off by placing it directly under the shower head so it collides with hot water. Hot water separates the whiskers and generates the steam that will keep the whiskers moist and vertical.

4

The shaver then applies his shave cream or gel. More is not better; shaving cream should be applied sparingly. The shaver should leave the cream on his face for a minute to really give his whiskers time to prepare for their fate. Here, another advantage of shaving in the shower becomes obvious: the shaver can wash the rest of his body while he lets the lather soak into his face.

5

COMMENTARY

1. The addition of the anecdote makes this a much more effective, even entertaining, introductory paragraph, one that does engage the reader's interest. The paragraph ends effectively with a short statement taken from the blueprint thesis in the second version.

2. Don has chosen to keep the four short, simple sentences at the end of the paragraph. They lack variety but they do help make the paragraph coherent. Repetition of sentence patterns is an effective way of establishing coherence within a paragraph, but it should not be overused.

3. Don has corrected the punctuation errors in the earlier version of this paragraph. Although this paragraph is quite short, it covers the information the readers need.

4. This is a well-developed paragraph full of interesting, specific detail supporting the topic sentence. Sentence structure is sound and variety is evident.

5. This is a fairly brief but effective paragraph. The step Don is describing is straightforward so a longer paragraph is not really necessary. Note the use of the colon in the last sentence to provide the explanation set up in the first half of the sentence.

Finally, skin meets steel. The shaver must draw his razor in short gentle strokes across his face, rinsing excess lather from the razor with hot water after every two or three strokes. The shaver must move his razor across his face in the same direction his whiskers lie. He must shave with the grain, so to speak. Many men, in an effort to get as close a shave as possible, shave against the grain. When they do this their beard and their razor are fighting against each other, just as a plane and a piece of wood would be if the carpenter planed against the grain of the wood. When a man shaves against the grain of his beard, he risks cuts, bumps, and ingrown hairs. 6

After his beard has been smoothly shaved away, the shaver must rinse off all excess lather, particularly that which collects around the ears. Even a company president loses dignity when he walks around with shaving cream stuck in his ear. Finally, the shaver needs to dry off his face with a clean towel and apply a light, unscented moisturizer. The moisturizer will replenish and revitalize the skin just as a cool glass of water revitalizes a body after a workout. Alcohol-based aftershave lotions should be avoided because they dry out the skin. Similarly, scented moisturizers usually contain alcohol, which cancels out the moisturizing benefits. 7

Getting a close, clean shave is not rocket science. With the right equipment, the right preparation, and the right technique, any man—even my roommate—can master this simple but satisfying art. 8

COMMENTARY

6. Don has corrected the sentence fragment, and now both the content and the style of this paragraph are effective. Notice how short the topic sentence (the first one) is. All the other sentences relate back to this sentence, establishing unity throughout the paragraph.

7. Don has added to this paragraph and has made it more interesting and readable, amusing even. He has added the joke about the company president and has also added a simile to the fourth sentence, which helps explain the effect of the moisturizer. He has inserted the comma between the coordinate adjectives.

8. Don has altered his concluding paragraph somewhat, including the phrase "even my roommate" in the first sentence. This is an effective technique in that it clearly and cleverly links his last paragraph back to his first. His last paragraph effectively summarizes the body of his essay and reiterates his thesis.

Overall Comments

Don has now improved his essay to the point where it is probably worth an A-, possibly even an A. Most markers would check-mark nearly all of the 21 items on the criteria list. The paper is entertaining and informative. The topic sentences in each paragraph are now quite well developed. Errors in grammar, spelling, and punctuation have been corrected. The style has been improved with better sentence variety and effective metaphors.

GLOSSARY

Abridged dictionary   one that does not include obsolete, archaic, or rarely used words.

Acknowledgement   credit given to the author of a quotation or idea used in an essay.

Active voice   verb form in which the subject, as opposed to the object, performs the action (i.e., "The Priest said a prayer," *not* "A prayer was said by the Priest").

Analogy   a comparison made with the subject of an essay to develop ideas to be used in that essay.

Anecdote   a brief story used to add interest to an informative or persuasive essay.

Antecedent   the noun that a pronoun refers back to.

Anthologized   refers to a poem, story, or essay that is printed in an "anthology," which is a book containing related works.

APA (American Psychological Association) method   a method, designed by an association of psychologists, of giving credit to original authors of quotes and ideas used in a research paper.

Bibliographies   a list at the end of an essay of all sources a writer has consulted.

Body paragraphs   paragraphs that follow the introductory paragraph and develop the essay's main idea.

Card catalogue   a list of all books contained in a library.

Case   the form (subjective, objective, or possessive) of a pronoun.

Cliché   a metaphor used so often that it has lost its original effect.

Coherence   the characteristic of a paragraph in which there is a smooth and logical connection between and among sentences.

Collective nouns   words such as "team," "orchestra," and "class" that refer to a common group of people.

Comma splice   (also called *run-on sentence*) a sentence error resulting from two sentences separated only by a comma.

Compare/contrast essay   a kind of informative essay that describes similarities and differences between two related objects or people.

Concise writing   writing that contains no unnecessary words.

Concluding paragraph   a paragraph that follows body paragraphs and that lets readers know that what was promised in the introductory paragraph has been delivered.

Conjunctive adverb   connecting word such as "however" and "therefore" that, when preceded by a semicolon, joins two sentences together.

Connotation   emotional meaning—what a word suggests or implies.

Content   the ideas, information, and arguments in an essay.

Coordinate adjectives   two words together modifying a noun and separated from each other by commas.

Coordinate conjunction   a short word ("and," "but," "or") that joins two sentences together when preceded by a comma.

Coordination   a method of combining sentences using coordinate conjunctions "and," "but," and "or."

Cumulative adjectives   two words together, the first of which modifies the second, which modifies a noun; they are not separated from each other by commas.

Dangling modifier   a phrase or clause that does not modify any noun in a sentence.

Database   information stored on a computer or computer system or network.

Date of access   the date, included in the Works Cited entry for an Internet document, on which the writer accessed that Internet document.

Denotation   the literal meaning of a word—what the dictionary says it means.

Dependent clause   a group of words that contains a subject and a verb but that cannot stand alone as a sentence. Also known as a *subordinate clause*.

Draft   a version of an essay before the essay is revised and complete.

Effects   a paragraph that describes the consequences, or results of the subject of the topic sentence.

Euphemisms   words or phrases that try to deflect complete truth and accuracy.

Expository essay   (same as *Informative essay*) informs readers about a subject using examples, details, definitions, comparisons, contrasts, causes, effects.

Expressive mode   a subcategory of written discourse that emphasizes the artistic aspect of language—includes creative writing such as poems and stories.

Faulty parallelism   characteristic of a sentence in which one of a series of phrases or clauses is not expressed in the same way as the others.

Feminine pronoun   "she," "her," or "hers."

Formal outline   a point-form list of ideas, arranged into a logical system of headings and subheadings, that will be developed in an essay.

Freewriting   brainstorming on paper to help a writer come up with ideas.

Gender-neutral plural pronoun pronouns such as "they" and "them," that could refer to men, to women, or to a combination of both.

Gender-specific noun word such as "fire*man*" or "actress" that refers specifically to either men or women.

Grammar the correct and appropriate arrangement of words to form sentences.

Homonyms words like "bear" and "bare" that sound the same but have different meanings.

Hyperbole exaggeration for rhetorical effect, not meant to be taken literally.

Indefinite pronoun words such as "each," "every," and "all" that identify unknown persons or things.

Independent clause a complete, properly structured sentence.

Informative essay see *Expository essay*.

Informative mode a subcategory of written discourse that presents factual information to the reader.

Internet 50 000 computer databases linked together.

Internet access number a number that helps Internet users retrieve a desired document.

Introductory paragraph one paragraph (in longer essays, more than one) that introduces an essay, usually stating the essay's topic and main idea.

Jargon specialized language shared by members of a profession or group.

Journal an inventory, written daily, of a writer's ideas, thoughts, questions, and observations.

Lack of unity describes a sentence that has two parts that do not seem related to each other.

Linear process a logical and deliberate step-by-step strategy by which an author composes an essay.

Linking verb a verb followed by a noun, pronoun, or adjective that establishes a relationship between the subject and the noun, pronoun, or adjective that follows.

Looping a second round of freewriting that focuses on key points emerging from the original freewriting.

Masculine pronoun "he," "him," or "his."

Metaphor a comparison between two objects to clarify the meaning of one or both objects and to add style to the writing.

Microfilm information such as back issues of magazines and newspapers stored on spools of film.

Misplaced modifier   a word, phrase, or clause that appears to modify something it does not.

Mixed metaphor   a blending together of two metaphors, creating a confusing effect for the reader.

MLA (Modern Language Association) method   a method, designed by an association of English educators, of giving credit to original authors of quotes and ideas used in a research paper.

Mnemonic device   a method used to remember something.

Non-restrictive clause   a word group *not* essential to the meaning of a sentence and, for that reason, separated from the sentence by commas.

Objective case   a class of pronouns that act as objects of verbs or prepositions.

On-line search   a search, done on a computer, for research material.

Organizational structure   the order in which the paragraph components of an essay are arranged.

Ostentatious synonyms   words that mean the same as a word you are replacing but that are too difficult or obscure for most readers to understand.

Paginated   the numbering of each page of a written document.

Parallel clauses   word groups with the same word patterns within a sentence.

Parallelism   the quality of two or more sentence elements or sentences being balanced.

Passive voice   a verb form in which object as opposed to subject performs the action. See *Active voice*.

Periodical index   a long alphabetical list in print or electronic form of articles available in magazines and journals.

Periodicals   weekly, monthly, bimonthly, or quarterly publications including popular magazines, specialized magazines, and academic journals.

Personification   a type of metaphor in which something not human is given human attributes.

Persuasive essay   a type of essay that tries to convince the reader that the writer's position on a controversial issue is valid.

Persuasive mode   a subcategory of written discourse that attempts to convince the reader that the writer's argument is valid.

Phantom verb   a verb without a subject, creating a confusing sentence.

Phonetically spelled word   a word spelled by "sounding out" the letters.

Phrase   a group of words that does not contain a subject or a verb and that modifies a noun or a verb.

Plagiarism failure to give credit to the author of a quote or idea, implying instead that the quote or idea is your own original work.

Preposition an often short word ("in," "on," "of," "to"), but sometimes longer word ("between"), that introduces a phrase that describes a noun or verb.

Pronoun a short word ("he," "him," "his") that stands in place of a noun.

Pronoun-antecedent agreement a grammatical principle that states that singular pronouns should identify singular nouns and plural pronouns should identify plural nouns.

Purpose the reason why a writer is writing a particular piece for a particular audience.

Recursive process the strategy of writing an essay in which the author does *not* work from an outline but develops content and shapes, revises, and refines the essay while writing drafts.

Redundancy useless repetition.

Reference book books such as encyclopedias or dictionaries that contain general information about a wide variety of topics.

References a list at the end of an essay of all sources a writer has cited within an essay.

Reiterate to restate using different words.

Restrictive clause a word group essential to the meaning of a sentence and so *not* separated from the sentence by commas.

Revision literally "reseeing"; rewriting a draft of an essay.

Rhetorical context refers to the language appropriate to the topic, audience, and purpose of a piece of writing.

Rhetorical modes the three subcategories into which written discourse can be divided.

Run-on sentence sentence error resulting from two sentences separated only by a comma. Also called *comma splice*.

Scratch outline a point-form list of ideas to be developed in an essay.

Secondary sources books, journals, magazines, and databases that contain information you might use in a research paper.

Sentence fragment a group of words punctuated like a sentence but not forming a complete sentence.

Sentence pattern the order of arrangement of the components of a sentence.

Sentence variety describes writing that uses sentences of differing lengths and structures.

Simile a type of metaphor that uses "like" or "as" to compare two things.

Spell check feature on most word-processing programs that allows writer to check the spelling of words used.

Stereotype a fixed, often biased, impression of a person or group.

Style the choice of words and sentence structures and use of figurative language to add pizzazz and flavour to writing; also, the level of vocabulary, the length, complexity, and structure of sentences that a writer uses.

Subjective case a class of pronouns that act as subjects of verbs.

Subordinate clause a group of words that contains a subject and a verb but that can not stand alone as a sentence. Also known as a *dependent clause*.

Subordinate conjunction a conjunction such as "when," "if," "while," "because," etc., that makes a clause subordinate to or dependent on the main clause of the sentence.

Subordination a method of combining sentences using subordinate conjunctions such as "because," "since," and "although" or relative pronouns "who," "whose," "that," and "which."

Synonyms two or more words with essentially the same meaning.

Syntax the way in which words are ordered in a sentence.

Thesis central or controlling idea of an informative or persuasive essay.

Tone refers to the attitude, ranging from light to formal, a piece of writing conveys.

Topic sentence a sentence that contains the paragraph's main idea.

Transitional expression a word or phrase that establishes a connection between sentences or paragraphs.

Transitional sentence usually the first sentence of a paragraph; it establishes connection with the last sentence of the previous paragraph.

Unabridged dictionary one that contains all the words in a particular language.

Unity the quality of a paragraph in which all sentences relate to one topic.

Works Cited the name of the list of sources (in the MLA method) used by a writer and mentioned in the text of his or her essay.

ANSWER KEY TO OBJECTIVE ASSIGNMENTS

Note: Writers can usually choose from a variety of effective methods for expressing themselves clearly and effectively. For this reason, answers are not provided for those assignments and exercises in *Lessons in Essay Writing* that have several acceptable answers. Your teacher will help you make sure you are on the right track with subjective questions and assignments.

Titles of works that would normally be italicized in published material are shown in the answer key with underlining. You may own a computer that provides an italic face, and if you have used that instead of underlining, the answer is still correct.

Lesson Three

ASSIGNMENT 3-1

1. Gittings has this to say about the sources of "La Belle Dame Sans Merci":

   > Wordsworth for the cadence of the poem, Coleridge for its nightmare quality, Spencer for its medieval setting, Burton for the melancholy of its hero, all contribute to, but none account for the intensity and underlying depth of a poem which brought Keats's darkest and most fundamental experiences to the surface. (Gittings 303)

   Works Cited

   Gittings, John. <u>John Keats</u>. Boston: Little, Brown, 1968.

2. As more and more athletes from what was once East Germany come forward with their confessions, the Olympic Committee "will be under increased pressure to review world records in several events" (Wasserman 97).

   Works Cited

   Wasserman, Eliot. <u>The Steroid Conspiracy</u>. 2nd ed. Vancouver: Paw Books, 1993.

ASSIGNMENT 3-2

1. Lu also believes that more research "which critiques portrayals of Basic Writers as belonging to an abnormal—traumatized or underdeveloped state" (910) is urgently needed.

   Works Cited

   Lu, Min-Zhan. "Conflict and Struggle: The Enemies or Pre-Conditions of Basic Writing." <u>College English</u> 54 (1992): 887-913.

2. Authorities in most African countries are reluctant to reveal accurate information, but there can be little doubt the infection rate is now higher than in any other continent (Kono 18).

Works Cited

Kono, Samual. "AIDS in Africa." <u>Journal of the World Health Society</u> 2.2 (1991): 3-21.

ASSIGNMENT 3-3

Davis and Strawberry wanted to be teammates ever since they played ball together as children on the playgrounds of Los Angeles (Fimrite 20).

Works Cited

Fimrite, Ron. ""Dodger Blues." <u>Sports Illustrated</u> 28 September 1992: 18-21.

ASSIGNMENT 3-4

The <u>Encyclopaedia of Religion and Ethics</u> defines confirmation as "an act, closely connected with baptism, in which prayer for the Holy Spirit is joined with some ceremony, through which the gift of the Spirit is believed to be conferred ("Confirmation").

Works Cited

"Confirmation." <u>Encyclopedia of Religion and Ethics</u>. 1971 ed.

ASSIGNMENT 3-5

Plath is uncompromising, explicitly comparing her father to a Nazi:

> Every woman adores a Fascist,
> The boot in the face, the brute
> Brute heart of a brute like you. (48-50)

Works Cited

Plath, Sylvia. "Daddy." <u>The HBJ Anthology of Literature.</u> Eds. Jon C. Stott, Raymond E. Jones, and Rick Bowers. Toronto: Harcourt Brace Jovanovich, 1993. 620-623.

ASSIGNMENT 3-6

Interestingly, director Tomas Pune sees Galileo not as a victim but as the architect of his own downfall (<u>Heavenly Bodies</u>).

Works Cited

<u>Heavenly Bodies</u>. Videocassette. Dir. Tomas Pune. Skywalker Productions, 1985.

ASSIGNMENT 3-7

Alcock makes a valid point when he notes that "if beach volleyball and the modern pentathlon can be olympic sports, why should ballroom dancing be excluded?" (65)

Works Cited

Alcock, Ralph. "New Events for the Atlanta Olympics." Onsport 2395.01 (28 Feb. 94): 24 pp. On-line. Internet. 10 June 94.

Lesson Four

ASSIGNMENT 4-1

1. Kirby and Ridge (1993) also believe that violence on television programs and films does influence teenage behaviour. Studies that indicate otherwise, they claim, are flawed because "studies of teen violence will refuse to make a connection between watching violence and committing violence unless 95% or more violent acts can be shown to be influenced by a violent film or TV program" (p. 201).

References

Kirby, H. & Ridge, M. (1993). Young offenders. Vancouver: Pever Press.

2. Needlecraft designs or "samplers" are very collectible now, ones made in the eighteenth century fetching prices at auction up to $600 (Watson, 1993, p. 137).

References

Watson, M. (1993). Attic treasures (2nd ed.). London: Leisure Books.

ASSIGNMENT 4-2

1. Lu (1992) also believes that more research "which critiques portrayals of Basic Writers as belonging to an abnormal-traumatized or underdeveloped state" (p. 910) is urgently needed.

References

Lu, M. (1993). Conflict and struggle: The enemies or preconditions of writing. College English, 45, 887-913.

2. Tobin and Tamsin (1993) argue that Kennedy's intervention will backfire, and that "public opinion will be against an American outsider criticizing Canadian logging practices" (p. 91).

References

Tobin, R. & Tamsin, B. The fight for the Carmanah Valley. Friends of the Earth Review, 7(3), 87-91.

ASSIGNMENT 4-3

Davis and Stawberry wanted to be teammates ever since they played ball together as children on the playgrounds of Los Angeles (Fimrite, 1992, p. 20).

References

Fimrite, R. (1992, September 28). Dodger blues. <u>Sports Illustrated</u>, pp. 18-21.

ASSIGNMENT 4-4

The <u>Encyclopaedia of Religion and Ethics</u> defines confirmation as "an act, closely connected with baptism, in which prayer for the Holy Spirit is joined with some ceremony, through which the gift of the Spirit is believed to be conferred" (Confirmation, 1971).

References

Confirmation (1971). <u>Encyclopaedia of Religion and Ethics</u> (Vol. 4, p. 1). New York: Scribeners.

ASSIGNMENT 4-5

Interestingly, Tomas Pune (1995) sees Galileo not as a victim but as the architect of his own downfall.

References

Pune, T. (Director). (1985). <u>Heavenly bodies</u> (Cassette Recording). Vancouver: Skywalker Productions.

Lesson Seven

ASSIGNMENT 7-1

The first sentence of the paragraph is the topic sentence. The first word in this sentence ("Another") establishes coherence between this paragraph, the paragraph that precedes it, and the essay's thesis. The key word in the topic sentence is "episode"; the other sentences all relate to the episode described. Coherence is also established by the repetition of another key word, "Athens" or "Athenian," mentioned in the second, third, and fourth sentences. Another key word is "soldier," also referred to as "messenger" and by the pronouns "he" and "his." "Unfortunately" is a transitional expression, signalling a change in focus from one sentence to the next.

Lesson Eleven

ASSIGNMENT 11-4

1. Change *canaliculated* to **grooved**.
2. Change *cacography* to **bad handwriting**.
3. Change *ensanguined* to **blood-stained**.
4. Change *immitigable* to **firm** or **rigid**.
5. Change *panegyric* to **speech**.

Lesson Twelve

ASSIGNMENT 12-1

1. Dr. Smyth certainly gave John and (me, him, her, you, them) a difficult assignment.
2. The community has accepted my family and (me, him, her, you, them).
3. The university admitted Charlotte but not (me, him, her, you, them).

ASSIGNMENT 12-2

1. At the Olympic Games in Lillehammer, my sister bought some wonderful pins for my brother and (me, him, her, you, them).
2. She says she will go to the games in Atlanta with her boyfriend and (you, her, me, them).
3. It makes no difference to my friend or (you, her, me, them).

ASSIGNMENT 12-3

1. Eric is quite a bit taller than (you, I, she, he, they).
2. She always liked her own family more than (you, I, me, she, him, he, her, they, them).
3. Most students didn't do as well on the test as (you, I, she, he, they).

ASSIGNMENT 12-4

1. The big winner was (you, she, he, I).
2. The detective is convinced that the murderer is (you, she, he, I).
3. The only one committed to the relationship is (I, he, she).

ASSIGNMENT 12-5

"Who" is the subjective case of the pronoun, and "whom" is the objective case. In sentence 1, "whom" is correct because it is the object of the verb "watched." In sentence 2, "whom" is correct because it is the object of the preposition "to." In sentence 3, "whom" is incorrect because the subjective case (who) is needed to be the subject of the verb "would be."

ASSIGNMENT 12-7

1. Your essay *is* interesting. The ideas in your essay *are* interesting.
2. Paragraph development *is* discussed in Chapter Two. Strategies for paragraph development *are* discussed in Chapter Two.
3. Your readers *need* to be stimulated. The interest of your readers *needs* to be stimulated.
4. My friends all *have* cars. One of my friends *owns* a Porsche.
5. An alliance *is* dangerous. An alliance with certain countries *is* dangerous.

ASSIGNMENT 12-8

1. Neither of these teachers *was* willing to help me.
2. Every one of my teachers *has* been willing to help me.
3. Most of your education *is* going to occur outside a classroom.
4. Most of your teachers *are* going to try to give you a good education.
5. None of the police officers *understands* why the Young Offenders Act can't be modified.

ASSIGNMENT 12-11

1. Born and raised in Rumania, I had difficulty learning English.
2. Flying over the Strait of Georgia, we saw Salt Spring Island shimmering in the early morning sun.
3. By attending college, we often achieve self-knowledge.
4. With a budget that mushroomed to two hundred million dollars, Waterworld drew the curiosity of the public, despite what the critics had to say.
5. Baseball fans were devastated by the death of Mickey Mantle, even though he was not always the greatest role model.

Lesson Thirteen

ASSIGNMENT 13-1

The list would include most words that contain "man": manpower, man-hours, foreman, man-made, marksman. It would also include words that use the prefix "ess": actress, seamstress, sculptress, etc.

ASSIGNMENT 13-2

1. Through their work, novelists try to give us some insight into human existence.
2. The ceremony was held at the tomb of the unknown soldier who sacrificed his life to preserve the freedom of his country.

3. An alternate juror will be assigned to the case. She or he will have to take a leave of absence from work, and she or he will have to agree to be sequestered, possibly for as long as three months.

4. Serious marathon runners will train at least five, usually six days a week. Usually, on those days they train, they will run twice, for at least fifteen kilometres, once in the morning and once in the evening. Obsessive marathoners will train seven days a week, and will run fifteen kilometres three times a day. Such intense training can pay dividends. Runners who train three times a day, seven days a week, can achieve their personal best within two months. Runners who train five days a week, twice a day, will take four months to reach their top fitness level. Without a rest day, however, runners increase twofold their risk of an injury serious enough to cause them to miss the race they are training for.

Lesson Fourteen

ASSIGNMENT 14-3

1. If a word ends in a "y," change the "y" to an "i" before adding a suffix: *beauty* becomes *beautiful*; *tricky* becomes *trickiest*. **Exception 1**: If a vowel comes before the "y," the "y" is not changed to "i." *Joy* becomes *joyful*. **Exception 2**: If the suffix is "ing," the "y" does not change. *Marry* becomes *marrying*.

2. If a word ends in a vowel-consonant pair, and if the accent is on the last syllable of the word, double the consonant before adding a suffix. *Forget* becomes *forgetting*; *refer* becomes *referred*.

3. If a word ends in a vowel-consonant pair, and if the accent is not on the last syllable, do not double the final consonant. *Abandon* becomes *abandoned*; *alter* becomes *altering*.

Lesson Fifteen

ASSIGNMENT 15-1

1. a. We planned to serve key lime pie, but my brother is allergic to citrus fruit.
   b. Tyson will be fighting an inexperienced opponent, and experts are predicting an early knockout.

2. a. Your essay should be double-spaced and should have one-and-a-half-inch margins on both sides of the page.
   b. He knew he had a strong case but decided not to press charges.

3. a. We couldn't serve key lime pie, because my brother is allergic to citrus fruit.

b. My uncle, who played basketball in college, taught me how to dribble behind my back.

4. a. Your essay should be double-spaced; it should also have one-and-a-half-inch margins on both sides of the page.

b. She decided to retire early; she could not handle the stress any longer.

ASSIGNMENT 15-2

The error is the comma before the conjunctive adverb "therefore." A comma is not a strong enough pause before a conjunctive adverb when that adverb is being used to join the two sentences together. A semicolon is required:

Ellis did not hand in two of his assignments; therefore, he did not get a passing grade in his sociology course.

A coordinate conjunction such as "and" could be used with the comma:

Ellis did not hand in two of his assignments, and he did not get a passing grade in his sociology course.

ASSIGNMENT 15-3

1. In 1992, Windsor Castle, the Queen's house on the banks of the Thames, was damaged by a serious fire.
2. Tia Maria, Drambuie, Benedictine, and Curacao are among the most popular liqueurs and are sold throughout the world.
3. The silver that is mined in Mexico is considered superior to the silver mined in Colorado.
4. The tern is a slender, gull-like bird, and with its long pointed wings and a deeply notched tail, it flies with grace and strength.
5. The upper limit of the biosphere, the part of earth where life can exist, is about 9000 metres above sea level; the lower limit is approximately 3000 metres beneath the surface of the ocean.

ASSIGNMENT 15-8

The sentence should be punctuated as follows:

Analyzing Keats's sonnet "Bright Star," Foster writes: "the repetition of the adverb, 'still,' is typical of Keats's style."

The title of the poem should be in quotation marks because it is a minor title. Quotation marks should be around all the material after the colon because this is a direct quotation from Foster's analysis. The word "still" is also a quotation, but it has to be in single quotation marks to distinguish it from the Foster quotation; it is a quotation within a quotation.

ASSIGNMENT 15-9

1. A portion of the play—the third scene of the final act, to be precise—was excluded to meet the two-hour time limit.

2. The anteater's tongue is covered with sticky saliva, which allows it to trap ants, termites, and other insects on which it feeds.

3. Dave's new interest is cybernetics, the science that, among other things, compares brain functions to the functions of machines, especially computers.

4. France lost Alsace and Lorraine to Germany in 1871 after a war in which the Germans, who were better prepared than the French, won nearly every battle.

5. The greyhound, wolfhound, and deerhound hunt by sight; the bloodhound, foxhound, and beagle hunt by scent.

6. Diabetics lack insulin, which controls the supply of sugar from the blood to the muscles; however, with proper insulin injections, diabetics can live a normal life.

7. Film adaptations of novels are usually disappointing, but the film version of Kinsella's Field of Dreams is better than the book.

8. Since the beginning of the century, the Nobel Prize has been awarded to men and women for outstanding contributions to the following fields: physics, chemistry, medicine, literature, peace, and economics.

9. As T.S. Eliot says in "Little Gidding," one of the poems in his Four Quartets: "What we call the beginning is often the end / And to make an end is to make a beginning."

10. Originally the word "tycoon," from the Japanese "taikun," referred to the commander-in-chief of the Japanese army, but now it's used, often in a derogatory sense, to describe a powerful, influential businessperson.

Lesson Sixteen

ASSIGNMENT 16-1

1. The separatist movement will lose some of its momentum if the Quebec Nordiques win the Stanley Cup.

2. Red Deer is located in the rich farmland midway between Calgary and Edmonton, a location that enhanced its development as an agricultural service and distribution centre.

3. Many comedians, including Rick Moranis, Martin Short, and John Candy, who got their start on SCTV, went on to star in American films.

4. William Beer, a dentist by profession, helped popularize lacrosse, spearheading a drive, in 1867, to have lacrosse accepted as Canada's national game.

5. After the Second World War, the demand for public education increased dramatically, mainly as a result of the baby boom.

ASSIGNMENT 16-2

1. Cats have excellent vision; they can see as well at night as they can during the day.

2. Leonard Cohen was an influential song writer, especially during the 1960s, when his songs were recorded by artists in several different countries.

3. A contract is an agreement between two people to allow for the exchange of goods and services. One person provides a product or a service, and the other person pays for it.

ASSIGNMENT 16-3

1. A black hole is a star that has so strong a gravitational force that nothing, including light, can escape from it.

2. A stable nuclide is one that has nuclear forces that are so strong that no particles escape from the nucleus.

ASSIGNMENT 16-4

1. With hundreds of tourists from all over the world enjoying the innovative architecture, the excellent art gallery, and the variety of shops, it is not surprising the streets of Vancouver are crowded.

2. Astronomers can study the outer layers of the sun and its corona when the light from the sun is obscured by the moon during an eclipse, and these astronomers are eager to travel across the world to do so.

3. An employer who refuses to pay minimum wage is guilty of unfair labour practice.

ASSIGNMENT 16-5

1. Newgate Prison was destroyed in the Great Fire of 1666 and was not rebuilt until 1778, only to be destroyed by fire again during the Gordon Riots of 1780.

2. People suffering from hypothermia become lethargic and eventually unconscious, and to recover, they need blankets and warm, non-alcoholic liquids.

3. Creon thought Polynices was a traitor, and refused to give him a state funeral, but Polynices's sister Antigone defied Creon and buried her brother with full military honours.

ASSIGNMENT 16-6

1. The Canadian dollar is weak compared with the American dollar, so it is economical for film companies to shoot feature films in Canada.
2. The forests on Texada Island have been cut down, and now the Island's economy depends on the mining of limestone.
3. The hawk is a diurnal bird of prey, but is not as common on the West Coast as is the eagle.

Lesson Seventeen

ASSIGNMENT 17-1

1. A "hand" is equal to four inches and is a unit of measure for calculating the height of horses.
2. A heat pump can save money in the long run, but it is costly to install.
3. The hemp plant is native to Asia, and it is now cultivated widely because of its strong fibre.

ASSIGNMENT 17-2

1. The Hippopotamus, which lives in herds, can be found throughout most of Africa.
2. Shrove Tuesday, the day to "shrive" or go to confession, is the day before Lent.
3. Archaeologists can use radiocarbon dating to gauge the radioactivity of organic materials and estimate the age of objects that were made 50 000 years ago.

Lesson Eighteen

ASSIGNMENT 18-3

1. She arrived dressed in jeans and a T-shirt and all the other women were dressed in suits.
2. Sports psychologists feel that some athletes take steroids not so much because they crave victory but because they have low self-esteem.
3. By the end of the movie, the main character has become quite unstable, losing his identity and, ultimately, committing suicide.
4. The company would either go bankrupt or be saved by a leveraged buyout.
5. You will write two kinds of exams in this course: subjective exams with a requirement to write essays and objective exams with a multiple-choice format.

6. Alan is planning to attend the local two-year college, Chris is going straight to the local university, while Jenny has chosen to work in her mother's business.

7. My essay will explore this question: Do humans have language because they can think, or can they think because they have language?

8. Literature can be entertaining, it can give us insight into human experience, and it displays the artistic dimension of language.

9. While he was Secretary General of the United Nations, Dag Hammarskjold worked tirelessly for peace in the Middle East and the Congo, and he was awarded the Nobel Prize for peace in 1962.

10. Under Shaughnessy's leadership, the CPR not only expanded its rail lines but also developed successful shipping and mining interests.

ANSWER KEY TO SUPPLEMENTARY EXERCISES

Note: Either italic type or underlining is a correct usage for the titles that are normally italicized in published material.

Lesson One

2. Identify the dominant rhetorical mode of the following essay topics. Place an "I" in the blank to indicate informative mode, a "P" to indicate persuasive mode, and an "E" to indicate expressive mode.

   a. Describe how the Trudeau government responded to the FLQ Crisis. I

   b. Do you think the Trudeau government's response to the FLQ Crisis was reasonable, too soft, or unnecessarily harsh? Support your answer. P

   c. Compare and contrast the personalities and political ideologies of Marx and Engels. I

   d. The fur traders of New France exploited the Native population. Discuss. P

   e. Where do you go to "get away from it all" and think about issues important to you? Describe the landscape and the surroundings of your "getaway" spot. E

   f. Compare and contrast cubism and post-impressionism. I

   g. Describe and explain the effects on a child's personality of three methods of parenting. I

   h. Was Dutch colonialism beneficial to Indonesians? P

   i. Describe three characteristics often found within dysfunctional families. I

   j. Windows '95 is not any better than the Mac software developed in the late 80s. P

Lesson Three

1. a. In an early article about Mahler's work, Cook argued that the composer's music was seriously flawed by "the unfortunate debt he owes to banal songs sung in Viennese beer halls" ("Popular Appeal" 46). But in his recent biography of Mahler, Cook has toned down the criticism and claims that Mahler "deserves credit for trying to write music which would have widespread appeal" (Life 321).

   b. There are, however, some educators who continue to insist that IQ tests are "accurate predictors of academic success" (Levin 81).

c. The complex interrelationship among the proteins, carbohydrates, and fats the body ingests is not yet completely understood, but it is clear that they do not function independently. Low-fat complex carbohydrates are the current darling of nutrition fanatics, but

> if the body ingests more carbohydrates than it needs, the excess will be stored as fat. Similarly, if the body ingests too much protein, but not enough carbohydrate, some of the amino acids that protein has produced will be converted into carbohydrate. (Davis 79).

2. Works Cited

"Aerobics." The Encyclopedia of Sport. 1994 ed.

Anderson, D.C., C.R. Crowell, Martin Donan, and G.S. Howard. "Performance Posting, Goal Setting, and Activity-Contingent Praise as Applied to a University Hockey Team." Journal of Applied Psychology 73 (1988): 87-95.

Atkinson, J.W. and John Raynor, eds. Motivation and Achievement. New York: Halstead.

Bar-Eli, M., N., Levy-Kolker, G. Tenenbaum, and Robert Weinberg. "Effects of Goal Difficulty on Performance of Aerobic, Anaerobic and Power Tasks in Laboratory and Field Settings." Journal of Sport Behaviour 16 (1993): 17-32.

Cox, R.M. Sport Psychology: Concepts and Applications. 3rd ed. Madison, WI: Brown and Benchmark, 1994.

Gould, D. "Goal Setting for Peak Performance." Applied Sport Psychology: Personal Growth to Peak Performance. 2nd ed. Ed. J.M. Williams. Mountain View, CA: Mayfield, 1993. 158-169.

Martens, R. Coaches Guide to Sport Psychology. Champagne, IL: Human Kinetics, 1987.

"Motivation." The Encyclopedia of Sport. 1994 ed.

Norbert, Mary. "Motivational Strategies for a New Diet and Exercise Program." Fitness World February 1994: 35-46.

Pemberton, C., and P.J. McSwegin. "Goal Setting and Motivation." Journal of Physical Education, Recreation, and Dance. 60.1 (1989): 39-41.

Singer, R.N., M. Murphey, and L. Tennant, eds. Handbook of Research on Sport Psychology. New York: Macmillan, 1994.

Weinberg, S. "Motivating Athletes Through Goal Setting." Journal of Physical Education, Recreation, and Dance. 53.9 (1982): 46-48.

Lesson Four

1. a. In an early article about Mahler's work, Cook (1975) argued that the composer's music was seriously flawed by "the unfortunate debt he owes to banal songs sung in Viennese beer halls" (p. 46). But in his recent biography of Mahler, Cook (1992) has toned down the criticism and claims that Mahler "deserves credit for trying to write music which would have widespread appeal" (p. 321).

    b. There are, however, some educators who continue to insist that IQ tests are "accurate predictors of academic success" (Levin, 1993, p. 81).

    c. The complex interrelationship among the proteins, carbohydrates, and fats the body ingests is not yet completely understood, but it is clear that they do not function independently. Low-fat complex carbohydrates are the current darling of nutrition fanatics, but

    > if the body ingests more carbohydrates than it needs, the excess will be stored as fat. Similarly, if the body ingests too much protein, but not enough carbohydrate, some of the amino acids that protein has produced will be converted into carbohydrate. (Davis, 1993, p. 79).

2. References

    Aerobics. (1994). The encyclopedia of sport. London: Perval.

    Anderson, D.C., Crowell, C.R., Donan, M. and Howard, G.S. (1988). Performance posting, goal setting, and activity-contingent praise as applied to a university hockey team. Journal of Applied Psychology, 73, 87-95.

    Atkinson, J.W. and Raynor, J.O. (Eds.), (1974). Motivation and achievement. New York: Halstead.

    Bar-Eli, M., Levy-Kolker, N., Tenenbaum, G., and Weinberg, R.S. (1993). Effects of goal difficulty on performance of aerobic, anaerobic and power tasks in laboratory and field settings. Journal of Sport Behaviour, 16, 17-32.

    Cox, R.M. (1994). Sport psychology: Concepts and applications (3rd. ed.), Madison, WI: Brown and Benchmark.

    Gould, D. (1993). Goal setting for peak performance. In J.M. Williams (Ed.), Applied sport psychology: Personal growth to peak performance (2nd ed. pp. 158-169), Mountain View, CA: Mayfield.

    Martens, R. (1987). Coaches guide to sport psychology. Champagne, IL: Human Kinetics.

    Motivation. (1994). The encyclopedia of sport. London: Perval.

    Norbert, M. (1994, February). Motivational strategies for a new diet and exercise program. Fitness World 5, 35-46.

Pemberton, C., & McSwegin, P.J. (1989). Goal setting and motivation. Journal of Physical Education, Recreation, and Dance, 60(1), 39-41.

Singer, R.N., Murphey, M., & Tennant, L.K. (Eds.), (1994). Handbook of research on sport psychology. New York: Macmillan.

Weinberg, S. (1982). Motivating athletes through goal setting. Journal of Physical Education, Recreation, and Dance, 53(9), 46-48.

Lesson Twelve

1. When painted, your car (house, etc.) will get a better price.
2. After waiting for over an hour, we were relieved when the concert finally began.
3. I was sorry one leg was not original because the antique was interesting.
4. The decision was not an easy one for Raj and me to make.
5. Lincoln, not Mckinley, was the President whom John Wilkes Booth assassinated.
6. Chrétien is one Prime Minister whom I think history will treat kindly.
7. I had to go along with the majority of the group who enjoy camping more than I (do).
8. Neither the senator nor the Member of Parliament on the committee is going to vote in favour of the bill.
9. A sentence fragment is a group of words that is missing a subject or a verb.
10. Every one of the players promises to vote against strike action.
11. The happiness of the children depends on which parent is going to get custody.
12. To survive a winter in Winnipeg, warm clothing and patience are essential.
13. Each of the students plans to bring along enough money to buy jewellery.
14. Fitch and Sons is a good place to buy fishing equipment.
15. Neither of them is willing to take the blame.
16. His so-called proof about the existence of UFOs has not convinced me.
17. A loaf of bread and jug of wine are essential for a romantic picnic.
18. In every town in the country, the candidate gave the same speech opposing Quebec separation.
19. I gave my old copy of the text, with all of the exercises completed, to my friend.
20. I thought I might be fired after I refused to pour, into their own mugs, coffee for the truckers.

21. On Friday, the professor collected all of the assignments about the civil war.

22. You can't take a suitcase that won't fit into the overhead compartment on the plane.

23. The bicycle we found at the dump can easily be repaired, even though it is missing its handle bars.

24. While trying to sneak into the house past curfew, I knocked over a vase which crashed to the floor.

25. An old man, whom I had never seen before, accompanied my wife.

26. Steve blamed Jennifer and me for his failing the exam, claiming we had not helped him study enough.

27. Nearly every Sunday afternoon, he and I play golf together.

28. The counsellor helped convince Raj and me to apply for admission to the Faculty of Engineering.

29. So many battered women feel there is no one who cares, no one whom they can turn to for help.

30. Alberta produces more oil than we (do), but we lead the country in agricultural production.

Lesson Fourteen

1. Her absence had a detrimental effect on my outlook on life.

2. When we analyze poetry in my English class, I'm always surprised by students' comments.

3. He apologized for the inconvenience, but I was still unhappy about the delay.

4. According to the college calendar, there are still ninety days of classes left.

5. Eighteen parking spaces have been allotted to staff, which is more than necessary.

6. Voting, I argued, is not a privilege but a right.

7. The professors on this campus have so many idiosyncrasies, it's a wonder we pay attention to them.

8. We will cover the rules of grammar in this course.

9. In Hong Kong, you can buy good jewellery for half the price you would pay here.

10. Mortgage rates will have to decline another point before we can afford to buy a house.

11. Parents always seem to embarrass their teenage children.

12. After my ballet class, my muscles are sore.

13. In February, they celebrate their ninth wedding anniversary.

14. In Flin Flon, there is a serious shortage of physicians.

15. It was a difficult manoeuvre, but its success would ensure victory.

16. Hamlet promises his father he will seek vengeance.

17. Elderly people are susceptible to colds and the flu.

18. The RCMP supersedes the local police in dealing with interprovincial crime.

19. She wrote me an outstanding letter of recommendation, but I still did not get an interview.

20. My niece is eligible for unemployment insurance, but she is reluctant to apply for it.

21. Sillitoe's The Loneliness of the Long-Distance Runner is not on our reading list.

22. He has a tendency to exaggerate, so he does not have a lot of close friends.

23. Iago deceives Othello right from the start of the play.

24. Every conceivable treatment was tried, but nothing seemed to work.

25. She is a business major, so they are suited to each other.

26. They very coolly entered the bank and produced their weapons.

27. The sweater was made of coarse cloth, and it was too itchy to wear.

28. Warring factions in the former Yugoslavia seem to be trying to annihilate one another.

29. I was on the horns of a dilemma because she is such a good friend, but I did not want to live in that dormitory.

30. Consistency is one mark of a good athlete.

Lesson Fifteen

1. I quit smoking fifteen years ago; now I can't be near anyone who smokes.

2. In Brandon, there are many interesting shops, and the shopkeepers welcome you, even if you just want to browse.

3. The plane will make a ninety-minute stop in Moncton, where you are free to disembark for thirty minutes; a twenty-minute stop in Toronto, where you must not disembark; and another ninety-minute stop in Calgary, where again you may disembark for twenty minutes.

4. According to the Daily Express, this season the Regina Theatre Company will produce the following plays: The Importance of Being Earnest, by Oscar Wilde; Trifles, by Susan Glaspell; and The Ecstasy of Rita Joe, by George Ryga.

5. Plato thought the world we see was a mere reflection, a "spume," to use Yeats's word, of the real world.

6. Tornadoes can reach speeds up to 60 km/h; the circling winds within the vortex of the tornado can reach speeds of 600 km/h.

7. Steroids enhance athletic performance but, to quote Professor W.A. Benson: "The short-term gain in strength is not worth the long-term health risks to which a steroid user exposes himself."

8. We think recycling is a progressive, new idea, but many reusable goods were recycled fifty years ago, during the war.

9. A Quisling (named after Vidkun Quisling, whom the Germans brought to power after they conquered Norway in 1940), is a term used to denote a fifth-columnist, a traitor, or a collaborator.

10. Flowers used in the making of perfume include the rose, jasmine, acacia, and violet; aromatic herbs that can also be used include rosemary, thyme, and lavender; fruit peel, especially from the citrus fruit, can also be used.

11. My mother's pearls came from the waters off the coast of Mexico, considered to be one of the finest places for pearl fishing.

12. Despite the protests, despite the dangers, Canada will need nuclear power plants to meet the energy needs of a growing population.

13. One of the poems, "Ode on a Grecian Urn," in the anthology Literature in English, ends with the lines: "Beauty is Truth Truth Beauty That is all / Ye know on earth and all ye need to know."

14. The reviewer in the Times gave Priscilla Queen of the Desert four stars, but I found it to be a dull, inane movie.

15. On November 21, 1945, at Nuremberg, an international military tribunal, consisting of four judges representing four different countries—America, France, Britain, and the Soviet Union—put twenty-four Nazi leaders on trial.

16. The teachers' staff room at my children's school has a brand new microwave oven.

17. The llama is a cousin to the camel, but llamas are smaller, they do not have humps, and they have a thicker coat.

18. Any mother who had to make the choice Sophie had to make would sooner sacrifice her own life; most fathers would feel the same way.

19. In the middle of the summer, a mountain covered with skiers is an unusual sight to see.

20. Over 90 000 moths and butterflies, characterized by large, colourful wings and scaly bodies, belong to the Lepidoptera order of insects.

21. "Libretto," the Italian word for booklet, is the text of an opera.

22. On January 10, 1920, the League of Nations, formed to promote international peace and security, held its first meeting in Geneva, Switzerland.

23. Alternative forms of medicine and therapy—acupuncture, meditation, and herbal, to name just a few—are becoming more popular.

24. Coleridge and Wordsworth lived in the Lake District in the northwest of England, where they wrote many of the poems included in their book <u>Lyrical Ballads</u>, including "Tintern Abbey" and "Kubla Khan."

25. The largest planet, eleven times the diameter of Earth, Jupiter is composed, like the sun, mainly of helium and hydrogen.

Lesson Sixteen

1. The Berlin Wall, dividing the eastern part of Berlin into a communist sector and the western part of the city into a capitalist sector, was built at the end of World War II.

2. The aardvark is a nocturnal mammal about 1.5 m long; it feeds on termites and ants.

3. Acid rain occurs when there is too much nitric and sulphuric acids in rain and snow.

4. Normally, rain would have a pH level of 5; however, in some areas of North America pH levels as low as 3 have been recorded.

5. Rain with a pH level of 3 has 100 times more acid than normal and gets into the soil, harming the fruit and leaves on trees.

6. We try to attend church during Advent, the four Sundays that precede Christmas.

7. Halloween is not celebrated in Jamaica, which explains why our neighbours were frightened by all the children in strange outfits.

8. George I was King from 1714 to 1727; his son George II was King from 1727 to 1760.

9. Queen Victoria was the granddaughter of George III, who apparently experienced a period of insanity.

10. The West Coast Trail is a paradise for hikers, but it is farther away than many tourists like to travel.

11. New episodes of <u>Friends</u> and <u>Melrose Place</u> are on this week, but I can't watch them because I have too much homework.

12. Federally, the Conservative party was reduced to two seats, but in Ontario the Conservative party won the election.

13. The wording of the referendum is controversial because it is not clear whether it asks for a vote on complete independence or sovereignty-association.

14. Although in the rural ridings there is widespread support for the Liberals, they might not get enough seats in total to form a government.

15. By looking through calendars, you can best determine which college or university is right for you.

16. A decrease in enrollment and an increase in tuition fees resulted in the demise of the music program.

17. Subject-verb agreement and pronoun case were the topics covered in the lesson in today's class.

18. Alliteration is a literary device in which a series of words begins with the same sound.

19. The hare has longer ears and legs than the rabbit, but hares do not burrow as rabbits do, relying instead for safety on their speed and ability to hide.

20. Thermodynamics is the study of the relationship of heat to work.

21. Thunder follows lightning because thunder is caused by the intense vibrations in the air that are the byproducts of the rapid heating followed by the rapid cooling of the air that the lightning has caused.

22. By tightly weaving together wool and cotton, gabardine, which is used in the making of raincoats, is produced.

23. Galleons are sometimes referred to as "treasure vessels," because precious minerals were transported in galleons from the South American colonies back to Spain.

24. Canada converted to the metric system years ago, but many Canadians still prefer to use the imperial system of measurement.

25. In Montreal, two rival motorcycle gangs, the Hell's Angels and Rock Machine, are fighting for control of drug trafficking and prostitution, creating, in the process, a wave of violence that is straining the resources of the Montreal Police Department.

INDEX